GLENCOE

English Workout
Language Skills for the Workplace

Glencoe McGraw-Hill

New York, New York   Columbus, Ohio   Woodland Hills, California   Peoria, Illinois

CONTRIBUTING WRITER

RITA MILIOS
Educational Consultant
Toledo, Ohio

REVIEWERS

DR. JOEL L. BAILEY
Instructor
Mountain Empire
 Community College
Big Stone Gap, Virginia

JEROME DUNN
Supervisor of Adult Education
Elizabeth, New Jersey

FRANCES K. FOSTER
Instructor
Wyoming State Penitentiary
Rawlins, Wyoming

SUE W. GRAHAM
Instructor
Cohn Adult Learning
 Center
Nashville, Tennessee

WAYNE G. PETERSON
Instructor
Butte Literacy Center
Butte, Montana

WILMA SHEFFER
Director
Workplace Literacy
 Services Center
St. Louis, Missouri

Glencoe/McGraw-Hill

A Division of The McGraw-Hill Companies

Send all inquiries to:

Glencoe/McGraw-Hill
936 Eastwind Drive
Westerville, OH 43081

ISBN 0-02-802813-9

Printed in the United States of America

2 3 4 5 6 7 8 9 045 04 03 02 01 00 99

Table of Contents

NOUNS AND PRONOUNS

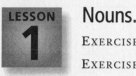

VERBS

SENTENCE PARTS

CAPITALIZATION AND PUNCTUATION

LESSON 15 Punctuation 161

WRITING SENTENCES

LESSON 16 Using Correct Vocabulary and Spelling 174

LESSON 17 Combining Sentence Parts. 185

LESSON 18 Independent and Dependent Thoughts. 196

LESSON 19   Using Descriptive Details in Sentences 205

LESSON 20   Improving Sentence Structure. 215

WRITING PARAGRAPHS

LESSON 21   Identifying Main Ideas. 230

LESSON 22 — Writing to Tell a Story 237

LESSON 23 — Describing People, Places, and Things 243

LESSON 24 — Writing to Influence Others. 258

To the Instructor

Glencoe English Workout: Language Skills for the Workplace is an adult basic education text that takes the student step by step through the essential elements of English grammar and usage. Starting with the simplest concepts, such as nouns and verbs, the text builds logically to include such skills as writing interesting and persuasive sentences and paragraphs.

This text includes enough instruction for students to work on the lessons and exercises alone or with a partner. The instructions at the beginning of each lesson give specific and thorough explanations covering all the grammar and usage questions that are asked on the exercises that follow. Most of the examples deal with situations in the workplace. At the end of each instruction section is a Workplace Application question. These questions are designed to be discussion starters, asking students for their opinions on various communication topics in the workplace.

The text starts at a low reading level and builds to progressively higher levels as students work through the lessons. The level of difficulty of the exercises also builds so that students will be able to write their own sentences and paragraphs. The exercises are literature-based, forming story lines so that student interest is maintained. Although many of the exercises have workplace themes, they also provide other themes and scenarios.

A pretest, *Check What You Know*, helps students determine the areas of grammar usage that give them the most difficulty. An evaluation chart provided after the answers to the pretest directs students to the lessons and exercises they need to study. The posttest, *Final Checkup*, helps students evaluate their progress after they have worked through the lessons and exercises.

The *Answer Key* at the back of the book provides answers to all exercises. However, answers to the *Workplace Application* are not provided because these questions are primarily given to spark discussion in the classroom.

Glencoe English Workout: Language Skills for the Workplace provides your students with tools for communication in the workplace. At the same time, students have an opportunity to improve their grammatical skills and writing so that they can advance academically. Thus, by gaining confidence in their ability to communicate, students can work more effectively and become more successful.

To the Student

Welcome to *Glencoe English Workout: Language Skills for the Workplace*. The goal of this book is to help you become more effective and successful at work and at home by improving your language skills. To communicate effectively, we must not only use the right words, we must also use words correctly and speak and write in grammatically correct sentences.

HOW TO USE THIS BOOK: Start by becoming familiar with the parts of the text. Look over the contents to preview the different kinds of lessons and exercises. Each of the twenty-four lessons contains several exercises. Notice that the exercises begin with work on basic language skills and build toward more difficult skills. The exercises help you develop specific grammar and usage skills. Some help you learn how to use correctly sentence parts like pronouns, verbs, and adjectives. Others explain how to combine or separate sentences and vary your writing. Still others teach you about writing persuasive and interesting paragraphs.

At the beginning of each lesson, the instructions explain the grammar skills used in the exercises that follow. As you work through the exercises, refer to the instructions if you need help with grammar rules, spelling, or the use of sentence parts. At the end of the instructions, *Workplace Application* questions are asked. The questions and their answers encourage you to think about your own workplace experience. These questions are designed for discussion with your teacher, a student partner, or a group of students.

Check What You Know and *Final Checkup:* Before starting the lessons, work through the pretest, *Check What You Know*. Answer all the questions in this test as best you can, but do not worry about answers you do not know. You are gathering information about the skills that you need to study and practice. To help evaluate what you know, check your answers in the answer key that follows the evaluation. Then use the *Check What You Know Evaluation Chart* at the end of this section to help identify areas in which you will need the most help.

After working through the lessons and exercises, take the posttest, *Final Checkup*, to see how much you have learned. Remember that improving your language and communication is a lifelong process. Continue to practice your new skills at home and at work.

✓ Check What You Know

Choose the correct noun, pronoun, or proper noun in each sentence below. Write your answer in the space provided.

1. (Ms. Jones, ms. Jones) is my supervisor. _____

2. Ms. Jones is my (supervisor, supervisors). _____

3. (She, Her) has an office on the second floor. _____

4. Tomorrow she will travel to (florida, Florida). _____

Choose the correct word in parentheses to complete each sentence below. Write your answer in the space provided.

5. (Your, You're) next in line for a promotion. _____

6. The (teams', team's) award was well deserved. _____

7. (It's, Its) time to go now. _____

8. (They're, Their) late for our meeting. _____

Choose the correct verb in parentheses. Write your answer in the space provided.

9. (Can, Are) you help me? _____

10. He (moved, moving) the desk to the basement. _____

11. It (was, were) like this when I got here. _____

12. Let's both (push, pushing) at the same time. _____

Choose the correct form of the following verbs or verb phrases in parentheses. Write your answer in the space provided.

13. The manager (has gave, has given) us an assignment. _____

14. He (told, tells) us about it yesterday. _____

15. He (teach, taught) the new employee the job skill. _____

16. The manager will (let, leave) me have some time off to attend a class.

_____

Add appropriate punctuation (period, question mark, or exclamation point) to each of the following sentences. Write your answer in the space provided.

17. Are you an employee _____

18. Yes, I am, sir _____

19. Tell me about this camera _____

20. I'd be delighted to _____

Complete the following sentences by adding appropriate connecting words. Write your answer in the space provided.

21. I could quit now _____ work a little longer. _____

22. Mr. Simpson wanted to stay, _____ he couldn't. _____

23. _____ I quit now, I'll just have to work harder tomorrow. _____

24. I guess I'll just stay _____ finish. _____

Choose the objects of the underlined verbs or connecting words. Write your answer in the space provided.

25. Juan <u>gave</u> the report. _____

26. He <u>listed</u> several opportunities for improvement. _____

27. The manager <u>took</u> Juan's suggestions seriously. _____

28. He took notes <u>in</u> his notebook. _____

Underline the complete subject once and the complete verb twice in the following sentences.

29. Employee satisfaction helps productivity.

30. Women in the workforce are more common than ever.

31. Female employees work just as hard as male employees.

32. Still, women often receive less pay than men do for similar work.

Choose the correct subject, object, or possessive pronoun in parentheses. Write your answer in the space provided.

33. Let (we, us) have a chance. _____

34. Sarah told (him, he) how to perform the task. _____

35. They helped (their selves, themselves) to coffee. _____

36. Jim and (me, I) won the award. _____

Match the correct subject with the correct verb in the following sentences. Write your answer in the space provided.

37. Pao, Steve, and Mario (are, is) in the cafeteria. _____

38. The work team (was, were) productive. _____

39. (Success, Successes) comes from hard work. _____

40. (Experience, Experiences) are also important. _____

Choose the correct indefinite pronoun in each sentence. Write your answer in the space provided.

41. (All, Each) of them is a member of this group. _____

42. Are (no one, none) excluded? _____

43. (Few, No one) writes longhand any more. _____

44. (Either, Neither) rain nor snow stops our postal service. _____

Choose the correct pronoun in parentheses. Write your answer in the space provided.

45. Different kinds of training are offered; (they, it) start at 3 P.M. _____

46. (These, That) supplies need replenishing. _____

47. Can you type (this, these) memos? _____

48. (These, This) is good work. _____

Choose the correct adjective or adverb for the sentences below. Write your answer in the space provided.

49. The (appropriate, appropriately) action was taken. _____

50. Look (careful, carefully) around you and tell me what you see. _____

51. After reconsidering, I (seriously, serious) think you may be right.

_____

52. This advertisement looks (good, well). _____

Choose the correct article in parentheses. Write your answer in the space provided.

53. (A, An) arrangement was made to keep him on the job. _____

54. Place (the, a) orders in the file. _____

55. She seems to be (a, an) honest person. _____

56. This gift was (a, an) premium for opening the account. _____

Choose the correct word in parentheses. Write your answer in the space provided.

57. This workshop is (better, best) than the last one. _____

58. The supervisor was the (angrier, angriest) that I've ever

seen her. _____

59. Please go help (this, these) customers. _____

60. Lauren did not feel (good, well) so she stayed home. _____

Circle the letters that should be capitalized.

61. I work at a greenhouse called pearl's plants. _____

62. My coworker smokes cuban cigars. _____

63. d. l. smith is the name of our lawyer. _____

64. I've never seen the atlantic ocean. _____

65. My favorite book is *war and peace*. _____

66. My favorite movie is *casablanca*. _____

67. Do you subscribe to *time* magazine? _____

68. I'm going to join the national organization for women. _____

Add commas to the following sentences to punctuate them correctly.

69. Mary please come here.

70. Flora writes for newspapers magazines and journals.

71. I need you to answer a question and I want you to be honest.

72. Do you like the pink the red or the blue one best?

Add the correct punctuation to the end of each sentence below.

73. I am so angry at you

74. Take this display to the front of the store

75. Is there another music store nearby

76. I don't think so

Add dashes or quotation marks to the following sentences to punctuate them correctly.

77. Barbara is over there at least she was a moment ago.

78. Come on, said Therese, let's go.

79. I'll be right there, Jolene answered.

80. This box the blue one must be mailed today.

Add semicolons and colons to the following sentences to punctuate them correctly.

81. These are the supplies we need stamps, invoices, photocopy paper, and time sheets.

82. Please pay with credit use this card.

83. The time is now 10.00.

84. The time clock was broken we latecomers got a break.

Choose the correct prefix or suffix to add to the words in parentheses. Choose from *i-*, *re-*, *in-*, *im-*, *un-*, *-ful*, *-er*, or *-ment*. Write the new word in the space provided.

85. We live in an (_____ perfect) world. _____

86. The meeting was (event _____). _____

87. Must I (_____ write) this today? _____

88. Pauline is a team (play _____). _____

Questions **89** to **100** refer to the paragraph below.

(1) Many successful businesspeople use an innovative way of thinking to help them get better ideas. (2) It is sometimes called creative thinking. (3) It is sometimes called lateral thinking, or "thinking out of the box." (4) Such thinking requires you to get out of your old, stuck, habitual ways of thinking. (5) And try out new ideas. (6) Ask yourself different questions. (7) Challenge existing frameworks. (8) Then you will adapt your new ideas to your present situation. (9) You might also find new ideas in unexpected places. (10) The daily newspaper can be a source of inspiration and innovation. (11) Perhaps a story you read will spark an idea. (12) Your idea may not be about the same thing. (13) But the process may be similar. (14) A story about a honey bee breeder may give you an idea about starting a fish breeding farm. (15) The key is to read with your mind open to new ideas. (16) Think while you read. (17) Look for the main idea in the story, but also consider what is new, unusual, puzzling, or interesting about what you are reading. (18) What questions does your reading bring up in your mind? (19) By taking the extra step and thinking beyond the obvious, you will help yourself become more innovative, and perhaps more successful.

89. Sentence 1. Many successful businesspeople use an innovative way of thinking to help them get <u>better</u> ideas. Which of the following is the best way to write the underlined word?

    a. better   **c.** more better

    b. best   **d.** most better   _____

90. Sentences 2 and 3. It is sometimes called creative thinking. It is sometimes called lateral thinking, or "thinking out of the box."

The most effective combination of Sentences 2 and 3 would include which of the following groups of words?

    a. ...called creative thinking. It is sometimes ....

    b. ...called creative. Thinking, it is sometimes....

    c. ...called creative thinking; it is sometimes....

    d. ...called creative thinking: it is sometimes....   _____

91. Sentence 4. Such thinking requires you to get out of *your* old, stuck, habitual ways of thinking. Which of the following is the best way to write the underlined segment of this sentence?

    a. yours   **c.** your

    b. their   **d.** my   _____

92. Sentences 4 and 5. Such thinking requires you to get out of yours old, stuck, habitual ways of thinking. And try out new ideas. Which of the following is the best way to write these two sentences?

    a. Such thinking requires you to get out of yours old, stuck, habitual ways of thinking. And try out new ideas.

    b. Such thinking requires you to get out of yours old, stuck, habitual ways. Of thinking, and try out new ideas.

    c. Such thinking requires you to get out of yours old, stuck, habitual ways of thinking: and try out new ideas.

    d. Such thinking requires you to get out of your old, stuck, habitual ways of thinking and try out new ideas.   _____

93. Sentence 6. Ask *yourself* different questions. Which of the following is the best way to write the underlined word?

    a. yourself   **c.** himself

    b. yourselves   **d.** theirselves   _____

94. Sentence 8. Then you will adapt your new ideas to your present situation. Which of the following is the best way to write this sentence?

    a. Then you will adapt your new ideas to your present situation.

    b. Then adapt your new ideas to your present situation.

    c. Then you had adapted your new ideas to your present situation.

    d. Then you will have been adapted your new ideas to your present situation.   _____

95. Sentences 12 and 13. Your idea may not be about the same thing. But the process may be similar. The most effective combination of Sentences 12 and 13 would include which of the following groups of words?

    a. ...the same thing, but the process ....

    b. ...the same thing because the process ....

    c. ...the same thing although the process ....

    d. ...the same processes, which are similar.   _____

96. Sentence 14. A story about a honey bee breeder may give you an idea about starting a fish breeding farm. What correction should be made to the sentence?

    a. For example, a story about a honey bee breeder may give you an idea about starting a fish breeding farm.

    b. In addition, a story about a honey bee breeder may give you an idea about starting a fish breeding farm.

    c. Although a story about a honey bee breeder may give you an idea about starting a fish breeding farm.

    d. Instead, a story about a honey bee breeder may give you an idea about starting a fish breeding farm.   _____

97. Sentences 15 and 16. The key is to read with your mind open to new ideas. Think while you read. Which of the following is the best way to write these sentences?

    a. The key is to read. With your mind open to new ideas. Think while you read.

    b. The key is to read with your mind open to new ideas; think while you read.

    c. The key is to read with your mind opens to new ideas. Thinking while you read.

    d. The key is to read with an open minds to new ideas. Think while you read.   _____

98. Sentences 16 and 17. Look for the main idea in the story, but also consider what is new, unusual, puzzling, or interesting about what you are reading. The most effective combination of Sentences 16 and 17 would include which of the following groups of words?

    a. Think while you read. Look for the main idea in the story, but also consider....

    b. Think while you read. While looking for the main idea in the story. But also consider....

    c. Think while you read, and look for the main idea in the story, but also consider....

    d. Think while you read, looking for the main idea in the story. But also consider....   _____

99. Sentence 18. What questions <u>does</u> your reading bring up in your mind? What is the best way to write the underlined portion of this sentence?

    a. does   **c.** don't never

    b. do   **d.** doesn't never

100. Sentence 19. By taking the extra step and thinking beyond the obvious, you will help yourself become more innovative, and perhaps more successful. Which of the following is the best way to write this sentence?

    a. You will help yourself become more innovative, and perhaps more successful.

b. By taking the extra step and thinking beyond the obvious you will help yourself become more innovative, although perhaps more successful.

c. By taking the extra step and thinking beyond the obvious, you will help yourself become more innovative—and perhaps more successful.

d. By asking the extra step and thinking beyond the obvious you will help yourself become more innovative perhaps: more successful.

Check What You Know Answer Key

1. Ms. Jones
2. supervisor
3. She
4. Florida
5. You're
6. team's
7. It's
8. They're
9. Can
10. moved
11. was
12. push
13. has given
14. told
15. taught
16. let
17. ? (question mark)
18. . (period)
19. . (period)
20. ! (exclamation point)
21. or
22. but
23. If
24. and
25. report
26. opportunities
27. suggestions
28. notebook
29. <u>Employee satisfaction</u> helps productivity.
30. <u>Women in the workforce</u> are more common than ever.
31. Female <u>employees</u> <u>work</u> just as hard as male employees.
32. Still, <u>women</u> often <u>receive</u> less pay than <u>men</u> <u>do</u> for similar work.
33. us
34. him
35. themselves
36. I
37. are
38. was
39. Success

40. Experiences
41. Each
42. none
43. No one
44. Neither
45. they
46. These
47. these
48. This
49. appropriate
50. carefully
51. seriously
52. good
53. An
54. the
55. an
56. a
57. better
58. angriest
59. these
60. well
61. Pearl's Plants (circle *p*, *p*)
62. Cuban (circle *c*)
63. D. L. Smith (circle *d*, *l*, *s*)
64. Atlantic Ocean (circle *a*, *o*)
65. *War and Peace* (circle *w*, *p*)
66. *Casablanca* (circle *c*)
67. *Time* (circle *t*)
68. National Organization for Women (circle *n*, *o*, *w*)
69. Mary, please come here.
70. Flora writes for newspapers, magazines, and journals.
71. I need you to answer a question, and I want you to be honest.
72. Do you like the pink, the red, or the blue one best?
73. I am so angry at you!
74. Take this display to the front of the store.
75. Is there another music store nearby?
76. I don't think so.

77. Barbara is over there—at least she was a moment ago.
78. "Come on," said Therese, "let's go."
79. "I'll be right there," Jolene answered.
80. This box—the blue one—must be mailed today.
81. These are the supplies we need: stamps, invoices, photocopy paper, and time sheets.
82. Please pay with credit; use this card.
83. The time is now 10:00.
84. The time clock was broken; we latecomers got a break.
85. imperfect
86. eventful
87. rewrite
88. player
89. a
90. c
91. c
92. d
93. a
94. b
95. c
96. a
97. b
98. c
99. a
100. c

Check What You Know Evaluation Chart

If you missed questions:	*Pay particular attention to:*
1–4	Lessons 1, 2, and 7
5–8	Lesson 3
9–16	Lessons 4, 5, and 6
17–28	Lesson 8
29–32	Lesson 4
33–36	Lesson 9
37–44	Lesson 10
45–56	Lessons 11 and 12
57–60	Lesson 13
61–68	Lesson 14
69–84	Lesson 15
85–88	Lesson 16
89–100	Lessons 18–24

1   Nouns

A **noun** names something. It can name a *person* (Mary, man, supervisor), a *place* (park, school, building), a *thing* (computer, desk, truck), or an idea (freedom, love). In the sentence, "John works at the Westmor Paper Mill on the south side of our town," the nouns are *John*, *Westmor Paper Mill*, *side*, and *town*.

Nouns can be **proper nouns**. Proper nouns name specific persons (Mary Smith, President Lincoln), places (Proctor & Gamble, New York), or things (Transportation Department, Highway Patrol). Other nouns are common nouns. Proper nouns begin with capital letters. Common nouns do not. In the sentence about John, the proper nouns are *John* and *Westmor Paper Mill*.

Nouns can be either *singular* or *plural*. A singular noun refers to one person, place, thing, or idea. A plural noun refers to more than one person, place, thing, or idea. Here are some rules for making nouns plural:

- **Rule 1**   Most nouns add *-s* to the end to become plural
  (*customer/customers; pen/pens; paper/papers*).
- **Rule 2**   When nouns end in *-ch*, *-o*, *-sh*, *-s*, or *-x*; add *-es* to make them plural
  (*church/churches; motto/mottos; dish/dishes; dress/dresses; tax/taxes*)
- **Rule 3**   When nouns end in *-f* or *-fe*, change the *-f* to *-v* before adding *-s* or *-es* (*half/halves; life/lives; wife/wives*).
- **Rule 4**   When nouns end in *-y*, change the *-y* to *-i* before adding *-es*
  (*city/cities; lady/ladies; copy/copies*). But when words end in *-ay* or *-ey*, add only *-s*
  (*essay/essays; attorney/attorneys; key/keys*).
- **Rule 5**   A few nouns do not follow the rules. Their plurals are made in different ways.
  Some plural nouns change the spelling of the noun when adding *-s* (*analysis/analyses; axis/axes*). Some plural nouns change their word spelling (*mouse/mice; tooth/teeth*).
  Others add an *-s* in places other than at the end (*mother-in-law/mothers-in-law*).

  A very few use the same word for singular and plural (*sheep/sheep; deer/deer; scissors/scissors*).

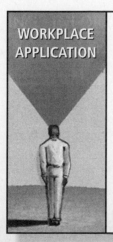

WORKPLACE APPLICATION

Mary sent the following memo to her boss:

To: Mr. Hill

From: Mary Miller

I will be at the 4 P.M. meeting. I will have my two sales report then.

What mistakes did Mary make in using proper nouns and singular or plural forms of nouns.? How do you think this affects Mr. Hill's opinion of Mary's job skills? _____

_____

EXERCISE 1

What Is a Noun?

A noun is a word that names a person, place, thing, or idea. A sentence may have more than one noun.

A. Find the nouns in the sentences. Draw one line under each noun that names a person. Draw two lines under each noun that names a place. Circle each noun that names a thing. Bracket each noun that names an idea.

Example: The businessperson took an umbrella to the office. [Freedom] is a good thing.

1. An employee is someone who works at a job.
2. An employer is someone you work for.
3. Some employers use humor to settle disagreements.
4. A boss, or supervisor, gives orders.
5. Some people work in plants or shops.
6. Bosses like workers to be on time.
7. Often, workers must use a time card.
8. Skills are needed in every workplace.
9. Some skills can be learned through job training.
10. Employers expect workers to be serious about their jobs.

B. Underline the nouns that name a person, place, or thing. Circle all the nouns that name ideas.

Example: John believes in honesty.

1. People who buy from a business are customers.
2. Sales to customers make money for a business.
3. Sales help pay for the salaries of workers.
4. All employees should treat customers well.
5. Communication is an important job skill.
6. Many workplaces have training.
7. Training may also be called classes or workshops.
8. Classes can teach workers communication skills.
9. A class may also teach how to use a telephone to make a sale.
10. Classes in computer training are popular today.

EXERCISE 2

Identifying Nouns

A noun is a word that names a person, place, thing, or idea.

A. Fill in the blanks in each sentence with nouns from the word list at the right.

Example: This is the ___*plot*___ of a new ___*movie*___ .

Word List	
airplane	movie
weekend	controls
pilot	landing
airport	storm
passenger	drive-in
plot	crew

1. I saw it at a _____ over the _____ .
2. An _____ got caught in a _____ .
3. The _____ and the _____ were hurt.
4. A _____ had to take the _____ .
5. She made a safe _____ at the _____ .

B. Underline the nouns in each sentence. The number of nouns is shown at the end of each sentence.

Example: <u>Airplanes</u> were not always comfortable.   (1)

1. Once the copilots served meals to the passengers.   (3)
2. Fifty years ago the first attendants flew on airplanes.   (3)
3. They flew from San Francisco to Chicago.   (2)
4. Even on a clear day, the flight still took twenty hours!   (3)
5. The early attendants were all nurses.   (2)
6. They had eighteen people to look after on each flight.   (2)
7. The excitement over their jobs did not last long.   (2)
8. The long trips and the hard work caused problems.   (3)
9. The journeys were difficult for the passengers.   (2)
10. The cabins did not provide much room or comfort.   (3)
11. There was one aisle that had one seat on each side of it.   (3)
12. Travel by air was very new in those days.   (3)
13. The crew and the travelers all needed courage.   (3)
14. Pilots flew low and followed landmarks on the ground.   (3)
15. Transportation in aircraft has changed since that time.   (3)
16. Today, a trip from New York to Los Angeles takes merely a few hours.   (4)
17. Some flights do not even provide full meals.   (2)

EXERCISE 3

Common and Proper Nouns

Nouns that name specific persons, places, or things are proper nouns. All other nouns are common nouns. Proper nouns start with capital letters. Common nouns do not.

A. Capitalize the proper nouns correctly, and write them on the lines.

Example: west germany   _West Germany_

1. new orleans   _____
2. doctor laura miller   _____
3. washington street   _____
4. city construction   _____
5. american red cross   _____
6. social security office   _____
7. president bill clinton   _____
8. rowe's housekeeping department _____

B. Write the proper nouns, capitalizing them correctly.

Example: Isn't yellowstone national park in wyoming?
            Yellowstone National Park   Wyoming

1. The sears tower is taller than the john hancock building.

   _____

2. The capital of missouri is jefferson city.

   _____

3. We enjoyed our business trip held near the pacific ocean last October.

   _____

4. We will visit ann's company in canada over christmas.

   _____

5. The spacecraft took photographs of io, a moon of jupiter.

   _____

6. General colin powell was a general during the gulf war.

   _____

EXERCISE 4

More Common and Proper Nouns

Nouns that name specific persons, places, or things are proper nouns. All other nouns are common nouns. Proper names begin with a capital letter, but connecting words (*in, on, of, the, etc.*) do not.

A. Circle the proper nouns.

Example: We went to see the (football)(hall) of (fame) in (canton), (ohio).

1. Our central office is in arizona.
2. Mr. phillips is the president of our company.
3. He will be visiting our plant in july.
4. Arizona plumbing makes plumbing supplies.
5. It is the largest supplier in the united states.
6. Must we wait until september for our bonuses?
7. The plant in memphis got bonuses last month.
8. I hope to visit new york this summer.
9. I want to see the statue of liberty.
10. I also want to visit the empire state building.

B. Capitalize the proper nouns and rewrite each sentence below.

Example: The ford motor company is a large automaker.

   The Ford Motor Company is a large automaker.

1. They have many plants in the state of michigan.

   _____

2. Henry ford made auto production easier.

   _____

3. The model t was one of ford's first cars.

   _____

4. You can see ford's early cars at the henry ford museum in michigan.

   _____

   _____

5. The fords today look much different from those henry ford made.

   _____

   _____

EXERCISE 5

Singular and Plural Nouns

Singular nouns name one person, place, or thing. Plural nouns name two or more. Most plural nouns are formed by adding *-s* or *-es* to the end of the singular noun. When nouns end in *-y*, preceded by a consonant, change the *-y* to *-i* before adding *-es*.

A. Write the plural form of each noun.

Example: splash _*splashes*_

1. bush _____
2. computer _____
3. copy _____
4. class _____
5. memo _____
6. bench _____
7. bakery _____
8. tax _____
9. city _____
10. ladder _____
11. disk _____
12. hero _____
13. lady _____
14. stapler _____
15. plank _____
16. baby _____
17. ticket _____
18. wrench _____

B. Write the plural of the noun in parentheses in the space provided.

Example: It is often a good idea to dress like ___*others*___ in your workplace.   (other)

1. If your boss wears _____, maybe you can, too.   (jean)

2. If everyone else wears _____, you should, too.   (tie)

3. If no one wears bright _____, you probably should not either.   (color)

4. _____ are worn in formal offices.   (suit)

5. Frills on _____ are usually not a good idea.   (dress)

6. Tennis _____ do not look right with a suit.   (shoe)

7. Dressing like your _____ helps you fit in.   (coworker)

8. People do not wear _____ in the office.   (hat)

9. He sometimes wears long sleeve _____.   (shirt)

10. Some _____ issue _____ to wear for work.   (business, uniform)

EXERCISE 6

Plural Nouns

A singular noun names one person, place, thing, or idea. A plural noun names more than one. Most nouns add an -s or -es to become plural. Some change an -f or -fe to a -v before adding -s or -es. Some plurals add their -s to the middle of the word.

Example: knife _____*knives*_____

1. clock   _____
2. loaf   _____
3. tomato   _____
4. fax   _____
5. piano   _____
6. crutch   _____
7. desk   _____
8. sister   _____
9. machine   _____
10. cabinet   _____

11. branch   _____
12. class   _____
13. movie   _____
14. self   _____
15. coin   _____
16. shelf   _____
17. half   _____
18. floor   _____
19. shoebox   _____
20. scarf   _____

B. Write the plural form of each noun in parentheses in the space provided.

Example: (Member) of the same family do not often work in the
                 same (office).   *Members*
                                                                            offices

1. Having (partner) in the office can cause (problem).   _____

                                                                           _____

2. (Husband) and their (wife) usually prefer to work at different jobs.   _____

                                                                           _____

3. Even (brother) or (sister) may find it difficult to work together.   _____

                                                                           _____

4. It is sometimes hard for (worker) to keep their home (life)   _____
   separate from their job.   _____

5. (Fight) at home could bring (trouble) into the office.   _____

                                                                           _____

6. (Battle) of the (sex) could easily occur.   _____

EXERCISE 7

Using Plural Nouns

Most plural nouns are formed by just adding -s or -es to the singular. Some nouns require a spelling change to form plurals.

A. In the sentences below change the word in the parentheses from singular to plural. Write your answers in the space provided.

Example: Rain made a pounding sound on our (window).   *windows*
                Many (woman) are trying to lose weight.   *women*

1. (Streak) of lightning lit up the sky.   _____

2. Great (clap) of thunder boomed like bells at (school).   _____

                                                                                    _____

3. Many (woman) and (child) began to come in out of the rain.   _____

                                                                                    _____

4. Most came to buy (umbrella) to keep their (foot) dry.   _____

                                                                                    _____

5. One man came in on (crutch).   _____

6. It was so cold their (tooth) were clicking.   _____

7. There was also a variety of different (style).   _____

8. Our (manager) were pleased with the unexpected business.   _____

9. (Clerk) rang up almost two dozen sales.   _____

10. (Customer) took their new (umbrella) and went back   _____
    into the rain.   _____

B. Write the plural form of the words below in the space provided.

1. man   _____   7. foot   _____

2. woman   _____   8. goose   _____

3. datum   _____   9. potato   _____

4. ZIP Code   _____   10. check   _____

5. strategy   _____   11. mouse   _____

6. curriculum   _____   12. idea   _____

EXERCISE 8

Other Plural Nouns

Some nouns are spelled the same way in their singular and plural forms. Other nouns require a spelling change.

A. Change the following sentences containing singular nouns to sentences that contain plural nouns. If no change is needed to make the noun plural, write "no change." Write your answer in the space provided.

Example: Marie has a child.   _Marie has two children._

1. There was a <u>crisis</u> in the office last month. _____
_____

2. I stood so long on the showroom floor that my <u>foot</u> began to ache.
_____
_____

3. This restaurant serves duck, quail, and other <u>fowl</u>. _____
_____

4. When it is in season, they also serve Copper River <u>salmon</u>. _____
_____

5. Yesterday a <u>deer</u> nearly ran into my car. _____
_____

6. They both wanted <u>trout</u>, but they wanted it baked, not fried. _____
_____

7. Someone once asked if we had <u>goose</u>-egg omelets. _____
_____

8. The cook laughed and said he had never cooked geese—or <u>moose</u>—but he could try. _____
_____

9. "The next thing you know," he said, "someone will ask me to cook an <u>ox</u>!"
_____
_____

10. That noise is from a <u>workman</u> repairing our roof. _____
_____

EXERCISE 9

Using Plural Nouns in Sentences

Some plural nouns are formed in unusual ways. These exceptions to the rules must be learned by practicing them.

A. Write the plural of each noun in the space provided. If you are not sure of a plural, look it up in a dictionary.

Example: policewoman   _policewomen_

1. daughter-in-law _____
2. analysis _____
3. great-uncle _____
4. encyclopedia _____
5. countryman _____
6. golf course _____
7. cactus _____
8. self-starter _____
9. double play _____
10. drive-in _____
11. forget-me-not _____

12. tooth _____
13. series _____
14. fungus _____
15. moose _____
16. salmon _____
17. goose _____
18. handful _____
19. woman _____
20. scissors _____
21. axis _____
22. chassis _____

B. Write the correct plural of the noun in parentheses in the space provided.

Example: There are fewer (specie) now.   _species_

1. My (great-grandparent) came from Italy. _____
2. Moon Lake is stocked with (trout). _____
3. Here come the (commander in chief). _____
4. Strep throat is caused by (bacterium). _____
5. The candidates are both (congresswoman). _____
6. Many (Chinese) work as farmers. _____
7. We carried two (armful) of folders. _____
8. Check in two (dictionary) for the correct spelling. _____
9. Two (fisherman) asked for directions. _____
10. The video provided too many (stimulus) for the senses. _____

2   Pronouns

Pronouns take the place of nouns. A pronoun is used to replace the noun when the noun is used a second time in the same sentence. Both nouns and pronouns often tell *what* and *who* the sentence is about. In the example below, the pronoun *he* takes the place of the noun *Manuel*. *He* stands for *Manuel*.

Example: Manuel drives a truck, and *he* enjoys it.

Pronouns can be personal, indefinite, or possessive.

Personal pronouns can be *singular* (one) or *plural* (more than one). They can be *subject pronouns*, as shown above, or they can be *object pronouns*. As object pronouns, personal pronouns are used with words that show the *action* (what is happening) or the *state of being* (no action) in a sentence. Object pronouns usually follow the action or state of being word in the sentence.

Example: The supervisor trained *me*. (Object pronoun *me* answers the question *trained whom?* and follows the action word, *trained*.)

Indefinite pronouns answer the questions *who*, *what*, or *which*. Both these pronouns and the nouns they replace are somewhat uncertain. Indefinite pronouns include *each*, *other*, *all*, *everyone*, *everybody*, *some*, *none*, *both*, *neither*, *someone*, *no one*, *anyone*, etc. Most indefinite pronouns are either singular or plural, but some can be both. The meaning of the sentence will tell you whether to use the singular or plural form.

Example: *Neither* of us is going. (Here *neither* shows one. The sentence could read *Neither one* of us is going. Note that in this sentence a singular state of being word is used to match the singular subject, *neither*.)

Example: *Neither* the boxes nor the crates are unpacked. (Here *neither* shows more than one, whether it means the boxes or the crates, the word to which *neither* refers is plural. Note that in this case, *are*, the plural form of the state of being word *is*, is used to match the noun it refers to.)

Possessive pronouns show *ownership*. Pronouns such as *my*, *mine*, *ours*, *hers*, *his*, and *theirs* are possessive pronouns. See the list below.

Example: This computer is *mine*. (*Mine* shows ownership of the computer.)

	Singular	Plural
Subject pronouns	I	we
Object pronouns	me	us
Possessive pronouns	my, mine	our, ours
Subject pronouns	you	you
Object pronouns	you	you
Possessive pronouns	your, yours	your, yours
Subject pronouns	he, she, it	they
Object pronouns	him, her, it	them
Possessive pronouns	his, hers, its	their, theirs

WORKPLACE APPLICATION

The following ad appeared in an interoffice newsletter:

HELP WANTED
Need assistance typing My computer or yous. Us can discuss hours and pay. Call Sam at 888-8888. Leave you number and him will call you back.

Do you think this advertiser needs help with more than typing? Perhaps grammar and spelling as well? Find and circle the four errors

What Is a Pronoun?

A pronoun is a word that takes the place of a noun or nouns. Words like *I, you, he, she, we, they,* and *it* can be used instead of names. Pronouns are less specific than nouns. Words like *them* and *their* are also pronouns.

A. Underline the pronouns in the sentences below.

Example: <u>We</u> are looking for jobs.

1. I know he is very interested in that job.

2. I talked to him about it yesterday.

3. She said this was her dream job.

4. The interviewers will ask them about their accomplishments.

5. They asked me to help them write résumés.

6. We included their personal strengths as well as job skills.

7. I think their résumés will help them get jobs.

8. "You will find a job if you don't give up," I told them.

B. Write the correct pronoun in the space provided and underline the noun that it replaces.

Example: A <u>job</u> interview need not be tense. _____*it*_____ can be a satisfying experience.

1. Interviewers are not the enemy. _____ want to identify qualified candidates for the job.

2. Interviews do upset many job-seekers. These people worry about _____.

3. An interviewer represents the company's interest. _____ will ask the job-seeker questions.

4. The questions concern the person's background and interests. _____ should be answered clearly and honestly.

5. Some people lie about their job experiences, but lying will only hurt _____ chances for the job in the end.

6. The job-seeker should also learn something about the job before the interview. _____ should be the right kind of job for the person.

EXERCISE 11

Personal Pronouns

Personal pronouns are used in place of nouns naming persons, places, or things.

A. Circle the twelve personal pronouns in these sentences.

Example: The employees saw that (they) were appreciated.

1. A national "suggestion" organization honored them.
2. They had made suggestions to employers.
3. Companies appreciate a good idea and use it.
4. Some companies reward an employee by promoting him or her.
5. Some employees are paid for an idea if the company uses it.
6. She is a mechanic who has made dozens of suggestions.
7. She has four more ideas and will announce them soon.
8. Companies belong to the organization and support it.
9. They gather to honor the "Suggesters of the Year."
10. Maybe a suggestion could make you famous.

B. Write the noun that the underlined pronoun refers to in the space provided.

Example: The winners said that <u>they</u> would pose for pictures.   _____winners_____

1. One official said that <u>she</u> was amazed at the good ideas.   _____
2. A reporter for a newspaper said that <u>she</u> was impressed, too.   _____
3. The organization admitted that <u>it</u> was pleased.   _____
4. The mechanic brought the blowers that a friend gave <u>her</u>.   _____
5. People at the ceremony decided that <u>they</u> would suggest
   things.   _____
6. The organization's president said that <u>he</u> would honor
   the winners.   _____
7. One man accepted an award and then dropped <u>it</u>.   _____
8. When the man dropped his award, <u>he</u> didn't seem to care.   _____
9. The audience liked the man and applauded <u>him</u> even more.   _____
10. The audience applauded the winners and praised <u>them</u>.   _____
11. The participating companies said that <u>they</u> were pleased, too.   _____
12. The suggesters were glad that <u>they</u> had helped.   _____

EXERCISE 12

Pronoun Agreement

A pronoun should agree with the noun it replaces. This means that both the noun and pronoun should be either singular (one) or plural (more than one).

A. Circle the correct pronoun in each sentence.

Example: Photographers use (his, (their)) cameras all the time. (*Photographers* is plural and indicates more than one. *Their* also indicates more than one.)

1. Harvey brought (his, their) camera on the trip.
2. Lois took all three of (her, their) cameras along.
3. Each person is taking (his or her, their) own photographs.
4. Harvey says (he, they) will photograph underwater.
5. Lois will shoot (her, their) pictures at night.
6. Neither of the boys want (his, their) picture taken.
7. Harvey and Lois develop (his, their) own pictures.
8. Each photographer will have (their, his or her) own exhibit.
9. Lois will display (her, their) pictures at George Hall.
10. Harvey will display (their, his) pictures at the Art Center.

B. Write a sentence using each pair of words. Make sure the noun and its pronoun are both either singular or plural.

Example: model, her _The model carefully combed her hair._

1. photos, their _____
2. lens, its _____
3. professionals, their _____
4. printer, her _____
5. snapshots, their _____
6. tripod, its _____
7. photographer, his _____
8. bracelet, her _____
9. toys, their _____
10. battery, its _____

EXERCISE 13

Indefinite Pronouns

Some pronouns are called *indefinite*. Indefinite pronouns are less specific in their reference. The nouns they refer to are also less specific. Indefinite pronouns may be singular or plural. Some of the indefinite pronouns are listed on page 21.

A. Circle each indefinite pronoun and underline the noun it stands for.

Example: Two <u>men</u> passed. (Both) stared at my feet.

1. People laughed. Everyone was looking at me.
2. My friends were there. Several pointed to my feet.
3. I had on two socks, but neither matched my outfit.
4. Jose and Lucinda laughed again. Both enjoyed my mistake.
5. I have many socks at home. Several are brightly colored.
6. My friends are proud of their clothes. All of them dress well.
7. My socks stood out. Each was a different shade of red.
8. I found two more socks. Both were the same color.
9. My friends were happy. All were glad that I had matching socks.
10. I must sort my socks. Many need mates.

B. Write the indefinite pronoun in each sentence in the space provided. Then write whether it is singular or plural in the second space.

	Pronoun	**Number**
Example: Someone asked about my socks.	*Someone*	*singular*
1. Many of my socks had holes in the toes.		
2. A few had holes in the heels.		
3. Everyone knows that is uncomfortable.		
4. Somebody always remarks on such things.		
5. I decided to buy others.		
6. Would anyone like to go to the store?		
7. I asked Lucinda and Jose, and both came.		
8. Each wore one red sock.		
9. Each also had on one green sock.		
10. Neither said a word about the socks.		
11. I finally said something to them.		
12. They said everyone was wearing them.		

EXERCISE 14

Possessive Pronouns

Personal pronouns have possessive forms. Possessive forms show ownership or possession.

A. Circle the fifteen possessive pronouns in these sentences.

Example: (My) customers loved (their) bargains.

1. The last sale was our best by far.
2. How old are your CDs and tapes?
3. Did your wife like her new electric toothbrush?
4. Is your husband having any trouble with his lawn mower?
5. My husband has owned the same model for ten years.
6. Its performance is outstanding.
7. Our lawn mowers are your best buy.
8. My other customers are usually happy with their purchases.
9. Tell your husband to try cutting his lawn again.
10. If the mower fails, his money will be refunded.

B. Write the correct possessive form of the personal pronoun in parentheses in the space provided.

Example: Please listen. May I have (you) ___*your*___ attention?

1. Welcome to my sale. This store is (I) _____.
2. You will save money. These bargains are (you) _____.
3. Patti wants a radio. This one can be (she) _____.
4. Al bought this bicycle. It is (he) _____.
5. They bought new clothes. (They) _____ hats look good.
6. We can all save money here. These bargins are (we) _____.
7. This is a great store. (It) _____ prices are low.
8. Do you like this CD? It can be (you) _____.
9. Buy that for your wife. It will be (she) _____.
10. Does Julio have one of these? It is (he) _____.
11. Erika and John saw that book first. It is (they) _____.
12. The store is small, but it is still (we) _____ best store.

3   Contractions, Possessives, and Plurals

A **contraction** is a single word made from two words. One or more letters are omitted when combining the two words. An **apostrophe** (') replaces the missing letters. The single word has the *same meaning* as the two original words.

Examples of Contractions

they are, they're   I will, I'll   cannot, can't   he is, he's

Possessive pronouns indicate ownership. Some possessive pronouns and contractions sound alike and can be spelled alike, but they have different meanings. A good way to tell if you should use a contraction or a possessive is to read the sentence with the contraction returned to its two word parts. If this does not change the meaning of the sentence, the contraction is correct. If not, a possessive is probably needed.

Example: (Their, They're work is done. (*They are* work is done is not correct.
The sentence should read *Their* work is done.)

Possessives and Troublesome Soundalikes

you're, your   it's, its   who's, whose   they're, there, their

Possessive nouns, like possessive pronouns, indicate ownership. Singular possessive nouns (indicating ownership by one) are made by adding -*'s* to the noun. Plural possessive nouns (indicating ownership by two or more) are made in one of two ways, depending on how the plural noun ends. (1) If the plural noun ends in -*s*, place an apostrophe after the -*s* (*typewriters'* ribbons). (2) If the plural noun does not end in -*s*, add -*'s* to the plural noun (*worker's* compensation).

Example: Lo Mei gathered the *report's* data. (data belongs to one report)
Damien sorted the *reports'* summaries. (summaries belong to more
than one report.)

Plurals (showing more than one) may often *sound* like possessives, especially if the plural ends in *-s*. Read the sentence and let its meaning tell you whether to use a plural or a possessive.

Example: The *time clocks* are broken. (more than one time clock—plural)
The *time clocks'* numbers all are still on 3 P.M. (indicates ownership of numbers by the clocks—possessive)

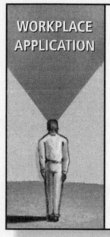

WORKPLACE APPLICATION

A report said:
"Our companies' sales grew by 20% this year."
Is this report about one company or more than one? How can you tell?

Pronouns in Contractions

A contraction is one word made from combining two words.
An apostrophe (') shows where a letter or letters have been left out.

A. Write each pair of words as a contraction.

Example: she + will _____*she'll*_____

1. he + is   _____
2. it + is   _____
3. we + had   _____
4. I + have   _____
5. she + will   _____

6. you + are   _____
7. I + would   _____
8. they + have   _____
9. I + will   _____
10. I + am   _____

B. Complete the crossword puzzle by writing the contraction for each word pair below. Remember to add the apostrophes. An example has been done for you.

Across

5. they + are
6. he + is
9. he + will
10. you + have

11. I + have
12. you + had
13. she + will

Down

1. it + is
2. we + are
3. we + would
4. you + will

7. she + is
8. they + would
11. I + will

EXERCISE 16

Using Contractions Correctly

A contraction is a shortened form of two words. An apostrophe (') replaces the omitted letter or letters.

A. Write the contraction for each item below.

Example: I am _____*I'm*_____

1. she had _____
2. they have _____
3. is not _____
4. were not _____
5. I will _____

6. it has _____
7. could not _____
8. you will _____
9. we have _____
10. did not _____

B. Each contraction below is incorrect because the apostrophe has been left out. First write the contraction correctly with the apostrophe. Then write the two words for which the contraction stands.

Example: wont _*won't—will not*_____

1. arent _____
2. hes _____
3. cant _____
4. wouldnt _____
5. its _____
6. dont _____
7. wasnt _____
8. havent _____
9. youre _____

C. Write sentences using three different contractions from the exercises above. Make sure you put the apostrophes in the right places.

1. _____
2. _____
3. _____

EXERCISE 17

Possessives and Contractions

Some words sound alike, but they have different meanings and are usually spelled differently. Do not confuse possessive pronouns with contractions.

A. Choose the word in parentheses that completes each sentence correctly. Think about the meanings of the words. Write your answers in the spaces provided.

Example: Businesses know (they're, their) success depends on
keeping customers happy.   *their*

1. Businesses make sure (their, they're) treating customers
   with respect.   _____

2. This is especially important if (you're, your) in a service
   business.   _____

3. (Their, There) is often training for new employees on
   customer service.   _____

4. (You're, Your) sure to learn about telephone skills.   _____

5. (It's, Its) very important to be polite to customers on the
   phone.   _____

6. Impolite salespeople are likely to lose (they're, their) sales.   _____

7. (Its, It's) harder to convince people to buy when (your, you're)
   not face-to-face.   _____

8. You must be even more careful to address (they're, their)
   needs.   _____

9. (Your, You're) conversation should also address (they're, their)
   likes and dislikes.   _____

10. The most important thing is to have (their, there) satisfaction
    as your goal.   _____

B. Make up sentences using each of the following words correctly.

1. its _____

2. it's _____

3. your _____

4. you're _____

5. their _____

6. they're _____

7. there _____

EXERCISE 18

Using Possessives and Contractions in Sentences

Some possessive pronouns and contractions sound alike, but they have different meanings and spellings.

Underline the correct word for each sentence.

Example: (They're, Their) participating in a motocross race.

1. The team from the Roanoke plant won (it's, its) first championship race.

2. The team members said that (they're, their) excited.

3. (Their, There) total time for the course was three hours.

4. "(You're, Your) bikes were not the best in the race," a spectator said.

5. He pointed to Eric Jacoby, (who's, whose) bike is quite old.

6. "(You're, Your) going to need repairs on that," said a concerned teammate.

7. "That bike has seen (it's, its) last race," said Eric.

8. The cyclists made (they're, their) way to the stand.

9. Now (they're, there) being presented with trophies.

10. The mayor was (they're, there).

11. "(You're, Your) a great team," said the mayor.

12. "(It's, Its) winning that makes the team feel good," said Kyle Jones.

13. A reporter asked the team members about (there, their) future plans.

14. "(Who's, Whose) going to race again?" he asked.

15. Neal Drake and Glen Linari aren't sure what (they're, their) going to do.

16. Kyle and Eric said (there, their) plans include entering three more races.

17. Rick Schmidt said (it's, its) doubtful whether he will be able to race again soon.

18. He is the person (who's, whose) knee has bothered him.

19. His doctor will check the knee next week to see whether (it's, its) condition has improved.

20. Joan did not see (there, their) car in the drive way.

21. (Who's, Whose) idea was it t ogo to the night ballgame.

22. I am sure (they're, there) going to be (they're, there) this afternoon.

What Are Possessive Nouns?

Possessive nouns indicate ownership. Singular possessive nouns are formed with an apostrophe and the letter *s* (*'s*) at the end of the word. Plural possessive nouns are formed with only an apostrophe or with *s'*.

A. Rewrite each phrase, making one noun a possessive.

Examples: the bracelet of the lad.   *the lady's bracelet*

                 the houses of the realtors   *the realtors' houses*

1. the atmosphere of the store   _____
2. the help of Mr. Haskins   _____
3. the choices of the student   _____
4. the color of the shirt   _____
5. the job for the clerk   _____
6. the design of the sweaters   _____
7. the inquiry of the man   _____
8. the floor for boys   _____
9. the toys for children   _____
10. the noise of the elevator   _____
11. the ringing of the telephone   _____

B. Find the noun that should be possessive in each sentence. Write its possessive form on the line.

Example: The shoppers faces were eager.   *shoppers'*

1. The clothes colors added sparkle to the display.   _____
2. One managers leadership was strong.   _____
3. The salespeoples enthusiasm was catching.   _____
4. All the boys jeans were on sale.   _____
5. Helens new sweater is purple.   _____
6. Jim bought his youngest sons new school outfit.   _____
7. His son liked Jims choices.   _____
8. Those dresses belts are all leather.   _____

Identifying Possessive Nouns

Possessive nouns indicate ownership. They are formed with an apostrophe and the letter _s_ ('s), or with only an apostrophe.

A. Write the possessive form of each noun in parentheses.

Example: (paper) edge ___*paper's edge*___

1. (elevator) doors _____
2. (man) wallet _____
3. (groups) timecards _____
4. (pilot) plane _____
5. (president) office _____
6. (visitors) tags _____
7. (twins) guitar _____
8. (employees) picnic _____
9. (door) sign _____
10. (heros) welcome _____

11. (computer) space _____
12. (assistant) duty _____
13. (editors) books _____
14. (women) voices _____
15. (son-in-law) gift _____
16. (oxen) load _____
17. (friend) letter _____
18. (club) dues _____
19. (group) decision _____
20. (seminar) leader _____

B. The underlined noun does not indicate possession. Rewrite the word, adding an apostrophe where needed, to indicate possession.

Example: <u>Painters</u> tools include brushes, paints, masking tape, and ladders. ___*Painters'*___

1. A chimney <u>sweeps</u> tools include brushes, ladders, duct tape, and extension poles. _____

2. A house <u>cleaners</u> tools may include brushes, a bucket, cleaning solutions, and a stepladder. _____

3. Some of these <u>jobs</u> tools are the same. _____

4. Still, very different skills are required for each <u>jobs</u> performance. _____

5. Some <u>peoples</u> perfect jobs allow them to work outside. _____

6. Other people prefer that their <u>works</u> requirements keep them inside. _____

7. Either way, it is the <u>employers</u> decision to make. _____

EXERCISE 21

More Practice With Plural or Possessive Nouns

An apostrophe is used to form a possessive noun. An apostrophe is *not* ordinarily used to form a plural noun.

A. Write the correct possessive noun in the space provided.

Example: A (wolves, wolf's, wolves') cry broke the silence.   *wolf's*

1. These two (copies, copy's, copies') look identical.   _____
2. One copies, (copy's, copies') cover was missing.   _____
3. All of the (copies, copy's, copies') covers were blue.   _____
4. Two (heroes, hero's, heroes') saved a drowning man.   _____
5. We admired both (heroes, hero's, heroes') courage.   _____
6. They were given a (heroes, hero's, heroes') welcome.   _____
7. That (women, woman's, women's) dress is very elegant.   _____
8. I am a designer of (women, woman's, women's) fashions.   _____
9. I design clothes for working (women, woman's, women's).   _____
10. These two (shelves, shelf's, shelves') are broken.   _____
11. Both (shelves, shelf's, shelves') books are missing.   _____
12. One (shelves, shelf's, shelves') paint is chipped.   _____

B. Each headline below has an incorrect plural or possessive noun. Write the correct word in the space provided.

Example: Three Thief's Trapped   *Thieves*

1. Zoos' New Birdhouse Opens   _____
2. Mexicos President to Travel Here   _____
3. Ten Thousand Runners' Enter Marathon   _____
4. Eight Workers Dreams Come True   _____
5. Horde's of Flies Invade City   _____
6. Two Players Injuries Hurt Team   _____
7. Grateful Mother's Plan Celebration   _____
8. Arnie Jones Wins Mens' Golf Classic   _____
9. Most Stocks' Soar on Wall Street   _____

EXERCISE 22

Using Plural and Possessive Nouns in Sentences

An apostrophe is used to form the possessive of a noun. It is not ordinarily used to form the plural of a noun.

A. Underline the correct form of the noun for each sentence.

Example: The (<u>candidates</u>, candidate's) debated.

1. The (ladies', ladies) worked during the election.
2. They put posters on the (streets', streets) lightposts.
3. Some teenage (boys, boy's) helped address envelopes.
4. The ballot (box's, boxes) were sealed.
5. A (workers, worker's) wallet was found on the floor.

B. Decide whether the underlined words are singular possessive, plural, or plural possessive. Write the answers in the space provided.

Example: Baseball's history is interesting.   *singular possessive*

Baseball in the United States came from (1) <u>England's</u> sports of cricket and rounders. Cricket (2) <u>players</u> used a bat to hit a pitched ball. However, cricket (3) <u>players'</u> bats were flat, not round. In rounders, (4) <u>hitters</u> used a bat and ball as well as (5) <u>bases</u>. The (6) <u>fielder's</u> job was to throw the ball in the (7) <u>runner's</u> path. If the fielder hit a runner with the ball, the runner was out.

Organized (8) <u>baseball's</u> first teams were made up of lawyers, doctors, bankers, and clerks. (9) <u>Historians</u> believe that the first organized team was called the Knickerbockers. Their experiments with the (10) <u>game's</u> rules resulted in (11) <u>today's</u> game. Once, the (12) <u>teams'</u> players numbered eight. After the (13) <u>shortstop's</u> position was added, there were nine players.

1. _____
2. _____
3. _____
4. _____
5. _____
6. _____
7. _____

8. _____
9. _____
10. _____
11. _____
12. _____
13. _____

EXERCISE 23

Review of Plural and Possessive Nouns

An apostrophe is used to form the possessive of a noun.

A. Write whether the underlined word in each phrase is a plural or a possessive noun. Write your answer in the space provided.

Example: the <u>janitor's</u> closet   <u>*possessive*</u>

1. an <u>electrician's</u> cap   _____
2. the five <u>carpenters</u>   _____
3. the <u>plumber's</u> tools   _____
4. the <u>painter's</u> ladder   _____
5. the busy <u>plasterers</u>   _____
6. a <u>mason's</u> job   _____
7. the alert <u>apprentices</u>   _____
8. a <u>roofer's</u> rope   _____
9. the <u>woman's</u> helper   _____
10. the good <u>drivers</u>   _____
11. <u>machinist's</u> oil   _____
12. <u>contractor's</u> job   _____
13. experienced <u>designers</u>   _____
14. day <u>laborers</u>   _____

B. Each sentence has an incorrect plural or possessive noun. Write the correct form of the noun in the space provided. Some plural nouns should be made possessive, and some possessives should be plural.

Example: Who has heard of Miss Farmers School of Cookery?   <u>*Farmer's*</u>

1. Student's learned to cook at the school.   _____
2. Fannie Farmer was known to her students and to other's.   _____
3. Miss Farmer wrote food article's for a magazine.   _____
4. For ten years, faithful readers' tried her recipes.   _____
5. In 1896 American cooks' were delighted to see her book.   _____
6. Some of the copies were printed at the authors expense.   _____
7. Fannie Farmer first cooked in her familys boarding house.   _____
8. Many people saw her cooking demonstration's.   _____
9. She used scientific methods' in her cooking.   _____
10. The measuring cup is only one of this teachers ideas.   _____
11. Even inexperienced cooks' could now work with ease.   _____
12. Bakers and chefs also followed this experts advice.   _____
13. Bakers' and chefs use her recipes today.   _____
14. Students recipes are often based on her recipes.   _____
15. Many modern recipe's are a result of her work.   _____

4 Identifying Verbs

A **verb** is a word that indicates *action* or *state of being* in a sentence. A verb can answer the question *what?* about the sentence topic or subject.

Example: The cookies *baked* in the oven. (*Baked* answers the question *what?* and indicates action.) The time *is* 2 P.M. (*Is* answers the question *time is what?* and indicates state of being.)

Action Verbs

talk	wash	sweep
buy	move	collect

Being Verbs

is	are	am
had	was	have

Verb phrases are made of *action* verbs and the *helping* verbs that appear with them. An action verb and its helping verb often indicate a *sense of timing* for the action. In other cases, helping verbs indicate *possibility*.

Example: You *tell* me. (Verb alone shows action that is about to occur but has not yet happened.)
You *are telling* me. (Verb with the helping verb *are* shows action that is happening at the moment.)
You *can tell* me. (Verb with the helping verb *can* shows the possibility of action.)

Verbs can be *active* or *passive*. An active verb is used when the subject is doing the action.

Passive verbs state the action directly. They emphasize another word in the sentence other than the subject that caused the action.

Example: Juanita *won* the Employee of the Month Award. (emphasizes Juanita)

Example: The Employee of the Month Award *was won* by Juanita. (emphasizes the award)

Examples of Helping Verbs

was	did	am	would	is
were	do	can	could	be
does	may	must	should	has

WORKPLACE APPLICATION

The following instructions were given to three workers.

1. Ted will bring parts in from the dock.

2. Rosetta will sort parts.

3. Angela will log in the numbers of any broken parts.

Name the action verbs and helping verbs in these instructions.

EXERCISE 24

What Is a Verb?

Some verbs show action. Other verbs link the subject with a word or words to show its state of being. State of being verbs include *is, am, was, were,* and so on.

A. Underline the verb in each sentence.

Example: Auto body mechanics <u>use</u> special tools on the job.

1. One such tool is a hydraulic machine.
2. A hydraulic machine repairs bent auto frames.
3. Some auto body mechanics cut through metal with torches.
4. Some hammer small dents with a special hammer.
5. Auto body mechanics may sometimes feel a little like sculptors.
6. Service station attendants also work with cars, sometimes making minor repairs.
7. An attendant may change a flat tire.
8. Some also tow stalled cars or trucks.
9. Attendants at this station check tire pressures.
10. They adjust the tire pressure if needed.

B. Write sentences using the words below as the subjects of the sentences.

Example: A mechanic   *A mechanic with special training may repair foreign cars.*

1. A dipstick _____
2. Service station managers _____
3. A hose _____
4. Dead batteries _____
5. The tires _____
6. His windshield wipers _____
7. A tune-up _____
8. The passenger side of the car _____
9. Her mechanic _____
10. The garage _____

Identifying Verbs

The verb in a sentence does one of two things. Some verbs indicate action. Other verbs link the subject with a word or words to show its state of being.

A. Underline the verb in each sentence.

Example: Archeologists <u>work</u> with very old things.

1. These "old things" are artifacts.
2. Artifacts were once used by people in the past.
3. This ancient vase is an artifact.
4. One archeologist found this old jewelry in a tomb.
5. It lay deep beneath the sands of the Egyptian desert.
6. Archeologists train for many years.
7. They attend college for four years or more.
8. They study archeology and other related fields.
9. Archeology students sometimes help with site excavation.
10. They gain valuable experience that way.

B. Complete the sentences with verbs from the verb list at the right.

Example: I ____*am*____ at the museum.

Verb List	
am	found
are	gather
was	touched
seem	buried

1. Crowds _____ outside the entrance.
2. The ancient treasures _____ a big attraction.
3. Archeologists _____ them in a pyramid.
4. The people _____ the objects with their pharaoh.
5. The objects _____ almost new.
6. The entrance to the tomb _____ a secret for thousands of years.
7. No one _____ these priceless objects in all that time.

EXERCISE 26

Action or State of Being

Some verbs tell what action is taking place. Other verbs join the subject to a word or words to show its state of being.

A. Underline the verb in each sentence.

Example: François-Eugene Vidocq <u>lived</u> a remarkable life.

1. François-Eugene Vidocq joined the police as an agent.
2. His occupation was a dangerous one.
3. Vidocq became extremely successful at this difficult work.
4. He used his talent for disguise.
5. He hid his identity.
6. Vidocq never looked suspicious to criminals.
7. Vidocq's masquerades fooled many thieves.
8. He was responsible for the capture of many criminals.

B. Write a complete sentence using each group of words listed below. The words can be used anywhere in your sentence. Underline the verb in each sentence.

Example: an old institution   *The Landmark Club is an old institution.*

   or   *An old institution in our town is The Landmark Club.*

1. many important activities _____

   _____

2. at the end of the week _____

   _____

3. talented employee _____

   _____

4. the smiling faces of coworkers _____

   _____

5. tall, imposing building _____

   _____

6. meetings with middle managers _____

   _____

EXERCISE 27

Identifying Verbs of Action or State of Being

Some verbs can be used to show either action or state of being.

A. Underline the verb in each sentence. The verb may indicate an action carried out by the subject, or it may show a state of being of the subject.

Example: The chef <u>tasted</u> his latest creation.   (action)

His unusual dish <u>tasted</u> wonderful.   (state of being)

1. A fire alarm sounded in our building.
2. Henry's excuse sounds unbelievable.
3. The aroma of fresh bread smelled delicious.
4. Thad smelled food cooking in the employee cafeteria.
5. Some of the truck drivers eventually grew sleepy.
6. We grow live plants in our office.
7. Come taste some of this delicious soup.
8. It tastes even better than the soup I make at home.
9. The breeze from the open window feels cool and refreshing.
10. Lionel felt bad about missing the meeting.

B. Write two sentences for each verb. Make the first verb indicate action and the second indicate a state of being.

Example: taste   *We each tasted a different salad.*

All of them tasted delicious.

1. grow _____

_____

2. sound _____

_____

3. smell _____

_____

4. feel _____

_____

Verb Phrases

A verb phrase is made up of a main verb and one or more helping verbs. Some helping verbs show past, present, or future. Others show different possibilities (can, should, must, etc.)

For each sentence below, underline the main verb once and the helping verb twice. Use the list of helping verbs at the right.

Example: The customers <u>are</u> <u>shopping</u> for groceries.

Helping Verbs
be
am
is
are
was
were
has
had
have
do
did
does
will
can
must
may
could
would
should

1. The employees had gotten to work early.
2. The store had just opened up for the day.
3. These customers were looking for several items.
4. Someone should help the customers.
5. They could not find either soup or spaghetti.
6. A clerk should know the right aisles for them.
7. They must ask him for some help.
8. The clerk is stacking cereal boxes on the shelf.
9. May I help you with something?
10. Would you direct me to the soup aisle, please?
11. The soups are shelved in the next aisle.
12. Does your store carry spaghetti too?
13. Sure, spaghetti is located right next to soups.
14. You have really helped us a lot.
15. The customers were turning the corner with their carts.
16. Did you get the soup and spaghetti yet?
17. We could look for them together.
18. Before long, the customers had found all their items.
19. They must now pay for the groceries.
20. The checker will add up their bills quickly.
21. She has already bagged the groceries.
22. One is handing the checker a ten-dollar bill.
23. They will be leaving here pretty soon.

EXERCISE 29

Identifying Verb Phrases

A verb phrase consists of a main verb and one or more helping verbs.

A. Underline the verb phrases in the sentences below.

Example: Scientists <u>are developing</u> new ideas.

1. Left-handed people were considered dangerous in the past.
2. Some people have come to use both hands equally well.
3. Which hand do you use most often?
4. Facts about hand choices are being studied.
5. Scientists have been discovering many interesting facts about this subject.
6. Sometimes a left-handed person is called a southpaw.
7. About 85 percent of the world's population is described as right-handed.
8. Left-handed people may perform better on tests of artistic ability.
9. This is supported by examples of many famous left-handers.

B. Add helping verbs to each main verb below, and write a sentence with the verb phrase. Use an office activity as the setting for your sentences.

Example: keyed _Marty has keyed the report._

1. arriving _____

    _____

2. entering _____

    _____

3. stayed _____

    _____

4. working _____

    _____

5. participated _____

    _____

Reviewing Verb Phrases

A verb phrase contains a main verb and one or more helping verbs. (Remember that some verbs and verb phrases have other words between them.)

A. Write the verb or verb phrase in the space provided. The number in parentheses indicates how many words are in the phrase.

Example: The Olympics began years ago. (1)   _____ *began* _____

1. The modern Olympics date back to the last century.   (1) _____
2. They were started by a French man in 1896.   (2)   _____
3. Winter games were not held until 1924.   (2)   _____
4. Today the Olympics have become a big business.   (2)   _____
5. They are shown on television all over the world.   (2)   _____
6. Many sports have been added to the games.   (3)   _____
7. Athletes from different countries can be seen.   (3)   _____
8. Americans have been participating for years.   (3)   _____
9. They are often found among the medal winners.   (2)   _____
10. The Olympics will remain popular.   (2)   _____

B. Underline each helping verb once and each main verb twice.

Example: Have you heard of fast-food restaurants?

1. Most people have eaten at such restaurants.
2. They are seen in every small town and large city.
3. Fast-food restaurants can be a good investment.
4. Owners have been known to make a lot of money.
5. Could you take an interest in a restaurant career?
6. Usually you must save enough money to buy a franchise.
7. You may also need courses in restaurant management.
8. You will have your hands full as an owner.
9. Even so, running a fast-food restaurant might be the career for you.

Active and Passive Verbs

Active verbs are used more often than passive verbs because they express action directly and naturally.

A. Underline the verb in each sentence. If the verb is active, write *A* on the line. If it is passive, write *P*.

Example: We <u>decided</u> to have a pancake breakfast to raise money.   *A*

1. The project was accepted enthusiastically by the Elks Club.   _____
2. First, we divided the big job into smaller jobs.   _____
3. Then we settled the question of work distribution.   _____
4. Ingredients for the pancakes were bought by one group.   _____
5. Flour, eggs, and milk were purchased in bulk.   _____
6. Another group looked for a breakfast location.   _____
7. The school gave us permission to use the cafeteria.   _____
8. Then the event was advertised by one of the work groups.   _____
9. They notified everyone, even the newspapers.   _____
10. The breakfast was cooked to perfection by our experts.   _____
11. It was served with grace by the members.   _____

B. Rewrite the sentences below, changing the passive verbs to active verbs.

Example: The breakfast was thought to be a success by everyone.
          Everyone thought that the breakfast was a success.

1. Any burnt food was thrown out by the cooks.

   _____

2. A review of the breakfast was conducted by our club.

   _____

3. A few improvements were suggested by several people.

   _____

4. The money was counted by the treasurer.

   _____

5. The breakfast was considered a triumph by the club.

   _____

5 Verb Tenses

Present, Past, and Future Verbs   Verbs are action words. Action can be taking place now, in the *present*. Actions may have taken place in the *past*. Actions may take place in the *future*. We call these action words present, past, and future verbs. They take place in present, past, or future **tense,** or *time*.

Verbs have **principal parts** from which the present, past, and future tenses are made. Changes in the verb form and its spelling indicate the verb's tense, or time.

A verb's principal part is the verb in its simplest form. Changes to the principal part may include adding helping verbs or endings to the principal part.

Principal Part	**Past**
pour	poured, have poured
change	changed, have changed
like	liked, have liked

Present	**Future**
pour, am pouring	will pour, shall pour
change, am changing	will change, shall change
like, am liking	will like, shall like

When writing sentences or paragraphs (several sentences with the same topic), it is important for all the verbs to be in the same tense. Look at the example on page 50:

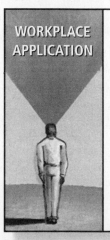

WORKPLACE APPLICATION

How do the errors in verb tense create problems in communication? Can you think of times when errors in verb tense have caused problems in communication in your job?

_____

_____

_____

Example: Clara <u>took</u> her apron out of the locker and <u>put</u> it on. She <u>combed</u> her hair.

She is <u>putting</u> on a hair net. The hair net <u>keeps</u> Clara's hair covered.

Clara <u>will go</u> to the kitchen. She <u>is ready</u> for her customers. She <u>went</u> to her station.

The above paragraph has eight verbs and verb phrases. Some are in the past tense, some in the present tense, and some in the future tense. Because the verbs use different tenses, we do not know when this action is or was really taking place.

A verb can indicate different times, or tenses: present, past, or future. When a verb changes to a different tense, it may also change its form and spelling. The changes are made to the principal part of the verb. The following rules explain how to write present, past, or future tense verbs.

Past Tense

- **Rule 1**   Add *-ed* to the principal part of most verbs to indicate past tense *(look, looked; print, printed; protect, protected)*.

- **Rule 2**   If a verb's principal part ends in *-e*, add *-d* to indicate past tense *(save, saved; bake, baked; place, placed)*.

- **Rule 3**   If a verb's principal part ends in *-y*, the *-y* almost always changes to *-i* before adding *-ed (carry, carried; hurry, hurried; try, tried)*.

- **Rule 4**   Some verbs change the spelling of the principal part to indicate past tense *(come; came; swim, swam; tell, told)*

Present Tense

- **Rule 1**   Many verbs use their principal part with *-s* for some forms of the present tense *(talk, talks; run, runs; find, finds)*.

- **Rule 2**   Some verbs add *-ing* or *-ing* with a helping verb to the principal part for some forms of the present tense *(talk, talking; is talking, am talking; find, finding, is finding, am finding)*.

- **Rule 3**   If the verb ends in *-n, -m, -p, -b, -g*, or *-t*, the *-n, -m, -p, -b, -g*, or *-t* is often doubled before adding *-ing* to the principal part for some forms of the present tense *(run, running, am running; hum, humming, am humming; clip, clipping, am clipping; sob, sobbing, am sobbing; log, logging, am logging; put, putting, am putting)*.

Future Tense

- **Rule 1**   Most verbs use *will* or *shall* as helping verbs to show future time *(will run, shall run; will clip, shall clip)*.

- **Rule 2**   A few verbs use *will* or *shall* with *be* to form a special form of future time which shows expectation. In these forms, the *-ing* form of the present tense verb may be used *(will be running, shall be running; will be clipping, shall be clipping)*. The past tense of the verb may also be used *(will be done, shall be done; will be gone, shall be gone)*.

WORKPLACE APPLICATION

Can you change the tense and the spelling of the principal part of this sentence to show the action in different time periods?

Example: Tom is working on his computer.

_____

_____

_____

Regular Verbs   Most verbs add *-ed* to show past tense. These verbs are called *regular verbs*. Some regular verbs also show a special form of the past. They show the past as seen from the present.

Regular verbs can use their principal parts with *have* or *has*. This shows that an action that took place in the past is now being remembered, or recalled, in the present. Sometimes the spelling of the principal part is changed when adding *have* or *has* to make this special form of the past tense.

Example: Janet <u>sent</u> her report to Mr. Jones. (*Sent* shows past tense.)

Janet <u>has sent</u> her report to Mr. Jones. (*Has sent* shows past tense as seen from, or recalled in, the present.)

Roberto <u>took</u> the day off. (*Took* shows past tense.)

Roberto <u>had taken</u> the day off. (*Had taken* shows past tense as seen from, or recalled in, the present.)

Have and *Has* With Regular Verbs

- **Rule 1**   To show the past tense as seen from the present, use *have* or *has* with the past tense of the verb (*have liked, has liked*).
- **Rule 2**   Follow the rules for forming past tense verbs from their principal parts when using them with *have* or *has* (*printed, have printed; baked, have baked; hurry, have hurried; enjoyed, has enjoyed; planned, has planned*).

Regular Verbs

Present	Past	Past With *Has, Have*
envy	envied	has (have) envied
snip	snipped	has (have) snipped
ski	skied	has (have) skied

Irregular Verbs   Verbs that do *not* add *-ed* to their principal part to show the past are called *irregular verbs*. Irregular verbs can show the past tense with or without *have* or *has*. But they are irregular because their spelling sometimes changes to show each of these forms.

Have and *Has* With Irregular Verbs

- **Rule 1**   To form the past tense and past tense with *have* for irregular verbs, you may have to change the spelling of the principal part of the verb.
- **Rule 2**   All three forms of irregular verbs may be different.

Irregular Verbs

Present	Past	Past With *Has*, *Have*
give	gave	has (have) given
swim	swam	has (have) swum
bring	brought	has (have) brought
teach	taught	has (have) taught
fly	flew	has (have) flown

WORKPLACE APPLICATION

This message was seen on a humorous poster:
Clean up your own mess. Your mother <u>have quit</u> working at this office.
She got tired of picking up after you!
Is the underlined verb used correctly? How might you change it to read differently?

_____

_____

_____

EXERCISE 32

Present, Past, and Future Verb Tenses

Active verbs can indicate action that is happening (present action), did happen (past action), or will happen (future action).

A. Underline the verb in each sentence. Write *present*, *past*, or *future* for the verb tense in the space provided.

Example: People <u>poured</u> into California in 1849.   _____*past*_____

1. Miners claimed land in the foothills.   _____
2. They all wanted to find gold.   _____
3. Most of these people remained in California.   _____
4. They considered it their home.   _____
5. Today people still look for California gold.   _____
6. First, they find a stream.   _____
7. They place sand from its rocky bed into a pan.   _____
8. Next, they add water to the sand and pebbles.   _____
9. They swirl the pan gently and slowly.   _____
10. Any flakes of gold will sink to the bottom.   _____
11. Who will discover some gold in their pans?   _____
12. Who will strike it rich?   _____

B. Rewrite each sentence, changing the verb tense to the time given in parentheses.

Example: Visitors enjoy "gold country."   (future)

   <u>Visitors will enjoy "gold country."</u>

1. Many people started their visit at Coloma.   (future)

   _____

2. Town names recalled miners' lives of long ago.   (present)

   _____

3. Rough and Ready will attract adventurers.   (past)

   _____

4. Only a few Gold Rush towns will remain.   (present)

   _____

EXERCISE 33

Using Verb Tenses

Verbs indicate the present, past, or future.

A. Underline each verb and write its verb tense in the space provided.

Example: Life <u>will change</u> in the future.   *future*

1. In the past, American families depended on coal.   _____

2. Today more families burn oil than coal.   _____

3. Energy experts worry about this fact.   _____

4. We import oil from foreign countries.   _____

5. The price of oil is high.   _____

6. Coal will cost much less.   _____

7. We have a great deal of coal right here in America.   _____

8. It lies beneath the surface of the land in many places.   _____

9. Some people say that coal will become more important
   to all of us.   _____

10. Years ago most homes had coal furnaces.   _____

11. Americans will heat their homes with coal once again.   _____

B. Complete each sentence. Write the verb and its correct tense in the space
   provided. Use the verb and tense indicated in parentheses.

Example: Coal _____*was*_____ important years ago.   (<u>be</u>, past)

1. Many houses _____ a window at ground level.   (<u>include</u>, past)

2. This window _____ above a bin in the basement.   (<u>be</u>, past)

3. Today there _____ no bins. (<u>be</u>, present)

4. A truck _____ the coal down a metal chute.   (<u>deliver</u>, past)

5. This chute _____ through the window into a coal bin.   (<u>pass</u>, past)

6. You _____ coal from the bin into the furnace.   (<u>shovel</u>, past)

7. Today home furnaces _____ oil or gas.   (<u>burn</u>, present)

8. Tomorrow, perhaps, they _____ coal again.   (<u>use</u>, future)

9. People _____ harder with these furnaces.   (<u>work</u>, future)

10. Our lives _____ like those of people years ago.   (<u>be</u>, future)

11. _____ coal mining _____ important again?   (<u>be</u>, future)

EXERCISE 34

Learning More About Verb Tenses

Verbs indicate the past, present, or future.

A. Underline the verb in each sentence. Then write *past*, *present*, or *future* for the correct verb in the space provided.

Example: I <u>collect</u> folk stories.   *present*

1. I started with my grandparents.   _____

2. They remember many old tales.   _____

3. You will recognize some of them.   _____

4. Some stories change over time.   _____

5. People substituted names and places.   _____

6. Usually the basic plot remains the same.   _____

7. My husband recorded the stories.   _____

8. I will photograph the storytellers.   _____

9. My grandfather uses gestures with his stories.   _____

10. He will tell us more stories tomorrow.   _____

B. In a paragraph, all the verbs should have the same verb tense—past, present, or future. Rewrite the paragraph using consistent tenses.

   Dark clouds filled the sky. The wind increases in speed. The lifeguard whistled the swimmers out of the lake. Large waves crash noisily on the beach. The first drops dotted the pale sand. People quickly scrambled for cover. With blankets over their heads for protection, they will run for their cars.

EXERCISE 35

Using Verb Tenses in Sentences

Verbs show present, past, or future action, or state of being.

A. Underline the verb in each sentence, and tell whether it indicates the past, present, or future.

Example: A geriatric aide <u>works</u> with elderly people.   _____*present*_____

1. Geriatric aides often work in nursing homes.   _____

2. Some are employed in retirement homes or day care
   centers for the elderly.   _____

3. My sister was a geriatric aide in a nursing home.   _____

4. She sometimes tells me stories about it.   _____

5. She cared for up to 20 patients at a time.   _____

6. Her typical day brought many surprises.   _____

7. One couple married at the nursing home.   _____

8. They will celebrate their fifth anniversary next month.   _____

9. They are planning a special party.   _____

10. The nursing home staff will provide decorations and
    a cake.   _____

B. Rewrite each sentence. Change the verb to the tense indicated in parentheses.

Example: My grandmother rides a bike every day.   (future)

       My grandmother will ride a bike every day.

1. She buys a new bicycle.   (past)

   _____

2. Grandmother wanted to keep fit.   (present)

   _____

3. She enjoys the scenery around her retirement home.   (future)

   _____

4. I go riding with her on weekends.   (future)

   _____

5. I will buy a used bike myself.   (past)

   _____

EXERCISE 36

Spelling Present and Past Verb Tenses

The spelling of some verbs changes when the verb tense changes to show differences in time—present, past, and future.

A. Write the past tense form of each verb below.

Example: learn _____learned_____

1. submit _____
2. like _____
3. mop _____
4. erase _____
5. try _____
6. handle _____

7. photocopy _____
8. gaze _____
9. flap _____
10. deny _____
11. apply _____
12. beep _____

B. Rewrite each sentence using the verb and tense shown in parentheses.

Example: Jim _____ about his coworker's health.   (<u>inquire</u>, past)

   Jim inquired about his coworker's health. _____

1. Meg _____ she must work more efficiently.   (<u>realize,</u> present)

   _____

2. Sometimes she _____ too much.   (<u>hurry</u>, present)

   _____

3. Then she _____ unnecessary mistakes.   (<u>make</u>, present)

   _____

4. Meg _____ to complete her project by Wednesday.   (<u>plan</u>, past)

   _____

5. She _____ about finishing it on time.   (<u>worry</u>, past)

   _____

6. Luckily, she _____ it on schedule.   (<u>complete</u>, past)

   _____

EXERCISE 37

Being Consistent With Verb Tenses

The verbs in a paragraph should be consistent in relationship to time—present, past, or future.

A. Rewrite the circled verbs in this business letter so that they are consistent with the underlined verbs in each sentence. Use the spaces provided below.

January 16, _____

Ali Nihm
Box 1234
Silver City Station, PA 18876

Dear Ali:

Congratulations on your appointment to the future Machine Design Committee. We were happy that you **(1)** are chosen. I hoped that I **(2)** can work with you someday. I **(3)** want to learn more about robotics, and I **(4)** know you were the person to ask.

(5) I know that you currently worked on a project involving robotics. Robotics **(6)** was an exciting field to be in. The future of our company **(7)** depends on learned how to work faster, safer, and more efficiently. Your experience with robotics is one thing we **(8)** hoped to learn from.

Our first meeting will be on March 12, and I **(9)** welcomed your participation. I **(10)** have sent you a memo that will tell you more about the meeting location and time.

Sincerely,

Sandra Smith
Superintendent of Operations

Paragraph 1	Paragraph 2	Paragraph 3
1. _____	5. _____	9. _____
2. _____	6. _____	10. _____
3. _____	7. _____	
4. _____	8. _____	

Two Forms of Past Tense Verbs

Verbs have different forms. One is present, one is past, and one is a special form of the past. It uses *have* or *has* before the verb. This indicates that the action happened more than once in the past. It can also indicate past action that is being related to the present.

A. Write the past form of the verb in parentheses with *has* or *have* in the space provided.

Example: Cassie (order) something by mail.   _____*has ordered*_____

1. Leon (ask) her what it was.   _____
2. We (guess) many times.   _____
3. A truck (deliver) Cassie's package.   _____
4. We (gather) around Cassie's desk.   _____
5. Cassie (open) the mysterious package.   _____
6. She (display) her new printer.   _____
7. We (enjoy) using the new printer.   _____

B. Write a sentence of your own with the form of the verb in parentheses.

Example: mention (past with *have* or *has*)
                 *Janet has mentioned several job openings.*_____

1. answer   (past) _____

   _____

2. hope   (past with *have* or *has*) _____

   _____

3. earn   (present) _____

   _____

4. reply   (past) _____

   _____

5. hurry   (past with *have* or *has*) _____

   _____

6. dip (past with *have* or *has*) _____

   _____

EXERCISE 39

Principal Parts of Regular Verbs

Verbs have basic forms called principal parts. These principal parts can be changed to show time changes in the action or state of being.

A. Complete the chart of principal parts of verbs by writing the missing present, past, or past with *has* forms.

Present	Past	Past With *Has*
Example: carry	carried	has carried
1. _____	*admired*	
2. *worry*		
3. _____		*has cleaned*
4. *shelve*		
5. _____	*prepared*	
6. *hurry*		
7. _____		*has stirred*
8. *stop*		
9. _____	*shipped*	

B. Write the principal part of the verb in parentheses in the space provided. Make sure to spell each correctly.

Example: Vic has _____*worked*_____ (work past with *has*) before.

1. Terri _____ (<u>drum</u>, past) her fingers on her desk.

2. Val and Ann _____ (<u>like</u>, present) my presentation.

3. We have _____ (<u>complete</u>, past with *have*) the project.

4. Joel has _____ (<u>mail</u>, past with *has*) my letter.

5. Dan _____ (<u>sip</u>, past) his coffee slowly.

6. The supervisors _____ (<u>call</u>, past) team meetings.

7. I have _____ (<u>push</u>, past with *have*) back the deadline.

8. The secretary _____ (<u>nudge</u>, past) Harold's desk.

EXERCISE 40

Using Principal Parts of Regular Verbs in Sentences

The present and past tense forms of a verb are made from its principal parts.

A. Underline the verb in each sentence. Then write the principal parts of that verb: the present, the present with *-ing* and a helping verb, the past, and the past with *has* or *have*.

Example: The swimmer <u>walked</u> to the pool.

<u>*walk   (is) walking   walked   (has, have) walked*</u>

1. She started her laps.

   _____

2. She continued her pace.

   _____

3. Her arms ached.

   _____

4. Still, she glided along.

   _____

5. Stamina helps in swimming.

   _____

B. Change the verb in parentheses to the past with *has* or *have* and write it in the space provided.

Example: The swimmer _____*has trained*_____ hard.   (train)

1. She _____ many times.   (succeed)

2. She _____ a few times, too.   (fail)

3. She _____ with each attempt.   (struggle)

4. Fans _____ her efforts.   (applaud)

5. They _____ her set records.   (watch)

6. She _____ daily.   (practice)

7. The athlete _____ from the cold.   (suffer)

8. She _____ pain.   (endure)

9. Her coaches _____ her.   (prepare)

10. They _____ about her.   (care)

EXERCISE 41

Irregular Verbs

Verbs that do not end in the letters -*ed* to show the past are irregular verbs. These verbs have special past forms. The spelling of these words can change slightly or entirely.

A. Write the correct form of the verb in parentheses in the space provided.

Example: My day _____*began*_____ with a problem.   (begin)

1. I have _____ one chewed sock.   (find)
2. It has _____ me a while to get dressed.   (take)
3. I _____ my breakfast in a hurry.   (eat)
4. I _____ our dog an angry look.   (give)
5. He has _____ to chew things lately.   (begin)
6. I have _____ to him several times.   (speak)

B. Circle the verb in parentheses that completes the sentence correctly.

Example: I (have given, have gave) her my new address.

1. Jerry (seen, saw) his old friend Tony across the room.
2. Mrs. Brown (has spoken, has spoke) to her boss.
3. Her boss (done, has done) what Mrs. Brown suggested.
4. I (have wrote, have written) a letter to my personnel manager.
5. His letter to me (come, came) in the interoffice mail yesterday.

C. Write a sentence for each verb, using the past tense with *has* or *have*.

Example: hear   _Dorothy has heard Dave's excuses before._

1. choose _____

   _____

2. teach _____

   _____

3. go _____

   _____

EXERCISE 42

Practice Using Irregular Verbs

Irregular verbs do not use -ed to show past tense. Sometimes the spelling of an irregular verb is different from the spelling of its principal part.

A. Underline the correct form of the verb in each sentence.

Example: My family once (run, <u>ran</u>) a greenhouse.

1. We (grow, grew) flowers, plants, and shrubs for the customers we served.
2. We (keep, kept) plants through the winter, because we had a heated greenhouse.
3. One day the motor on our furnace (blow, blew) up.
4. My father (drive, drove) to town to get a new motor.
5. He (bring, brought) the new motor into the basement and replaced the old motor.
6. His quick work (keep, kept) all our plants alive.
7. Mom (say, said) that if he had been longer, many of the plants would have died.
8. I (know, knew) my dad would not let us lose our business.

B. Underline the verb in each sentence. Then write three sentences using the present tense, past tense, and past tense with *have* or *has*.

Example: We lifeguards <u>swim</u> as a part of our job.

1. _I swim in a pool._
2. _You swam in the ocean._
3. _I have swum every day this summer._

1. Some children run around the pool.

   _____

   _____

2. In the summer, the sun sets at about 9 o'clock at night.

   _____

   _____

3. At the beach, we hear the seagulls overhead.

   _____

   _____

EXERCISE 43

More Irregular Verbs

The past tense forms of some verbs are irregular. They do not end in -ed. Many have spellings different from their present tense form.

A. Complete the chart of principal parts of irregular verbs by writing the missing forms. Be sure to spell them correctly. Use *has* with the special past form in the third column.

Present	Past	Past With *Has*
Example: drive	*drove*	*has driven*
1. take		
2. speak		
3. choose		
4. know		
5. grow		
6. fly		
7. find		
8. think		
9. bring		

B. Write the form of the underlined verb given in parentheses.

Example: The cat <u>fly</u> out the door.   (past)   *flew*

1. I <u>give</u> the cat a glare.   (past with *have*)   _____
2. I <u>say</u> a few unkind words.   (past)   _____
3. She <u>choose</u> not to listen.   (past with *has*)   _____
4. The cat <u>break</u> another vase.   (past)   _____
5. I <u>find</u> all of the pieces.   (past with *have*)   _____
6. It <u>take</u> me hours to locate them.   (past)   _____
7. At first, I <u>think</u> about fixing it.   (past)   _____
8. Soon I <u>grow</u> weary from the task.   (past)   _____

Review of Irregular Verbs

The past tense forms of some verbs are irregular. They do not end in *-ed*. Some of them have different spellings.

A. Underline the correct past tense form of the verb in parentheses in each sentence.

Example: I was (chose, <u>chosen</u>) to give a speech at Sam's retirement party.

1. At first I eagerly (dive, dove) into the task.

2. My enthusiasm faded when I (had realized, realized) I did not know how to write a speech.

3. I (began, begun) to panic when, two days before the party, I still had no speech.

4. I had almost (given, gave) up, but on the last day I got an idea.

5. I (written, wrote) about Sam as a person, not just an employee.

6. Sam (gave, given) his all to his job, and he was an excellent worker.

7. But it was Sam's personality that everyone (felt, feeled) was his greatest asset.

8. Sam (forsaken, forsook) his own pleasure to give pleasure to others.

9. He (bringed, brought) flowers to coworkers' homes when they were sick.

10. He (held, holded) positions on committees to which no one else wanted to be appointed.

11. Sam always (putted, put) others first.

12. In my speech, I (gave, given) Sam the respect and appreciation he deserved.

B. Complete each sentence with the correct past tense form of the verb in parentheses.

Example: Our supervisor _____*found*_____ someone to work the evening shift. (find)

1. He had _____ hard to convince me to do it, but I just could not. (fight)

2. My best friend had _____ in from Chicago.   (fly)

3. I had _____ us tickets to the championship game.   (get)

4. I was happy things had _____ out for both myself and my supervisor. (work)

6   Using Verb Forms Correctly

It is important to use verb forms correctly. Verb forms indicate timing. Their incorrect use changes the meaning of the sentence and results in poor communication.

Some verbs, like irregular verbs and the verb *to be*, use different forms to show their tense or time. In some of these forms, a second verb is added to indicate the tense. This second verb is called a *helping verb*. Verbs like *will, shall, have, has, had*, etc., are helping verbs. Other forms of the verb *to be* follow no special rules. You will need to become familiar with the forms of the verb *to be* by using them in sentences.

The Verb *to Be*

Present	Past	Future	Past With *Have, Has*
am	was	will be	have been
are	were	shall be	has been
is			

The Verb *to Have*

Present	Past	Future	Past With *Have, Has*
have	had	will have	have had
has		shall have	has had

The Verb *to Do*

Present	Past	Future	Past With *Have, Has*
do	did	will do	have done
does		shall do	has done

Verb Contractions With *Not*   Many forms of the verb *to be* with a helping verb can be used as *contractions* (a single word made from two words, by adding an apostrophe to replace the omitted letters). When you make contractions for these verbs, remember to use the form of the verb *to be* that shows the correct meaning of the sentence. Make the form of the verb agree with the subject of the sentence.

Example: This machine (don't, <u>doesn't</u>) work properly. (The noun in the sentence, *machine,* is singular. In the verb contraction, use the form of *do* that agrees with singular nouns [*does*], not the form that agrees with plural nouns [*do*].)

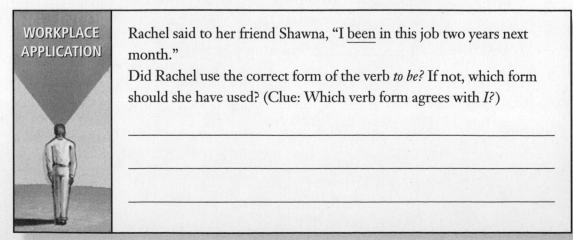

WORKPLACE APPLICATION

Rachel said to her friend Shawna, "I <u>been</u> in this job two years next month."
Did Rachel use the correct form of the verb *to be?* If not, which form should she have used? (Clue: Which verb form agrees with *I?*)

_____

_____

_____

Forms of the Verb *to Be*

The verb *to be* can be used as a main verb or as a helping verb to modify or change the main verb. Helping verbs are often used to indicate tense.

A. Underline the verbs and the verb phrases below that are, or include, forms of *to be*. Then write whether the form *to be* is a *main verb* or a *helping verb*.

Example: Meetings <u>are</u> turning into a way of life for many   *helping verb*
businesspeople.

1. Many employees are spending several hours or more per day in meetings.   _____

2. Some are improving the quality of the time they spend in meetings.   _____

3. One way they do this is by listening more carefully.   _____

4. They are listening for ideas, not just words.   _____

5. Evaluating and judging are left for later.   _____

6. These employees are striving to resist jumping to conclusions.   _____

7. Each one is careful to allow the meeting leader to make his or her point before asking questions.   _____

B. Circle the correct form of the verb in parentheses.

Example: A new break room (being, (is being) built for our office.

1. There (be, will be) a meeting in McKnight's office.

2. The benches and the chairs (are, be) in the basement.

3. More file cabinets (being, are being) installed.

4. I (been, have been) wanting to go on lunch break.

5. I (am, be) taking my youngest daughter to the doctor.

6. There you (be, can be) listening to music while waiting.

7. That young man (is, be) just starting to prepare the meeting room.

8. If I (am, be) quick, I can make it back from the doctor in time for the meeting.

EXERCISE 46

Using Different Forms of *to Be*

Use the forms of the verb *to be* correctly. Refer to the chart on page 66 to help you make each choice.

A. Choose the correct form of the verb *to be* in parentheses, and write it in the space provided.

Example: That (be, is) an interesting zoo.   _____is_____

1. (Are, Is) you planning to bring your children soon?   _____
2. You (be, will be) surprised at some of the changes.   _____
3. The animals (is, are) no longer in cages.   _____
4. Such treatment (be, was) not healthful for the animals.   _____
5. The zoo (been, has been) building natural enclosures.   _____
6. Each enclosure (be, will be) a different environment.   _____
7. Many new homes (been, have been) finished already.   _____
8. There (be, is) plenty of room for each animal.   _____
9. The animals (were, was) very cramped in the old cages.   _____
10. The monkeys (are, is) living in synthetic-made valleys.   _____
11. The lions (is, are) roaming across an artificial plain.   _____
12. The animals (are being, being) treated very well.   _____

B. Write a sentence for each form of the verb *to be*.

1. am _____
2. is _____
3. are _____
4. was _____
5. were _____
6. will be _____
7. are being _____
8. was being _____

EXERCISE 47

More Practice Using Forms of *to Be*

Use the forms of the verb *to be* correctly, use the correct verb tense, and use the proper verb number (singular or plural).

A. Underline the verb in parentheses that completes each sentence below correctly.

Example: Employers (is, <u>are</u>) interested in hiring the best person for a job.

1. Most employers (are, be) looking for certain work skills and traits.
2. One such skill (were, is) communication.
3. (Am, Are) the person's speaking and writing skills adequate?
4. If they (ain't, aren't), the employer may not hire that person.
5. (Being, Been) able to set goals and complete tasks is another needed skill.
6. The ability (to be, to have been) flexible and get along with others is also important.

B. Rewrite each sentence using the correct form of *to be*.

Example: This employer are interested in hiring very creative people.

   This employer is interested in hiring very creative people.

1. Her company had always been known for finding solutions to unusual problems.

   _____

   _____

2. She were also looking for someone with leadership qualities.

   _____

   _____

3. She found that person; José have just been offered the position of project manager.

   _____

   _____

4. In addition to creativity, the ability to work independently will certainly have been important in this job.

   _____

   _____

EXERCISE 48

The Verb Forms of *to Have*

Use the forms of the verb *to have* correctly.

A. Underline the verb that completes each sentence correctly.

Example: (Has, <u>Have</u>) you ever strung an archer's bow?

1. My friend (has, have) set up the round archery target.
2. I (hasn't, haven't) mastered the bow, but I'm learning.
3. My friend (has, have) had me use his protective glove.
4. My lower arm (has, have) been protected by a leather sleeve.
5. Now I (has, have) the tight string on my fingertips.
6. I (has, have) practiced my position many times.
7. "You (has, have) plenty of time," Matt told me.
8. "I (has, have) moved the target closer to you," he said.
9. I (haven't, hasn't) been this nervous in a long time.

B. Rewrite each sentence, using the correct form of *to have*.

Example: Target arrows has rounded tips.

Target arrows have rounded tips.

1. I think I should of worn my glasses.

   _____

2. My friend Matt have given me valuable hints.

   _____

3. Each shot have a different quality.

   _____

4. I has heard the sounds of arrows.

   _____

5. Some arrows has a hiss like a snake.

   _____

6. My whole arm have begun to tremble.

   _____

7. My arrow must of landed by the target.

   _____

EXERCISE 49

The Verb Forms of *to Do*

Use the forms of the verb *to do* correctly.

A. Underline the verb in parentheses that completes each sentence below correctly.

Example: He (don't, <u>doesn't</u>) know much about Benjamin Franklin.

1. What (do, does) Rico know about Benjamin Franklin?
2. (Didn't, Doesn't) he live during the eighteenth century?
3. Yes, he (do, did) live during an important era in history.
4. (Do, Does) you know that he was a writer and an inventor?
5. His education (do, did) not end when he left school.
6. He (didn't, don't) concentrate on only one kind of work.
7. Instead, he and his friends (had done, had did) many things.
8. Franklin (did, do) sign the Declaration of Independence.
9. (Does, Do) Stan know that Franklin signed the Constitution?
10. Stan (don't, doesn't) know that!

B. Write *do*, *does*, *did*, or *done* in the space provided.

Example: Franklin ____*did*____ organize the first American hospital.

1. What else _____ you know about Franklin?
2. Benjamin Franklin _____ some work as a printer.
3. His family _____ live in Philadelphia.
4. We _____ know that he invented bifocals.
5. He had _____ that to help people see better.
6. _____ you know what bifocals are?
7. _____ he also invent the lightning rod?
8. Today Franklin's picture _____ appear on stamps.
9. I _____ believe Franklin was a civic leader.
10. I think Franklin _____ serve as a deputy postmaster.
11. _____ he serve as our ambassador to France?
12. Franklin had _____ much for his nation.

EXERCISE 50

Forms of the Verbs *to Do* and *to Have*

Use the correct forms of *to do* and *to have*.

A. Underline the correct verb form in each sentence.

Example: They (are having, having) a fish boil.

1. Ken Koch (done, has) caught a lot of fish.
2. He (has, have) a fish boil for his friends every year.
3. His wife (done, did) the menu planning.
4. The fish, potatoes, and vegetables (having, have) been put into a huge kettle of boiling water.
5. The fire under the kettle (has, did) a very high temperature.
6. Kevin and Gordon (done, were doing) the cooking.
7. The fish and vegetables (have done, have) boiled for several hours.
8. Ken said he (had, having) two helpings of food.
9. I know that Ken (did have, done had) three helpings.
10. Everyone (did, done) work hard.
11. The sky (has, did) gotten darker.
12. We all (have, having) to go inside.
13. The rain (did, has) started.

B. Complete each sentence below using the verb in parentheses. Remember to use helping verbs when needed.

Example: (done)   They ____*have done*____ all the work.

1. (did)   We _____ the best we could.
2. (having)   Who _____ trouble?
3. (had)   Tanya _____ her hands full.
4. (done)   She _____ everything so well.
5. (does)   She _____ like parties.

EXERCISE 51

Verb Contractions With *Not*

A contraction is one word made from two words. Most contractions are formed by adding the ending -*n't* to the principal part of the verb.

A. Write contractions for the following verbs and *not*.

Example: is not _____*isn't*_____

1. cannot _____
2. will not _____
3. would not _____
4. have not _____
5. were not _____
6. is not _____
7. does not _____

8. are not _____
9. do not _____
10. did not _____
11. could not _____
12. had not _____
13. has not _____
14. was not _____

B. Write a contraction that will change each sentence to an opposite meaning.

Example: The plane did leave on time.   _____*didn't*_____

1. We were surprised.   _____
2. The fog did lift for several hours.   _____
3. The planes are very large.   _____
4. Some of them do have radar.   _____
5. The trip to the coast is far.   _____
6. Still, you can get there easily by car.   _____
7. We have been delayed often.   _____
8. Our friends will worry.   _____
9. The fog does bother them.   _____
10. We should have long to wait.   _____
11. I was a bit worried.   _____
12. The pilot had seemed concerned.   _____
13. Thunderstorms were around us at that time.   _____

7   Troublesome Verb Pairs

Some verbs seem to have "twins." These "twins" may look or sound alike, but they are not the same. They have different meanings. It is important to recognize **troublesome verb pairs** and to choose the correct verb for the meaning of each sentence.

It is often helpful to think of interesting ways to remember troublesome verb pairs; for example, lay means "to put down"; *lie* means "to recline," or "to tell a falsehood."

Another example is the verb *set*. It is often confused with the verb *sit*. (*Sit* means "to rest on." *Set* means "to be placed.") But over time has gained new meanings, some of which are similar to the verb *sit*. Can you think of some things that *set?*

To use troublesome verb pairs correctly, use a dictionary. Look up the meaning of each verb in the pair. You may want to write the verbs and their meanings in a notebook to keep for reference. Practice using each verb correctly in a sentence. Examples of proper usage for some troublesome verb pairs are shown below.

Troublesome Verb Pairs

affect, effect	adapt, adopt	accept, except
ensure, insure	teach, learn	let, leave
lay, lie	bring, take	rise, raise
can, may	lend, borrow	set, sit

Bring me the report, please. (*Bring* means "to cause to come to or toward.")

I will *take* the report to the meeting. (*Take* means "grasping *or* carrying.")

Can you get this work done on time? (*Can* indicates ability.)

May I go with you? (*May* indicates possibility and asks permission.)

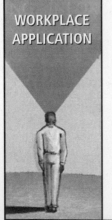

WORKPLACE APPLICATION

You have been offered a new job. Congratulations! But first, you will have to either *accept* or *except* it. Which will you do? Choose carefully. The choice of verb you use will be very important to you.

_____

_____

_____

Troublesome Verb Pairs

Some verb pairs are confusing because they have similar meanings or because they look alike.

A. Underline the verb in parentheses that completes each sentence correctly.

Example: The merchandise (<u>lay</u>, lie) on the counter.

1. The customer (set, sat) down another item.
2. She (lays, lie) the camera next to the film.
3. She (let, left) the counter to look for a special camera lens.
4. The clerk (leave, let) her try out a sample lens.
5. The woman's baby (set, sat) quietly nearby in a stroller.
6. Finally the woman (laid, lain) out all her purchases.
7. "(Leave, Let) me have these for now," she said. "I will be back for more."
8. After paying, the customer (let, left) with her baby and her purchases.

B. Use the correct form of the verb in parentheses to complete each sentence.

Example: <u>Let</u> me see that sales receipt.   (let)

1. The clerk _____ the receipt on the desk.   (lay)
2. Are you _____ up the tripod display?   (set)
3. I've _____ out all the equipment.   (lay)
4. Oh, I almost forgot. I _____ one tripod in the storeroom.   (leave)
5. I was going to bring it out. Then I _____ down to write
   out this receipt, and I forgot it.   (sit)
6. I should _____ right now and go take care of it.   (leave)

EXERCISE 53

Practice Using Troublesome Verb Pairs

Don't confuse verb pairs that look alike or have similar meanings. (Look up the words in a dictionary if you need help.)

A. Circle the verb that fits the meaning of the sentence. The word list at the right may help you.

Example: Why must Al (sit, set) in the dugout?

Present
lay(s)
lie(s)
raise(s)
set
sit

Past
laid
lay
rose
set

Past with *has* or *have*
laid
lain
risen
set

1. He will (sit, set) out the rest of the game.
2. Al has (laid, lain) down because of a sprained ankle.
3. The doctor may (sit, set) it if it gets worse.
4. A pinch hitter has (raised, risen) from the bench.
5. He will (rise, raise) his team's spirits.
6. His practice bat (lays, lies) on the ground.
7. The fans (sit, set) motionless in the stands.
8. The batter has (sat, set) his feet in the batter's box.
9. He (raises, rises) his bat off his shoulder.
10. The pitcher (lay, laid) his warmup jacket on the bench.
11. The ball (rose, raised) in the air after a loud crack.

B. Write a sentence for each verb in the numbered pairs.

1. lay (present) _____

    lie _____

2. sit _____

    set _____

3. rise _____

    raise _____

4. (has) risen _____

    (has) raised _____

EXERCISE 54

More Practice With Troublesome Verb Pairs

Some verbs look similar or have similar meanings. Use the meaning of the sentence to tell which verb to use.

A. Choose the verb that fits the meaning of the sentence, and write it in the space provided.

Example: We (taught, learned) about reading charts at yesterday's   _learned_
training meeting.

1. (Let, Leave) me try to give you some examples of what we learned.   _____

2. We learned that the use of graphics (lets, leaves) you explain
   directions in much less space.   _____

3. By showing instead of telling, you can (let, leave) out a lot of words.   _____

4. A lot of explanation about equipment parts can be (leaved, left) out.   _____

5. A picture (teaches, learns) you what the parts are and how they
   fit together.   _____

6. Maybe you'd like to (teach, learn) more about reading charts.   _____

7. I can (lend, borrow) you my notes and handouts.   _____

8. First, I'll have to get them back from Carlita. She (lended, borrowed)
   them this morning.   _____

9. Yes, I'd like to (teach, learn) about reading charts.   _____

10. Thank you for helping. You've (learned, taught) me something
    about it already.   _____

11. I don't think you (leaved, left) out anything important.   _____

B. Write a sentence for each verb in the numbered pairs.

1. let _____

   leave _____

2. lend _____

   borrow _____

3. taught _____

   learned _____

4. (has) let _____

   (has) left _____

Review of Troublesome Verb Pairs

Some verb pairs are confusing, but each verb has its own meaning in a sentence.

A. Underline the verb in parentheses that completes each sentence below.

Example: The man (<u>sat</u>, set) down to write fortunes for fortune cookies.

1. Soon he (lay, laid) down his pencil.

2. He (set, sat) the empty page on the desk in front of him.

3. He (rose, raised) from his chair and sighed.

4. His boss (borrowed, lent) him a pen so he could begin writing.

5. (Let, Leave) your true self come to the surface.

6. Beware of those who (sit, set) while others work.

7. Your mistakes (learn, teach) you much.

8. Don't (lay, lie) down until the job is finished.

9. Those who have (lent, borrowed) money to others have less money themselves.

10. (Let, Leave) your good fortune always be shared.

11. When trouble comes, (rise, raise) your face to the sun.

B. Write the verb form needed to complete each sentence in the space provided. Use the time and verb given in parentheses.

Example: Connie _____*took*_____ out the paper.   (past of <u>take</u>)

1. She _____ her fortune down.   (past of <u>lay</u>)

2. "It _____ me nothing," she said.   (past of <u>teach</u> with <u>has</u>)

3. She _____ the fortune there.   (past of <u>leave</u>)

4. She _____ not to trust fortunes.   (past of <u>learn</u> with <u>has</u>)

5. Connie _____ from her chair.   (past of <u>rise</u>)

6. Then she _____ down again.   (past of <u>sit</u>)

7. "Maybe I really can _____ something," she said.   (present of <u>learn</u>)

8   Sentence Basics

A **sentence** is a group of words that expresses a *complete thought*. The subject, or topic, of the sentence tells *who* or *what* the sentence is about. The verb tells what the subject *is* or *does*. There are four kinds of sentences: *statements, questions, commands,* and *exclamations*.

Statements simply *tell* about something that is happening, did happen, or will happen. They end with a period **(.)**.

Questions *ask* about something. They ask about something in the present, something from the past, or something in the future. They end with a question mark **(?)**.

Commands *order* or demand. They are "strong" sentences. They end with a period **(.)**.

Exclamations are strong sentences, too. Their strength lies not in their orders, but in their sense of *urgency* or *excitement*. Exclamations "exclaim" or say something with strong feeling. They end in an exclamation point **(!)** to show their urgency or excitement.

Here are some examples of the four different kinds of sentences.

Statement:	The meeting will be held in room 144.
Question:	Is the meeting to be held in room 144?
Command:	Sue, attend that meeting in room 144.
Exclamation:	I can hardly wait for the meeting in room 144!

Sentences must have both a subject and a verb. Subjects explain what the sentence is about. Verbs indicate the action or state of being. Both subjects and verbs can be complete or simple in their form. Sometimes the subject is not listed but only understood, for example, "Go!" or "Jump!": *You* is the understood subject. Therefore a sentence may consist of just one word.

The **complete subject** contains the whole subject, or topic, of the sentence, not just the main noun word.

Example: *Unread newspapers* covered his desk. (The noun phrase *unread newspapers* is what this sentence is about. It shows the entire topic.)

The **simple subject** contains only the main word, or noun, in the topic.

Example: Unread *newspapers* covered his desk. (The noun *newspapers* is the main
                word in the complete subject of this sentence.)

The **complete verb** contains the whole verb, not just the main verb or verb phrase
(the verb with its helping word).

Example: Ms. Sanchez *asked for our feedback*. (The verb phrase *asked for our feedback*
                indicates the complete action that took place.

The **simple verb** contains only the main verb, which may or may not use a helping
verb to indicate the action or state of being.

Example: Ms. Sanchez *asked* for our feedback. (The verb *asked* is the main action verb
                in the sentence.

Sometimes **verb phrases** may be separated into two parts, with other words between
the verb and its helping word. The action of the sentence is indicated by the words
in the verb phrase. The added words may *alter* or *add emphasis* to the meaning of
the verb.

Example: We *could* almost *make* another team. (The verb phrase *could make* is sepa-
                rated by the word *almost*, which alters the meaning of the verb slightly.)

In some cases, part of a *contraction* may be used as a "word" that separates the verb
phrase.

Example: If he *doesn't pick* up the stamp machine, please let me know. (The verb
                phrase *does pick* is separated by the contraction *-n't* standing for the
                word *not*.)

Subjects, like verbs, can also be separated into two parts. Separated subjects often
contain more than one noun or more than one topic. The word *and* is most often
used to connect multiple subjects. Other connecting words may also be used.

Example: *Pens, pencils,* and *markers* were in the container. (The multiple subjects—
                pens, pencils, markers—are separated by commas and the connecting word
                and.)

And or other connecting words can also be used to connect multiple verbs or verb
phrases.

Example: We *swept, mopped,* and *waxed* the showroom floor. (The multiple verbs—
                swept, mopped, waxed—are separated by commas and the connecting
                word *and*.)

Connecting words, like the word *and* join words or groups of words. Some connect multiple nouns. Some connect multiple verbs or verb phrases. Others connect whole thoughts.

Connecting Words

and	as	so	both . . . and
but	for	yet	either . . . or

Objects are other important parts of sentences. An object is a word or phrase that answers the question *who?* or *what?* after a verb or a connecting word. Objects often indicate who or what the action verb refers to.

Example: Maria received a *good evaluation.* (In this sentence, *good evaluation* answers what? about the verb *received.*)

Objects can also be used with state of being verbs.

Example: Ms. Pi is *our supervisor.* (The words *our supervisor* answer the question who? or what? *is*)

When objects are used with connecting words, they answer who? or what? after the connecting word.

Example: I filed those papers for Janel. (The word *Janel* answers who? after the connecting word *for.*)

Subjects usually appear first in sentences, followed by the verbs or verb phrases. Some sentences, however, appear in reverse order. In these sentences, the verb or verb phrase comes first, followed by the subject. These sentences have **inverted order.** Sentences may be written in inverted order to add variety or to emphasize a point.

Question sentences often use inverted order to emphasize the questioning.

Example: *Are* those *disks* full? (The verb *are* comes before the noun subject *disks* to make the sentence a question.)

In exclamation sentences, inverted order adds more emphasis or excitement.

Example: Faster and faster *came* the *orders!* (Using the verb *came* before the noun *orders* adds variety and interest to this sentence and emphasizes the point demonstrated by the word *faster.*)

Example: Never *will I understand* that rule! (Part of the verb phrase *will understand* comes before the subject, *I.* This helps make the exclamation stronger by emphasizing the word *never.*)

WORKPLACE
APPLICATION

Can you find examples of the four kinds of sentences in this speech?

Address to Sales Staff

This week, 1427 crates of produce were sold to 16 stores in District Twelve. This reflects an 11 percent gain!

_____

_____

_____

Our sales force spent an average of 22 minutes talking with the produce managers of each store in the district. Customer service questionnaires reveal that an overwhelming 92 percent of our vendors are pleased with our service.

_____

_____

_____

But I think we can do better. What do you think? I think we can sell 2000 crates and gain a 98 percent approval rate. I want you to do just that. I'm telling you to do it. Don't just try. Do it!

_____

_____

_____

EXERCISE 56

What Is a Sentence?

A sentence is a group of words that expresses a complete thought. The subject of a sentence indicates who or what the sentence is about. The verb tells what the subject is or does.

A. Read each group of words. Write *sentence* in the space provided if the words express a complete thought. Write *not a sentence* in the space provided if the words do not express a complete thought.

Example: Ron and Joy went to a meeting.   <u>   *sentence*   </u>

1. Enjoyed the company picnic.   _____

2. A few late arrivals.   _____

3. Listened to a good speech.   _____

4. The speaker was Ron's cousin.   _____

5. They served hamburgers for dinner.   _____

6. Left for home very late.   _____

B. Draw a vertical line between the complete subject and the complete verb.

Example: I | watched an exciting neighborhood soccer game last Saturday.

1. Two men's teams played in the park.

2. They passed the ball to each other very quickly.

3. The coaches shouted directions to the players.

4. My friend Juan played goalie.

5. My brother was a defender.

6. On the sidelines everyone cheered with enthusiasm.

7. My brother's team won the game.

C. Make three sentences with the group of words below. Use at least two of the groups in each sentence and select each group at least once.

the manager   a lesson   my worst assignment

_____

_____

_____

Four Kinds of Sentences

A sentence is a group of words that expresses a complete thought. There are four different kinds of sentences: statements, questions, commands, and exclamations. Each sentence begins with a capital letter and ends with a period (.), a question mark (?), or an exclamation point (!).

A. Write the correct end punctuation in the first blank after the sentence. Then identify what kind of sentence each is in the second blank.

Example: Laura is single ____ .   _____*statement*_____

1. Does he work for the doctor _____   _____
2. What an unusual job she has _____   _____
3. Many people work out of their homes _____   _____
4. How funny these old manuals are _____   _____
5. Mike can spot mistakes easily _____   _____
6. Help me move this equipment _____   _____
7. Where did I put those nails _____   _____

B. Identify which word groups are complete sentences and rewrite them using correct capitalization and punctuation. There are six in all. One has been done for you as an example.

Example: how old are these statues
                 *How old are these statues?*_____

they look very costly	found it for me
up in this musty attic	brought here from Cuba
how beautiful they still are	should we insure them
covered with dust and cobwebs	belonged to my in-laws
hold them carefully	the wood beams in the ceiling
don't bump your head	

1. _____

2. _____

3. _____

4. _____

5. _____

Identifying the Four Kinds of Sentences

A sentence may be a statement, question, command, or exclamation.

A. Read each sentence below. Put the correct end punctuation mark on the line after each sentence. Write whether the sentence is a statement, question, command, or exclamation.

Example: Have you ever tried this coffee ___?___   _____*question*_____

1. Follow my lead _____   _____

2. Use your head to get ahead in life _____   _____

3. Good managers listen to employees _____   _____

4. Wow, this is exciting _____   _____

5. We call this sport "shooting the rapids" _____   _____

6. Your vote can make a difference _____   _____

7. Oh no, we're going to crash _____   _____

8. When do we leave for the meeting _____   _____

9. Bring me the files on the desk _____   _____

10. I'd like to do this again _____   _____

B. Write four sentences about television. Write one of each kind of sentence: statement, question, command, and exclamation.

statement _____

_____

question _____

_____

command _____

_____

exclamation _____

_____

Using Different Kinds of Sentences

A sentence may be a statement, question, command, or exclamation.

A. Read these sentences and write what kind each one is.

Example: Ghostwriters do not write about Halloween.   _statement_

1. Some of the best writers in the world are "ghosts."   _____

2. Do not look for these ghosts in haunted houses.   _____

3. Ghosts are people who write for other people.   _____

4. Did you know that about ghosts?   _____

5. Pick up just about any sports autobiography.   _____

6. It was probably written by a ghostwriter.   _____

7. Did you know that many politicians have speech writers?   _____

8. These speech writers are real live ghosts!   _____

B. Rewrite each sentence. Change it to the kind of sentence indicated in parentheses.

Example: Was his book written by a ghostwriter?   (statement)
       His book was written by a ghostwriter.

1. Ghostwriting existed in ancient Rome.   (question)

   _____

2. Is there still a need for ghostwriters?   (statement)

   _____

3. Some businesspeople need ghostwriters to write their speeches.   (question)

   _____

4. You might consider being a ghostwriter yourself.   (command)

   _____

5. Could I make a lot of money ghostwriting?   (statement)

   _____

6. I don't think that is possible.   (exclamation)

   _____

Simple and Complete Subjects

All the words in the subject make up the complete subject. The most important word in the complete subject is the simple subject. The simple subject names the specific person, place, thing, or idea that the sentence is about.

A. Underline the complete subject once. Underline the simple subject twice.

Example: Forgetful <u>Ken</u> lost the keys to his car.

1. The unhappy young man gazed hopelessly around his studio apartment.
2. The keys lay somewhere in this mess.
3. Piles of books filled the room's corners.
4. Some dirty shirts hung from a chair.
5. Old papers covered Ken's desk.
6. Cards from last night's game were scattered on the rug.
7. The room reminded him of an obstacle course.
8. A giant cleanup job was begun.
9. His work was finally rewarded.
10. The object of his search fell out of an old shoe.
11. A weary Ken slumped on his chair.
12. The enormous task took several hours.
13. His old dog let out a weary sigh.
14. Ken cleans his apartment regularly now.

B. Write two sentences using these complete subjects. Then circle the simple subject in each sentence.

my least favorite work assignment   the problem with commuting

_____

_____

_____

_____

Finding the Simple and the Complete Subject

A sentence has a complete subject. The most important word in the complete subject is the simple subject.

Write the complete subject of each sentence in the blank. Then circle the simple subject.

Example: The library in our town is quite popular.

The (library) in our town

1. This library was constructed over one hundred years ago.

   _____

2. People of all ages borrow books every day.

   _____

3. Many adults come to read the newspapers and magazines.

   _____

4. Groups of teenagers often meet their friends on the front steps.

   _____

5. Pictures by local photographers hang in the lobby.

   _____

6. A famous artist painted the mural in the hallway.

   _____

7. Several local clubs use the auditorium in the evenings.

   _____

8. Travel films about faraway places are shown once a week.

   _____

9. The library loans videotapes for three days at a time.

   _____

10. A community volunteer conducts story hours for children.

    _____

11. Old and new CDs can also be checked out.

    _____

EXERCISE 62

Simple and Complete Verbs

The complete verb indicates what the subject does or is. The most important word in the complete verb is the simple verb. The simple verb is the action or state of being word.

A. Draw a vertical line between the complete subject and the complete verb in each sentence. Underline the simple verb.

Example: The <u>job</u> of bricklaying | is not for everyone.

1. It requires strength and stamina.
2. You are lifting bricks all day long.
3. Your hands and arms may become tired.
4. Detailed precision work is part of the job.
5. Bricklayers sometimes create elaborate patterns with bricks.
6. Some people may call bricklaying an art form.
7. Bricklayers are also called masons.
8. Masons, as a group, also include tile layers and cement masons.
9. Some brick, tile, and cement masons are working as independent contractors.
10. They pay all their own expenses up front.
11. Their fees are paid once the entire job has been completed.

B. Write five sentences using these simple verbs. When you have finished, underline the complete verb in each sentence.

completed   invented   collected   worked   started

_____

_____

_____

_____

_____

Finding the Simple and the Complete Verb

The complete verb indicates what the subject does or is. The most important word in the complete verb is the simple verb. Sometimes the simple verb has more than one word. This is called the verb phrase. Both verbs and verb phrases show the action or state of being in the sentence.

Write the complete verb of each sentence in the blank. Then circle the simple verb or verb phrase.

Example: Scientists are studying faces.

(are studying) faces

1. A research team identified 80 facial expressions.

2. Different smiles are signs of different feelings.

3. Friends share many kinds of smiles and expressions.

4. A good joke will trigger a broad smile.

5. Games cause some very interesting grins.

6. Some smiles express fear or surprise.

7. We use smiles for courtesy and respect, too.

8. One researcher has proven a connection between feelings and posture.

9. Sad or ill people walk with a slouch.

10. Busy people on their way to their jobs have straighter posture.

11. A happy child will skip along lightly.

EXERCISE 64

Separated Parts of the Simple Verb

The words in a verb phrase are often separated by other words. The action of the sentence is still indicated by the words in the verb phrase.

Underline the complete verb in each sentence. Then write the verb phrase in the space provided.

Example: The moon has just risen.

has risen

Helping Verbs
be
am
is
are
was
were
has
had
have
do
did
does
will
can
must
may
could
would
should

1. Its shape doesn't change every night.

   _____

2. The moon's surface is actually reflecting sunlight.

   _____

3. We could barely see the moon last night.

   _____

4. A thin crescent was dimly glowing in the night sky.

   _____

5. The clouds had nearly made the moon invisible.

   _____

6. It didn't rise until very late.

   _____

7. I have never seen an eclipse of the moon.

   _____

8. The earth's shadow will sometimes cover the moon's surface.

   _____

9. The moon can also cast a shadow over the earth.

   _____

10. Eclipses of the earth have often frightened people.

    _____

11. They could not understand this strange occurrence.

    _____

More Simple Subjects and Verbs

A sentence has a simple and a complete subject and verb.

A. Draw a vertical line between the complete subject and the complete verb in each sentence. Then underline the simple subject once and the simple verb twice.

Example: <u>Numbers</u> | <u>are counted</u> daily.

1. An abacus is the oldest kind of calculator.

2. An abacus has counters on rods.

3. The counters are used for adding, subtracting, multiplying, and dividing.

4. Many ancient civilizations used some form of an abacus.

5. The Egyptians, the Chinese, and the Romans counted with an abacus. (Hint: There is more than one subject.)

6. An abacus is a kind of computer.

7. Computers became widespread after World War II.

B. Write sentences for each of the verbs and subjects below.

Example: Use <u>my friend from work</u> as a complete subject.
    My friend from work walked home with me today.

1. Use <u>work</u> as a simple verb.

   _____

2. Use <u>employee</u> as a simple subject.

   _____

3. Use <u>has taught</u> as a simple verb.

   _____

4. Use <u>the happiest day in my career</u> as a complete subject.

   _____

5. Use <u>drove safely to the warehouse</u> as a complete verb.

   _____

6. Use <u>dispatcher</u> as a simple subject.

   _____

EXERCISE 66

A Review of Subjects and Verbs

A sentence has a simple and a complete subject and verb.

A. Draw a vertical line between the complete subject and the complete verb.

Example: Rodeos | are full of action.

1. A big rodeo takes place in July.
2. This event is held in Alberta.
3. It is the Calgary Exhibition and Stampede.
4. This festival lasts ten days.
5. More than 850,000 people come to Calgary.
6. Rodeo champs from all over participate.
7. Everyone marches in a parade.
8. Many events are scheduled during the rodeo.
9. Races with chuck wagons are popular.
10. Tourists enjoy rope throwing too.

B. Draw a vertical line between the complete subject and the complete verb. Then underline the simple subject once and the simple verb twice. Some sentences have two or more subjects or verbs.

Example: The <u>audience</u> and <u>performers</u> | <u>have</u> fun.

1. The biggest and most famous rodeo is held in Calgary.
2. Great rodeo performers rope steers and ride bucking horses.
3. Newspapers, radio stations, and television networks cover the events.
4. Visitors watch events and wander around.
5. They eat at the many restaurants and buy souvenirs.
6. Tourists and locals enjoy the sights and sounds.
7. Many performers have colorful saddles and fancy outfits.
8. Performers and spectators find opportunities for dancing.

C. Write a new sentence as directed.

Example: The spectators came.   (Add a second verb.)
         The spectators came and watched.

1. The clerk stocks.   (Add a second verb.)   _____
2. Computers help.   (Add a second subject.)   _____
3. The team discusses.   (Add a second verb.)   _____

What Is Inverted Order?

In most statements, the subject comes before the verb. In most questions, all or part of the verb comes before the subject. This is an example of inverted order.

A. Read the sentence pairs. Then draw one line under each simple subject and two lines under each simple verb.

Example: Are you studying geography for the GED test?

               You are studying geography for the GED test.

1. Is the Mississippi River used for transportation?

   The Mississippi River is used for transportation.

2. Is Mount Kilimanjaro located in Africa near Kenya?

   Mount Kilimanjaro is located in Africa near Kenya.

3. Is Rainbow Bridge, a natural bridge, located in Utah?

   Rainbow Bridge, a natural bridge, is located in Utah.

4. Is the Verrazano Narrows Bridge a suspension bridge?

   The Verrazano Narrows Bridge is a suspension bridge.

B. Rewrite each statement as a question or rewrite each question as a statement. Underline the simple subject once and the simple verb twice in each sentence you write.

Example: A good education is helpful.

               Is a good education helpful?

1. The management listens to new ideas.

   _____

2. Did the telephone ring this morning?

   _____

3. This store will close at 6 P.M.

   _____

4. Are you going to the store?

   _____

5. Gary is a transfer student.

   _____

EXERCISE 68

Inverted Order in Sentences

In some sentences the complete subject does not come before the complete verb. This happens most often when the sentence is a question. In other sentences the complete verb comes before the complete subject to add emphasis or strength to the sentence.

A. Rewrite each question in the form of a statement. Underline each simple subject once and each simple verb twice.

Example: Are heavy thunderstorms expected again today?

Heavy <u>thunderstorms</u> <u><u>are expected</u></u> again today.

1. Did large hailstones fall last night?

    _____

2. Have you seen darker thunderclouds than these?

    _____

3. Are they getting closer and closer?

    _____

4. Was that tree struck by lightning?

    _____

5. May I listen to the weather report?

    _____

B. Write the simple subject and the simple verb to each inverted sentence in the blanks at the right.

		Simple Subject	Simple Verb
Example:	Never have I heard such thunder!	_I_	_have heard_
1.	Lower and lower came the dense clouds.	_____	_____
2.	Do these storms usually occur in the spring?	_____	_____
3.	Down beat large raindrops against the windows.	_____	_____
4.	Was Joan caught outside in it again?	_____	_____

EXERCISE 69

Verbs and Subjects in Sentences With Inverted Order

In some sentences, the complete subject does not come before the complete verb.

A. Underline the verb or verb phrase in each sentence. Circle the subject.

Example: Does (anybody) really know the time?

1. Will you please tell me the time?
2. Why does he want the time?
3. Is it four o'clock yet?
4. Has she missed her appointment?
5. Is your watch very accurate?
6. Do you have a watch of your own?
7. Will you buy me one?
8. Why should we do that?
9. Where is my watch?
10. Have I lost my new watch?

B. Circle the subject and underline the verb in each sentence.

Examples: Here is Rosa's (watch) on the ground.   There are (people) watching.

1. A loud shout came from the street.
2. My sister ran to the window.
3. Below the window stood Rosa.
4. In her eyes were tears.
5. In her hand lay her watch.
6. There was a problem with the spring.
7. There was no other watch like it.
8. On the back were her initials.
9. At the corner was a repair shop.
10. Quickly Rosa ran toward it.

C. Rewrite each sentence by changing the order of the subject and the verb.

Example: Is Jane a friend of yours?

Jane is a friend of yours.

1. Around the corner raced Jane.

_____

2. Jane was late for work.

_____

3. Jane's boss stood in her office.

_____

4. Was Jane in trouble?

_____

EXERCISE 70

Finding the Verb Object

A verb object answers the question *who?* or *what?* after a verb. Verb objects are always nouns or noun phrases.

A. Draw a line under the object of the verb in each of the following sentences. Draw two lines under the verb that the object refers to.

Example: Sam <u><u>took</u></u> <u>the apron</u> off the hanger.

1. Sam put the apron on.

2. He took out some flour.

3. He took out some milk.

4. He took out other ingredients.

5. Sam mixed the flour and milk.

6. He added the other ingredients.

7. Sam made some bread.

8. Sam set the oven at 350°.

9. He baked the bread.

10. Juanita helped Sam.

11. Juanita cooled the bread.

12. Then Juanita wrapped the bread.

B. Fill in the blanks in the sentences below by adding a word that can be used as the object of the verb in the sentence.

Example: Gretchen took _____*orders*_____.

1. Gretchen helped a _____.

2. The customer asked a _____.

3. Do you have _____?

4. We do not have that, but we have _____.

5. I'll take _____ of those.

6. Would you also like _____?

7. Yes, I want _____ on my toast.

8. You can also have _____ for your toast.

What Is a Connecting Word?

A connecting word joins words or groups of words. Some connect nouns or noun phrases, some connect verb or verb phrases, and others connect complete thoughts.

A. Circle the connecting word in each sentence. Then underline the words, phrases, or thoughts that it joins.

Example: Will you help me with the sorting (or) with the stocking?

1. Jim and Donna work at the bakery.
2. Jim helps with the baking, and Donna serves the customers.
3. The equipment is either in the basement or in the pantry.
4. Jim likes working in the kitchen and in the dining area.
5. Joe fixed my hard drive last spring, but it needs work again.
6. Everyone has a favorite task or activity.
7. Melissa's interests are photography and volleyball.
8. She spends her time at the gym or in her darkroom.
9. Andy is a good artist, but Marnie is even better.
10. She sketches and draws well.
11. I like to eat in the cafeteria, but my friend prefers to bring her lunch.
12. Do your friends ride the bus or drive cars to work?

B. Write two sentences for each connecting word—*and*, *but*, and *or*. Join words, phrases, and entire thoughts.

Example: but   *I watered the plants, but they need more.*

1. and _____
2. but _____
3. or _____
4. and _____

_____

5. but _____

_____

6. or _____

_____

EXERCISE 72

Using Connecting Words

A connecting word joins words or groups of words. Some connecting words come in pairs.

A. Complete these sentences with connecting words. Choose from the words in the word list.

Example: Some roses are delicate, _____ so _____ they are grown with care.

1. In Bulgaria, perfume _____ roses go together.

2. Roses grow elsewhere, _____ one kind of rose grows only there.

3. This rose is used in perfumes, _____ it is valuable.

4. It needs sunlight, _____ otherwise it must be protected from the weather.

5. Cold spells are bad, _____ cold damages these roses.

6. They _____ die _____ grow poorly.

7. Perfume makers crush the flowers of this rose _____ use the remaining oil.

8. The scent is _____ strong _____ sweet.

9. This rose thrives in Bulgaria _____ nowhere else.

10. It is picked by 10:00 A.M. _____ not at all.

11. This rose is famous, _____ there are perfumes made from it everywhere.

12. _____ politics _____ economics can lessen its fame.

Word List	
yet	and
but	so
or	because
both . . . and	
either . . . or	
neither . . . nor	

B. Circle the connecting words in the sentence. Remember to look for pairs. Some sentences have two or three connecting words.

Example: (Both) roses (and) gold are valuable in Bulgaria.

1. Kazanlik, Bulgaria, has the perfect soil and climate for roses.

2. Both nature and science help them grow there.

3. The oil can be either sold or stored away like gold.

4. Gold is valuable, but rose oil is also precious.

5. Neither time nor effort is spared in improving the flowers.

6. The growing methods are kept secret, so the industry stays protected.

7. Both Bulgaria and India make perfume from oils.

9 Pronouns as Subjects and Objects

Pronouns are words that replace nouns in sentences. Pronouns can be subjects or objects of sentences, just like nouns.

Pronoun subjects can be singular or plural.

Examples: I joined the union.   (singular)

                 We joined the union.   (plural)

Pronoun verb objects can be singular or plural. They answer the question *who?* or *what?* after the verb.

Examples: José asked me to stock the shelves.   (singular)

                 José asked us to stock the shelves.   (plural)

Pronouns

Singular Subject	Plural Subject	Singular Object	Plural Object
I	we	me	us
you	you	you	you
he, she, it	they	him, her, it	them

Pronouns can be used as multiple subjects. Multiple subjects can have several singular subjects or several plural subjects. But the subject pronoun should always agree with the noun number (singular or plural).

Example: Alice took the money to the bank. Now *she* is able to write checks. (*She* is a *singular subject pronoun*. It agrees with the *subject, Alice*.)

Example: The secretaries and salespeople are here; now *they* can go to the conference. (*They* is a *plural subject pronoun*. It agrees with the *plural subjects, secretaries* and *salespeople*.)

Pronouns can also be the objects of other words in sentences besides verbs. These words are used to connect sentence parts. The pronouns that follow these connecting words answer the question *who?* or *what?* for the connecting word. Use the object form of the pronoun and the correct singular or plural form.

Example: Sheila left the office with Rose and her. *Her* is the object form of the pronoun. It answers the question *whom*. Sheila left with *Rose and her*.

Connecting Words That Use Pronouns as Objects

with	behind	of	by	for
between	besides	near	in	to

The pronouns *I* and *me* and *we* and *us* are often used incorrectly. Remember, *I* and *we* are subject pronouns. *Me* and *us* are object pronouns.

Example: *I* (or *we*) would like an evaluation. (not *me* or *us*—use subject pronoun)

Example: Please give *me* (or *us*) an evaluation. (not *I* or *we*—use object pronoun; object of verb *give*)

Example: Please give an evaluation to *me* (or *us*). (not *I* or *we*—use object pronoun; object of connecting word *to*)

Example: That is between *you* and *me*. (not *I*—object of the preposition *between*)

Some pronouns end with *-self* or *-selves*. These pronouns are *always* used as objects. They can be singular (*-self*) or plural (*-selves*). Always make a *-self* or *-selves* object pronoun agree with its subject (*either* singular *or* plural). Remember: *hisself* and *theirselves* are not words.

Example: We can do it *ourselves*. (The subject, *we*, is plural; use the plural *ourselves*.)

Example: John made *himself* a sandwich for lunch. (The subject, John, is singular; use the singular *himself*.)

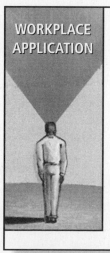

WORKPLACE APPLICATION

Bart said to Rodney, "You and me should finish this report soon. Then us can go to lunch with Sara and Monica. Them invited us when I saw they at break."

How many mistakes in pronoun usage can you find in this conversation? How would you correct them? Write your corrections below.

_____

_____

EXERCISE 73

Pronouns as Subjects

Some pronouns are subjects of sentences.

A. Write a subject pronoun for each underlined subject in the sentences below.

Example: <u>Charles and Lauren</u> went to an art exhibit.   _____*They*_____

1. <u>The exhibit</u> was a Currier and Ives show.   _____

2. <u>Currier and Ives</u> were artists in the 1800s.   _____

3. <u>These artists</u> painted lithographs.   _____

4. <u>Each lithograph</u> illustrates nineteenth-century
   America for us.   _____

5. <u>Nathaniel Currier</u> was born in Massachusetts,
   but his first prints were of New York City.   _____

6. <u>James Ives</u> joined him in printmaking.   _____

7. <u>The partners</u> were reporters and historians.   _____

8. <u>Lauren</u> likes Currier and Ives prints.   _____

9. <u>Charlie</u> knows many of them by name.   _____

B. Draw a circle around the correct word or words in parentheses that serve as the
   subject of each sentence.

Example: (Us, We) saw events of the 1800s in the prints.

1. (Lauren and I, Lauren and me) saw how people dressed, too.

2. (She, Her) and (me, I) learned that the lithographs were printed in the
   newspapers.

3. (Charlie and she, Charlie and her) like the old locomotives in one print.

4. (He and me, We) like the ice-skating scene.

5. (They, Lauren and him) read a booklet about Currier and Ives prints.

6. (Charlie and I, Me and Charlie) bought a copy of a Currier and Ives print.

EXERCISE 74

Pronouns as Objects of Verbs

Some pronouns serve as objects of action verbs. The pronoun answers the question *who?* or *what?* the action is referring to.

A. Circle the correct object pronoun for the underlined nouns and pronouns.

Example: Andy took <u>Sara and Bob</u> (us, we, (them)) to lunch.

1. Cy Fernandez will drive <u>you and me</u> (we, us) to work.
2. Does he know <u>Sheila, Juanita, and me</u> (we, us, them)?
3. Will he recognize <u>Kimberly</u> (she, her)?
4. Mr. Karpov hired <u>Sara and him</u> (them, us) to do some yard work.
5. Mr. Shapiro asked <u>Ken and me</u> (we, them, us) to work at the polls.

B. Circle the correct pronoun.

Example: Marcia met Judy and (I, (me)) after work.

1. Kelvin invited Harry and (I, me) to his garage.
2. He then introduced (we, us) to his mechanics.
3. The staff welcomed (we, us) warmly.
4. Pedro saw you and (I, me) at the site.
5. The police officer allowed the tractor and (I, me) to pass.
6. The team leader divided (they, them) into two groups.
7. If everything goes well, the boss will give you and (I, me) raises.
8. The rain forced Peter and (they, them) to go home early.
9. The committee selected Takeo and (she, her).
10. The county board elected Rafael and (he, him) officers.
11. Mr. Huang is training (he, him).
12. Please direct (they, them) and Mrs. Cruz to my office.
13. Nothing seems to bother (she, her).

Pronouns as Objects of Other Words

Some pronouns are used as objects of other words. Some of these words are prepositions, like *in*, *on*, and *by* that are place words. Others are prepositions like *for*, *of*, and *to*. A noun or pronoun always follows these words.

A. Choose the correct pronoun in parentheses, and write it in the blank.

Example: The letter was for my husband and (I, me).   _____*me*_____

1. I went to the meeting with Todd and (he, him).   _____
2. Besides (we, us), there are eight others in the office.   _____
3. The choice was between (she, her) and (I, me).   _____
4. You will scarcely hear a peep out of (she, her) or (I, me).   _____
5. The exhibit seems very large to the women and (he, him).   _____
6. The memo was from (they, them) and (I, me).   _____
7. Many people were in line behind (we, us).   _____
8. Some new offices already had roofs on (they, them).   _____
9. The work was done by (she, her) and (I, me).   _____
10. Judy works near you and (he, him).   _____

B. Circle any errors made with pronouns. Then rewrite the sentence correctly. If a sentence has no pronoun error, write *correct* on the line.

Example: Between you and I, that movie wasn't very good.
         Between you and me, that movie wasn't very good.

1. Besides she and I, no one else knew the secret.

   _____

2. Nadia was meeting with they and I.

   _____

3. More packages came for you and we.

   _____

4. Here are some responses from she and they.

   _____

5. Between you and me, I have had enough evaluations.

   _____

EXERCISE 76

Subject and Object Pronouns

Subject pronouns are used as subjects of sentences. Object pronouns can be used as objects of verbs or other words in sentences.

A. Write the pronoun that can be substituted for the underlined word or group of words.

Example: <u>Sarah</u> has read many of Zane Grey's stories.   _____*she*_____

1. <u>Zane Grey</u> wrote about the Old West.   _____

2. Grey's stories made <u>Grey</u> a well-known author.   _____

3. Action and thrills characterize <u>his stories</u>.   _____

4. Grey received a dental degree, but <u>Grey</u> wanted to write.   _____

5. Grey received <u>the dental degree</u> in 1896.   _____

6. Grey and <u>Lina Elise Roth</u> were married in 1905.   _____

7. Zane Grey's wife encouraged <u>Grey</u> to write his books.   _____

8. Historians know that <u>his wife</u> helped Grey in many ways.   _____

9. <u>Grey</u> wrote more than 60 books.   _____

10. <u>Grey's books</u> were very popular.   _____

B. Underline the correct form of the pronoun in parentheses.

Example: Bob and (<u>I</u>, me) saw the new buses yesterday.

1. The bus company gave Bob and (I, me) a preview of the buses.

2. (They, Them) and some vans were ordered several months ago.

3. A manufacturer delivered (they, them) and the vans last week.

4. To Bob and (I, me), the new buses are a big improvement.

5. Bob and (I, me) asked when the buses would be used.

6. The bus company's president talked to some other visitors and (we, us).

7. (He, Him) and the drivers hope to use the buses next week.

8. We asked (he, him) and a manager what would be done with the old buses.

9. "Most of (they, them) and a van will be sold for scrap metal," the manager said.

10. We thanked (he, him) and the president for the preview.

EXERCISE 77

I and *We*, *Me* and *Us*

The pronouns *I* and *we* should be used as subjects. The pronouns *me* and *us* should be used as objects.

Rewrite each sentence, choosing the correct pronoun in parentheses. Remember that the subject does not always come first in a sentence.

Example: Phyllis and (I, me) went to the concert.

Phyllis and I went to the concert.

1. Her boss gave concert tickets to (us, we).

2. The couple in the second row were Phyllis and (I, me).

3. (We, Us) watched the musicians tune their instruments.

4. All of (us, we) couldn't wait for the concert to begin.

5. Between the stage and (I, me) stood an usher.

6. The people who play trumpets sat closest to Phyllis and (me, I).

7. Phyllis and (I, me) enjoyed the concert.

8. The orchestra played the *Grand Canyon Suite* for (us, we).

9. The music sounded very pleasant to (I, me).

10. The next day (her, she) told her boss about the concert.

EXERCISE 78

Pronouns With -*self* and -*selves*

Some pronouns end with -*self* or -*selves*. These pronouns are used as objects.

A. Circle the pronoun ending in -*self* or -*selves*, and write the noun or pronoun to which it refers in the blank.

Example: Leo lifted (himself) into his wheelchair.   _____Leo_____

1. The printer had jammed itself again.   _____
2. Have you given yourselves time off?   _____
3. The women treated themselves to lunch.   _____
4. I stopped myself at the door to his office.   _____
5. Has Bob painted himself into another corner?   _____
6. We arranged ourselves around the conference table.   _____
7. The group gave itself a round of applause.   _____
8. Mrs. Zack prepared herself for the bad news.   _____
9. I dragged myself up the stairs to my office one last time.   _____
10. The citizens govern themselves in a democracy.   _____
11. The carpenter familiarized himself with the blueprints.   _____
12. My boss threw herself into a tizzy.   _____

B. Choose the correct pronoun in parentheses and write it in the blank.

Example: My uncle taught (hisself, himself) to sail.   _____himself_____

1. We reminded (ourselves, ourself) of the time.   _____
2. Todd dressed (himself, hisself) for work.   _____
3. My sons made (theirself, themselves) dinner.   _____
4. The customers let (themselves, theirselves) in through
   the front door.   _____
5. We have introduced (ourselves, ourself) already.   _____
6. The winners of the award congratulated
   (theirself, themselves).   _____
7. Tom made (hisself, himself) a sandwich.   _____
8. Jo and I saw (ourselves, ourself) on the news.   _____

10   Subject-Verb Agreement

A sentence should always have **agreement** between its subject and verb or verb phrase. This means that a *singular noun subject* should have a *singular verb* or *verb phrase*. A *plural noun subject* should have a *plural verb* or *verb phrase*.

Examples: The photocopy *machine was* broken. The photocopy *machine has been* fixed. (singular subject; singular verb or verb phrase)

The photocopy *machines were* broken. The photocopy *machines have been* fixed. (plural subject; plural verb or verb phrase)

A *singular pronoun subject* should have a *singular verb* or *verb phrase*. A *plural pronoun subject* should have a *plural verb* or *verb phrase*.

Examples: *He walks* to work. *He is walking* to work. (singular pronoun subject; singular verb or verb phrase)

They walk to work. *They are walking* to work. (plural pronoun subject; plural verb or verb phrase)

Indefinite pronouns are unclear about the nouns they replace. Some indefinite pronouns can be *either singular* or *plural*, according to their meaning in a sentence, but *indefinite pronouns* and *verbs* always agree. Use *singular verbs* or *verb phrases* with *singular indefinite pronouns*. Use *plural verbs* or *verb phrases* with *plural indefinite pronouns*.

Examples: *No one types* faster than Steve. (singular indefinite pronoun—refers to a single person; use singular verb)

Few (people) have typed as fast as Steve. (plural indefinite pronoun—refers to plural noun, *people*; use plural verb phrase)

None of the money *was* raised. (singular indefinite pronoun—refers to singular noun, *money*; use singular verb)

Both of us *have given* to United Way. (plural indefinite pronoun—refers to plural pronoun, *us*; use plural verb phrase)

Indefinite Pronouns

Singular			Plural	Singular or Plural
one	nobody	anyone	few	most
no one	anybody	everyone	both	none
each	anything	everybody	many	either
something	someone		others	neither

Pronouns and verbs in a sentence agree even when the subject and verb are separated by other words or phrases.

Examples: Jim *does* only what *he* likes. (Use singular pronoun *he* with singular verb *does*.)

We—no matter how large we grow—*are* still a single team. (Use plural pronoun *we* with plural verb *are*.)

Pronouns and verbs agree even if the sentence is written in inverted order.

Examples: *Is he* a customer? (Use singular verb *is* with singular pronoun *he*.)

Are they some of our customers? (Use plural verb *are* with plural pronoun *they*.)

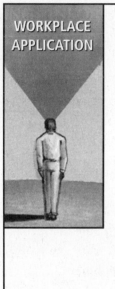

WORKPLACE APPLICATION

Jim was given the following instructions.

Jim: Empty the cooler. Then throw out the old produce. You is to put it in the bin outside. The trash collectors is coming in the morning. They is already told about the produce.

Can you find three errors in agreement between pronouns and verbs in this instruction note? Do these errors hurt or help Jim as he tries to do a good job?

_____

_____

_____

EXERCISE 79

Subject-Verb Agreement

The subject and verb of a sentence should always agree. A singular subject agrees with a singular verb. A plural subject agrees with a plural verb.

A. Circle the verb form that completes each sentence.

Example: Jilda (name, (names)) her favorite objects.

1. Jilda (call, calls) her car "Wheels."
2. Parts (move, moves) quickly along the conveyor belt.
3. Gifts (say, says) something about the givers.
4. Only Harry (know, knows) the truth.
5. Some people (laugh, laughs) at others' problems.
6. Sometimes your excuses (sound, sounds) silly.
7. Comics sometimes (imitate, imitates) the president.
8. Mr. Flynn (call, calls) his client in Germany every month.
9. The Boysons (refer, refers) their clients to us.

B. Underline the correct verb form that agrees with the subject and write it in the space provided.

Example: Parents often _____*give*_____ their children nicknames.   (give, gives)

1. A baby _____ the name Red because of the color of its hair.
   (get, gets)
2. Most people _____ their nicknames.   (enjoy, enjoys)
3. Sometimes people _____ them unpleasant.   (find, finds)
4. Once in a while a nickname _____ famous.   (become, becomes)
5. Nicknames _____ the public.   (interest, interests)
6. A nickname also _____ us.   (amuse, amuses)
7. Usually people _____ unusual names better.
   (remember, remembers)

EXERCISE 80

More Practice With Subject-Verb Agreement

A singular indefinite pronoun requires a singular verb. If a pronoun is plural, it requires a plural verb. Some pronouns are confusing. They sound plural but really refer to a single person. You must look to the meaning of the sentence to decide.

A. Underline the correct singular or plural verb in parentheses.

Example: Kay (<u>drives</u>, drive) to the airfield.

1. The glider (looks, look) very fragile to me.
2. The two pilots (leads, lead) me to the cockpit.
3. The seats inside (is, are) very small and hard.
4. A long cable (lies, lie) on the field near the glider.
5. The attendants (picks, pick) up the end of the cable.
6. One pilot (walks, walk) to a small airplane.
7. The plane's engine (roars, roar) ahead of me.
8. The cable (is, are) the link between us.
9. The glider's runners (bumps, bump) over the runway.
10. Suddenly our two aircraft (rises, rise) into the sky.

B. Follow the directions for **A.**

Example: The airplane and the cable (pulls, <u>pull</u>) the glider.

1. Both the airplane and the glider (glides, glide) upward.
2. Neither the sun nor the valley (seems, seem) far away.
3. Both the cable and the wings (is, are) whistling in the air.
4. The towplane and its cable (takes, take) us higher and higher.
5. The glider and its passenger (soars, soar) in the morning sky.
6. The challenge and freedom (is, are) so appealing.
7. Longer wings and a streamlined design (helps, help) it glide through the air.
8. Neither heavyweight materials nor an engine (is, are) found on a glider.
9. Brian and Kris (uses, use) gliders for recreation.
10. Either Tony or Mike (constructs, construct) gliders.

EXERCISE 81

Pronoun-Verb Agreement

The subject pronoun and verb of a sentence must always agree.

A. Choose the verb in parentheses that agrees with the subject. Then write it in the space provided.

Example:　　She often (plan, plans) our summer party.　　　*plans*

1. They (send, sends) out the invitations early.　　_____

2. We (attend, attends) the block party every summer.　_____

3. Usually he (bring, brings) his whole family.　　_____

4. It (begin, begins) with races and contests.　　_____

5. Sometimes we (win, wins) the tug-of-war.　　_____

6. She never (arrive, arrives) until lunchtime.　　_____

7. I (cook, cooks) the hamburgers on the grill.　　_____

8. They (stay, stays) until sunset.　　_____

9. We (has, have) a wonderful time every year.　　_____

B. Circle the incorrect verb in each sentence, and write the correct present tense verb in the space provided. If the sentence has no verb error, write *correct* instead.

Example:　　I usually (comes) to the block party.　　　*come*

1. We gladly welcomes people new to the neighborhood.　　_____

2. I, without fail, eats my weight in deviled eggs.　　_____

3. He barbecues chicken and ribs on an extra large grill.　　_____

4. It make everyone within a mile hungry.　　_____

5. They closes off the entire street to traffic.　　_____

6. We sets up a platform in the middle of the street.　　_____

7. He play drums with the group every year.　　_____

8. She dress in a denim skirt and a white shirt.　　_____

9. They dance much better than we do.　　_____

10. She practices dancing once in a while.　　_____

11. We likes the chance for a neighborhood get-together.　　_____

EXERCISE 82

Agreement With Indefinite Pronouns

An indefinite pronoun does not always refer to a particular noun. Therefore, indefinite pronouns may be singular or plural. Read the sentence to determine whether the indefinite pronoun is singular or plural.

A. Underline the indefinite pronoun in each sentence. Then write whether it is singular or plural in the space provided.

Example: Anybody can whistle a tune.   *singular*

	Singular
1. No one was listening to my report.	someone
2. Has everybody left the meeting?	anyone
3. Few have stayed until the end.	everyone
4. Several tried to move the cabinet.	something
5. Somebody has given me this mail.	somebody
6. Others can be found in the next room.	anybody
7. Everyone in the store offered me help.	everybody
8. Many know the owner of this building.	no one
9. Someone sent me a fax from Rome.	**Plural**
10. Both took more than a day to arrive.	few
	both
	many
	several
	others

B. Choose the verb in parentheses that agrees with the indefinite pronoun. Then write the correct verb in the space provided.

Example: Someone (is, are) at the door.   *is*

1. Few (knows, know) the value of these documents.   _____
2. Many (fits, fit) along this wall.   _____
3. Something (knocks, knock) over our trash cans.   _____
4. Now both (is, are) in our backyard.   _____
5. No one ever (sees, see) the culprit.   _____
6. Everyone usually (arrives, arrive) on time for lunch.   _____
7. Several (brings, bring) their own sandwiches.   _____
8. Others (buys, buy) their lunch.   _____
9. Somebody (sings, sing) in the shower.   _____
10. Everybody (plays, play) the game tic-tac-toe.   _____

EXERCISE 83

Practicing Agreement in Sentences With Indefinite Pronouns

When an indefinite pronoun is used as a subject, the verb in the sentence must agree with it.

Underline the subject of each sentence once. Then underline the verb in parentheses twice that agrees with it.

Example: Neither of the two (knows, know) much about water.

1. Everyone (has, have) heard the expression "solid citizen."

2. None of us would (thinks, think) of saying "liquid citizen."

3. Everyone (is, are) composed of a great deal of water.

4. Most of the world's males (is, are) approximately 70 percent water.

5. Few of the females (contains, contain) that much water.

6. All of the water in a woman (equals, equal) about half her body weight.

7. Of infants, many (is, are) 85 percent water.

8. Each of us (has, have) to replenish his or her body's water daily.

9. One (needs, need) to drink approximately three quarts of liquids per day.

10. Each of us (use, uses) a good deal of water daily.

11. Anybody without a daily supply of water (is, are) in trouble.

12. All of the parts of the human body (need, needs) water.

13. No one (think, thinks) of muscles and brains as water.

14. Yet both (is, are) three-quarters water.

15. Neither (has, have) as much water as blood has.

16. Everyone (require, requires) water.

17. No one (is, are) able to survive without water.

18. Most of the water in the world (is, are) salt water.

19. Many of the world's people (waste, wastes) much water.

20. Some of us (uses, use) less water than others.

21. Everyone should (learns, learn) how to conserve water.

EXERCISE 84

Review of Agreement in Sentences With Indefinite Pronouns

When an indefinite pronoun is used as a subject, the verb in the sentence must agree with it.

A. Circle the correct form of the verb for each sentence.

Example: Both of us (work) works).

1. Each of us (works, work) for a different company.
2. Everyone in the family (helps, help) at home.
3. Everybody (takes, take) turns cooking.
4. One of my sons (is, are) responsible for the vacuuming.
5. Most of his friends (has, have) jobs at home, too.
6. No one (is, are) free until after dinner.
7. Neither of my daughters (do, does) boring jobs.
8. One (is, are) a secretary by day and a student by night.
9. Both (works, work) for a travel agent.
10. All of us (travels, travel) together frequently.

B. Write either *has* or *have* in the space provided.

Example: Everyone _____*has*_____ vacation plans.

1. No one in the family _____ much extra money.
2. Some of us _____ worn-out luggage.
3. Everyone still _____ fun on our trips.
4. Neither of my daughters _____ much spare time.
5. Both of them _____ new jobs.
6. Each of us _____ a favorite way of traveling.
7. Both of my daughters _____ many vacation ideas.
8. Most of us _____ many souvenirs.
9. Each of my sons _____ collected mementos.
10. One son _____ posters from many places.

EXERCISE 85

Agreement When Subjects Are Separated From Verbs

Agreement between subject and verb is not affected by words or phrases that come between the subject and the verb.

A. Underline the correct verb in parentheses. Remember to make the verb agree with the noun that is the subject of the sentence, not the noun that is an object.

Example: Riders of motorcycles often (carries, <u>carry</u>) maps.

1. A map of the 50 states often (shows, show) parts of Mexico.
2. The boundaries of this town (is, are) on this map.
3. A special guide for campers (is, are) at the store.
4. Landmarks of general interest (is, are) on this map.
5. Travel without any maps (is, are) sometimes risky.
6. Many of the best trips in the world (requires, require) careful planning.
7. The trail between the mountains (is, are) a favorite route.
8. Sea lions in California (attracts, attract) many tourists.

B. Rewrite the sentences. Correct the agreement mistakes.

Examples: Maps in an atlas is very useful.

Maps in an atlas are very useful.

1. Maps of this state shows all the important roads.

_____

2. Many people in our town does not travel far from home.

_____

3. Bicycles with ten gears appears frequently.

_____

4. The use of bicycles have increased recently.

_____

5. A bicycle rider without proper skills are dangerous.

_____

More Practice With Agreement When Subjects Are Separated From Verbs

Agreement between subject and verb is not affected by words or phrases that come between the subject and the verb.

A. Write *S* over each subject and *V* over each verb. Draw a line under any word that comes between the subject and the verb.

Example: Jobs, for some people, provide fun as well as financial gain.

1. Jobs for outgoing types include costumed telegram delivery, and flower or balloon delivery.

2. Zany costumes, some homemade, can replace uniforms.

3. Smiles, as well as money, are part of the payment.

4. Children, especially young ones, love clowns.

5. Clowns—with sad or funny faces—will be welcomed at most children's parties.

6. Clowns, on their off days, may entertain their own children at home.

7. Almost anyone with a sense of humor can become a costumed delivery person.

8. Few people, believe it or not, make really good clowns.

B. Circle the correct form of the verb in parentheses.

Example: A curb painting service for homeowners (is, are) an inexpensive business to start.

1. The costs, even with quality supplies, (is, are) minimal.

2. A painting kit with the following items (helps, help) you get started.

3. Spray paint, masking tape, paintbrushes, a ruler, and a numerical stencil—which you can buy at any office supply store—(puts, put) you in business.

4. Neighborhoods, with lots of homes close together, (makes, make) your job easier.

5. A good idea, just to be safe, (are, is) to review your community's rules before starting your business.

6. Laws, old or new, (require, requires) your compliance.

7. You, of course, (wants, want) to obey all laws concerning community property.

EXERCISE 87

Agreement of Verbs in Sentences With Inverted Order

The position of a subject in a sentence does not affect subject-verb agreement.

A. Underline the correct form of the verb in parentheses.

Example: How (<u>do</u>, does) you get a patent?

1. What (is, are) patents?
2. In Washington (is, are) an office that grants patents.
3. There (seem, seems) to be inventors everywhere.
4. Why (does, do) these inventors seek patents?
5. How (does, do) a patent protect an invention?
6. There (is, are) a patent law for the rights of the inventor.
7. Here (is, are) some devices that have been patented.
8. There once (was, were) a patented lip-shaping machine.
9. (Is, Are) there any special inventions for dieters?
10. Here (is, are) an electric calorie-counter.

B. Underline the subject in each sentence. Then identify the seven sentences with mistakes in subject-verb agreement. Write the correct verb in the space provided. Write *correct* if the correct verb is used.

Example: Does <u>you</u> know of more inventions like these?   _____*Do*_____

1. There has been patents for dog-food flavors.   _____
2. Here is some dogs now.   _____
3. Is they ready to taste the different flavors?   _____
4. There is a collie with a napkin in its collar.   _____
5. Into the room come a hungry bulldog.   _____
6. Do these dogs have delicate tastebuds?   _____
7. Is they good judges of dog food?   _____
8. How do we find out?   _____
9. There are no way to ask them.   _____
10. Why doesn't we watch what they eat?   _____

EXERCISE 88

Using Sentences With Inverted Order

The position of a subject in a sentence does not affect the agreement between the subject and the verb.

A. Circle the subject and underline the verb in each sentence.

Example: <u>Do</u> (you) <u>know</u> about exotic fruits?

1. Have you heard of a rambutan?
2. Is it really from Southeast Asia?
3. Does it actually have little whiskers?
4. What is this fruit called?
5. Have you eaten a mineola?
6. Does it look like an orange?
7. Is this fruit egg-shaped?
8. Is this a kiwi?
9. How tasty is this fruit?
10. Should it be eaten cold?

B. Complete each sentence below with either *here* or *there* plus a verb showing the present time.

Example: ___There are___ some plantains over there.

1. _____ a fruit called the naranjilla.
2. _____ a place in the Andes where it grows.
3. _____ some South American tree tomatoes.
4. _____ many strange plants in the world.
5. _____ one from Africa.

C. Rewrite each sentence so that the subject is first and the verb agrees with the subject.

Example: Beneath the desk lies the lost documents.

Lost documents lie beneath the desk.

1. Inside the drawer was money and receipts.

_____

2. Above the bookshelves is a plaque.

_____

3. Alongside the desk is a cabinet and a wastebasket.

_____

4. Down the hall is my colleagues.

_____

11   Words That Describe Nouns or Pronouns

Adjectives are words that describe nouns or pronouns. They answer the questions, *What kind? How many? Which one?*

Examples: The *red* folders contain new customer orders. (*Red* answers the question, What kind of folders?)

Several orders are missing. (*Several* answers the question, How many orders?)

His *first* order was misplaced. (*First* answers the question, Which order?)

Some adjectives are **proper adjectives**. They are special adjectives formed from proper nouns, which name a *specific* person, place, or thing. Proper adjectives, like proper nouns, are always *capitalized*.

Examples of Some Proper Adjectives

Mexican	Jamaican	Canadian	Korean
Swiss	Danish	African	Asian
Greek	Turkish	Spanish	Egyptian

Articles are also words that describe nouns. Words like *a*, *an*, and *the* come before the noun or adjective. There are a few simple rules for using articles:

- **Rule 1**   Use *a* before nouns or adjectives that have a consonant sound.
- **Rule 2**   Use *an* before nouns or adjectives that have a vowel (a, e, i, o, u) sound.
- **Rule 3**   *A* and *an* are used with singular nouns and adjectives.
- **Rule 4**   *The* can be used with singular or plural nouns or adjectives. *The* shows a nonspecific amount.

There are a few exceptions to these rules (for example, a university; an RCA television, etc.)

The adjective pairs *this* and *that* and *these* and *those* are often misused. *This* and *that* are singular adjectives; *these* and *those* are plural. Use *this* and *that* with singular nouns and pronouns. Use *these* and *those* with plural nouns and pronouns.

Examples: *This* uniform is too tight. (singular noun; use *this*)

These aprons are starched. (plural noun; use *these*)

Adjectives describe nouns and pronouns. Adjectives can also be used to compare things. When adjectives are used to compare, they change their form to show comparison between two or more things.

Examples: This memo is *long*. (Simple adjective describing the noun *memo*)

This memo is even *longer*. (Adjective changes form to describe two things—*this memo* and another one.)

This memo is the *longest* I've ever seen. (Adjective changes form to describe three or more things—many memos.)

There are four rules for using adjectives to compare:

- •**Rule 1**   Most adjectives add *-er* to compare two things and *-est* to compare three or more (*bright, brighter, brightest; soft, softer, softest*).
- •**Rule 2**   Some adjectives use more or most with the adjective to show comparison (*gifted, more gifted, most gifted; talented, more talented, most talented*).
- •**Rule 3**   When an adjective ends in *-y*, it often changes the *-y* to *-i* before adding *-er* or *-est* to show comparison (*pretty, prettier, prettiest; healthy, healthier, healthiest*).
- •**Rule 4**   Some adjectives follow no rules. Each comparison form is spelled *differently*. Below are some examples of these *irregular comparisons*.

Irregular Adjective Comparisons

much	more	most
little	less	least
bad	worse	worst
good	better	best

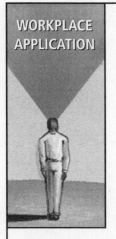

WORKPLACE APPLICATION

The following conversation was overheard on the way to a lunchroom:

"Come on, Sally," Anthony said. "Let's eat. I'm more hungrier than I've ever been."

"Slow down, Anthony," Sally said. "We'll get there. It's only 10:45. This is the earlier we've eaten in three years of working together."

Can you find two mistakes in using comparison adjectives?
(Clue: An adjective follows *either* Rule 1 or Rule 2, but not both.)

_____

_____

What Is an Adjective?

Adjectives help describe nouns or pronouns. They tell what kind, how many, or which one.

A. Underline the adjectives in the sentences below.

Example: Sasha wore a <u>beautiful</u> <u>new</u> scarf to work.

1. The scarf was made of fine blue wool.
2. Her husband had given this warm gift to Sasha.
3. Friends admired the three vivid green stripes on the end.
4. On Monday Sasha wore this favorite item to work.
5. That day she lost the lovely scarf.
6. A sorry Sasha hunted for this special scarf.
7. Helpful coworkers joined the search.
8. Two clerks looked through several rooms.

B. Find the adjectives in each sentence and underline them. Next circle the noun the adjective describes. Then write whether the adjective tells *which one* or *what kind*.

Example: An <u>unhappy</u> (Sasha) went home.   _____*what kind*_____

1. That night Mr. Moss checked the offices.   _____
2. The kindly custodian saw a scarf by a table.   _____
3. The next morning he called to Sasha.   _____
4. He handed her the woolen scarf.   _____
5. The happy woman thanked Mr. Moss.   _____
6. Later Sasha bought a thank-you card.   _____
7. She gave it to the thoughtful Mr. Moss.   _____

C. Write an adjective for each noun under the headings. The first one is done for you.

Which One	What Kind	How Many
1. ___*second*___ shift	_____ letter	_____ employees
2. _____ factory	_____ fax	_____ supervisors
3. _____ union	_____ memo	_____ managers

EXERCISE 90

Proper Descriptive Adjectives

Some adjectives are formed from proper nouns and are often spelled a little differently than the proper noun they came from. Both proper nouns and proper adjectives are always capitalized.

A. Rewrite the following list. Change the proper nouns to adjectives. Choose from these words: *Egyptian, Greek, Turkish, Swiss, Australian, Arabian, Canadian, Danish,* and *Spanish.*

Example: art from Africa   _African art_

1. horses from Arabia   _____
2. lumber from Canada   _____
3. lace from Spain   _____
4. beef from Australia   _____
5. furniture from Denmark   _____
6. jewelry from Egypt   _____
7. carpets from Turkey   _____
8. watches from Switzerland   _____
9. sandals from Greece   _____

B. Rewrite each sentence so that the proper adjectives are capitalized.

Example: The american diplomat had a party.
              The American diplomat had a party.

1. Two german officials met the english consul.

   _____

2. The hostess wore indian jewelry and chinese silk.

   _____

3. The peruvian guests liked the alaskan salmon.

   _____

4. The european visitors heard puerto rican music.

   _____

5. He liked canadian bacon with his eggs.

   _____

More Proper Descriptive Adjectives

Some adjectives are formed from proper nouns. These adjectives are always capitalized.

A. Write the proper adjective in each sentence correctly in the space provided.

Example: The korean songs sounded familiar.   _____Korean_____

1. These are unusual chinese cymbals.   _____

2. Do you like spanish guitar music?   _____

3. Listen to Tedsu play his hawaiian ukulele.   _____

4. Lou Ackerman plays the french horn.   _____

5. Is it difficult to master the indian sitar?   _____

6. The ukrainian dancers all wore boots.   _____

7. Most of the men in the welsh choir are miners.   _____

8. I love italian operas.   _____

9. Can you name some american composers?   _____

10. A russian ballet troupe will visit our city.   _____

B. Rewrite each phrase, changing the proper noun to one of the adjectives at the right.

Example: art from Nigeria   _____Nigerian art_____

1. baskets from Ecuador   _____

2. a kilt from Scotland   _____

3. a rug from Sweden   _____

4. a team from Ireland   _____

5. lakes in Canada   _____

6. cars from Germany   _____

7. a river in Egypt   _____

8. jewelry from Mexico   _____

9. minerals of Bolivia   _____

10. singer from Jamaica   _____

Word List
- - - - - - - - -
Canadian
Bolivian
Swedish
Ecuadoran
Egyptian
Jamaican
Scottish
Mexican
German
Irish

Using Adjectives

Some words describe nouns or pronouns.

A. Write an adjective before each noun below. Then use each group of words to write a sentence with a workplace setting as the background.

Example: _____gift_____ shop _We work in a gift shop._

1. _____ books   4. _____ storeroom   7. _____ poster

2. _____ ornaments   5. _____ audiotape   8. _____ dolphin

3. _____ seashells   6. _____ customer   9. _____ wall

10. _____

11. _____

12. _____

13. _____

14. _____

15. _____

16. _____

17. _____

18. _____

B. Underline the proper adjectives. Circle any other adjectives. You will find 11 in all.

Example: (That) woman is a (talented) American athlete.

1. She is a skillful player.

2. She plays in many European tournaments.

3. She has won tournaments in several nations.

4. She plays against famous English athletes.

5. An Australian coach helped her greatly.

6. She won a British championship.

7. She has won North American titles, too.

8. Her colorful style inspires young people.

EXERCISE 93

Review of Adjectives

Some words describe nouns or pronouns.

A. Write an adjective for each noun.

Example: _____*blue*_____ wall

1. _____ day   5. _____ music   9. _____ weather
2. _____ paper   6. _____ bus   10. _____ vacation
3. _____ time card 7. _____ building   11. _____ salary
4. _____ customer 8. _____ lobby   12. _____ check

B. Circle the proper adjectives in the sentences. Underline all the other descriptive words.

Example: Three (Greek) divers found an old shipwreck near Greece.

1. They discovered ancient pots and parts of a wooden ship.

2. Were those fine relics from an ancient Grecian culture?

3. The American divers had scientific backgrounds.

4. For many years they had examined numerous clues from the past.

5. Several clues provided new information.

6. The divers had discovered beautiful Roman pottery and jewelry.

7. They had uncovered important European carvings and tools.

8. Other scientists have contributed to this historical study.

C. Complete each sentence by adding *-ful*, *-able*, *-less*, or *-ish* to the word in parentheses.

Example: Archaeologists spend _____*endless*_____ hours seeking relics.   (end)

1. They find _____ things.   (remark)

2. Some discoveries are _____.   (price)

3. A major find makes them _____.   (joy)

4. Searchers rarely take _____ chances.   (fool)

5. Sometimes the search seems _____.   (hope)

6. Archaeologists travel to _____ places.   (wonder)

7. They sometimes find _____ relics.   (value)

Articles

A, *an,* and *the* are special kinds of words called articles. Articles are placed before nouns or before words that describe nouns. Articles are used to show amounts that are nonspecific, or not definite. Use *a* before an adjective that begins with a consonant. Use *an* before an adjective that begins with a vowel.

A. Complete each sentence with a correct article.

Example: The woodcarver made _____*a*_____ beautiful statue.   (a, an)

1. His statue is _____ soaring eagle.   (a, an)

2. The statue is _____ exact copy of a real eagle.   (a, an)

3. _____ eagle has huge wings.   (The, A)

4. You can see every feather on _____ eagle.   (a, the)

5. Have you watched _____ eagle soar in the sky?   (a, an)

6. It's _____ magnificent sight!   (an, a)

7. The carver also made _____ old-fashioned ship.   (an, a)

8. This little ship has _____ smallest sails that you have ever seen. (a, the)

9. Everything on _____ ship is carved in exact detail.   (a, the)

10. It is _____ authentic model of ships that sailed the oceans in the 1800s.   (an, a)

B. Using the given nouns, write sentences using the articles *a*, *an*, and *the*.

Example: key _The key has a shiny gold color._

1. showroom _____

_____

2. auditor _____

_____

3. recommendation _____

_____

_____

4. hospital _____

_____

EXERCISE 95

Using *This, That, These,* and *Those*

The words *this* and *that* are singular. The words *these* and *those* are plural. Use *this* and *that* to indicate one (singular). Use *these* and *those* to indicate more than one (plural).

A. Circle the word in parentheses that completes each sentence correctly.

Example: (This, (These)) days offices require more than secretaries and file clerks.

1. I like (this, these) kinds of jobs more than where I used to work.
2. A desktop publisher does the job that (this, these) secretary used to do.
3. (This, These) extra duties were added, however.
4. Working with graphics and page layouts are among (that, those) duties assigned.
5. (That, Those) kind of technology has come to the workplace to stay.
6. Computers made quick work of (this, these) spreadsheet calculations.
7. Files from (that, those) file cabinets were put onto a single computer desk.
8. One electronic database organizes all (this, these) office's data.
9. A computer network connects all (this, these) computers.
10. Employees from several different areas use (this, these) same printer.

B. Rewrite each sentence, using *this, that, these,* or *those* correctly.

Example: This here tape recorder belongs to me.

This tape recorder belongs to me.

1. Them fax machines are broken.

_____

2. That there electronic dictionary holds over 10,000 words.

_____

3. I hope to buy one of that small laptop computers.

_____

4. I'd like to have some of this new technologies in my house.

_____

5. The boys from those team are on the bus.

_____

More Practice Using *This, That, These,* and *Those*

This and **that** are singular. **These** and **those** are plural. Each one must be used in agreement with the verb of a sentence.

A. Write the correct word in parentheses in the space provided.

Example: Look at (this here, this) old album I inherited.   _____*this*_____

1. (Those, Them) photos were taken by my uncle.   _____

2. He visited all of (these here, these) places.   _____

3. (This, This here) picture is of Latourell Falls.   _____

4. (Them, Those) waterfalls are very tall.   _____

5. Have you ever visited (this here, this) area?   _____

6. (That there, That) river has some thrilling rapids.   _____

7. The river's source is in (those, them) rugged cliffs.   _____

8. (These here, These) hills are huge sand dunes in Colorado.   _____

9. (Those, That) person looks almost like a tiny speck.   _____

10. Now take a look at (these, this) scene!   _____

11. (Them, Those) mountains are certainly beautiful.   _____

B. Rewrite the sentences using *this, that, these,* or *those* correctly.

Example: Them ships are huge oil tankers.
   Those ships are huge oil tankers.

1. Personally, I prefer these here sailboats.

   _____

2. This here harbor is very busy.

   _____

3. Have you ever ridden on one of them ferries?

   _____

4. I once took a boat to that there island.

   _____

5. Look at them oyster boats docked at the pier.

   _____

Review of *This, That, These,* and *Those*

This and **that** are singular. **These** and **those** are plural.

A. Underline the correct word in parentheses once. Draw two lines under the noun it identifies.

Example: "(This, These) eggs are too hard," said the fussy man.

1. "I thought you liked them (that, those) way," said the waiter.
2. "Please tell (that, those) cooks of yours to soften them."
3. "(These, these here) eggs cannot be softened, sir."
4. "(This, These) restaurant is terrible," the fussy man said.
5. "(That, Those) customers are staring," the waiter said.
6. "I should have stayed home (this, these) morning."
7. The waiter said, "Let me correct (this, these) problem, sir."
8. At (that, those) moment, the waiter had a bright idea.
9. "(This here, This) customer doesn't know what he wants."
10. "I'm sure he ordered (them, those) eggs cooked hard."
11. "Why do you want (that, that there) plate?" the cook asked.
12. "I'll put (this, these) hard eggs on it," the waiter replied.
13. "I'll put (that, those) soft eggs on the same plate."
14. "Now (this, these) eggs are delicious!" said the fussy man.
15. "(This, These) kinds of eggs are cooked just the way I like them."

B. Write *this, that, these,* and *those* to complete each sentence correctly.

Example: I'll buy _____*that*_____ hat over there.

1. _____ hat on my head is too big.
2. _____ people out there aren't wearing hats.
3. Maybe I should buy _____ gloves that are right here instead.
4. _____ pair of gloves I have on fits well.
5. The gloves match _____ scarf I'm wearing.
6. How much do _____ scarves over there cost?

Showing Comparisons of Things

Some adjectives change form when they are used to compare two or more items. Many add -er to compare two. They add -est to compare three or more. A few add more or most in front of the word to show comparison.

A. Add the missing forms of each word. Remember to make spelling changes and to use *more* or *most* when needed. The first one is done for you.

Descriptive Word	Comparing Two Things	Comparing Three or More Things
large	larger	largest
nervous		
	smoother	
		most splendid
		shiniest
	more intelligent	
rough		
		widest
		earliest
creative		

B. Complete each sentence with the correct form of the word in parentheses.

Example: This tie is _____*longer*_____ than this one.   (long)

1. The other tie is _____ than this one.   (narrow)

2. This is a _____ tie than that one.   (pretty)

3. These are the _____ patterns of all.   (nice)

4. The _____ person to shop for is my father.   (difficult)

5. The _____ tie he has is his red one.   (attractive)

6. Which of these two ties is _____?   (expensive)

7. Her baby is the _____ in the nursery.   (small)

8. Karen writes _____ than her sister.   (neat)

EXERCISE 99

Additional Comparisons of Things

Adjectives can compare two or more things. They have different forms for each comparison.

A. Complete the chart by writing in the correct adjective. The first one is done for you.

Description	Two Things	Three or More Things
1. hungry	hungrier	hungriest
2. brilliant		
3.	tidier	
4.	angrier	
5.	more athletic	
6. huge		
7.		kindest
8. delicious		
9.	thinner	
10. simple		

B. Fill in the blank with the correct form of the word in parentheses.

Example: Your joke is much (funny) than mine.   _____funnier_____

1. Gus was once the (gloomy) guy.   _____

2. The old mill on the hill is (mysterious) than

    any other.   _____

3. The (windy) day of the year was yesterday.   _____

4. Put all but the (shabby) dish towels in this pile.   _____

5. The younger employee is (ambitious) than his

    older coworker.   _____

6. I want this office staff to be (cheerful) than

    ever before.   _____

7. A coat of paint has made the employee

    lounge (sunny) than it was.   _____

EXERCISE 100

Irregular Forms for Comparisons

Some adjectives change forms in irregular ways to compare things. If you are not familiar with these forms, you need to look them up in a dictionary to use them correctly.

A. Complete the chart by writing in the correct forms of the adjectives. The word list at the right helps you. Use a dictionary if necessary.

Description	Two Things	Three or More Things
1. much		
2. far		
3. little		
4. bad		
5. good		

Word List
- - - - - - - - - -
worse
better
least
more
farther
farthest
most
best
less
worst

B. Fill in the blank with the correct form of the word in parentheses.

Example: Your ad is (good) than mine.   *better*

1. Who has (much) money, you or me?

2. The bus stop is (far) away than I thought.

3. Of all the workers, Pat Ryan has the (little) difficulty.

4. My legs feel (good) today than they did yesterday.

5. This training video is the (good) one we've seen yet.

6. Unfortunately, this is the (bad) assignment of all for beginners.

7. Anne and Rich live (far) away than the rest of us.

8. My computer is in (bad) condition than I thought.

9. This is the (far) distance I have ever driven a truck.

10. That programmer can key the (much) words per minute.

11. I am doing a lot (little) work than I used to.

12. This looks like the (good) warehouse of all to rent.

13. There is (much) gossip in our office now than in the past.

More Irregular Comparisons

Adjectives change form to compare two or more things.

A. After each adjective, write its forms to compare two things and more than two things.

Example: small, _smaller, smallest_

1. tall, _____
2. happy, _____
3. easy, _____
4. careful, _____
5. high, _____
6. keen, _____

7. little, _____
8. bad, _____
9. loyal, _____
10. clean, _____
11. sturdy, _____
12. curious, _____

B. In each sentence write the correct form of the word in parentheses. You will not need to change some of the words.

Example: Sharks have the _____ _worst_ _____ reputation of all fish. (bad)

1. The shark is _____ than a whale. (ferocious)

2. Sharks have _____ teeth than killer whales. (sharp)

3. A shark's tail is _____ than a whale's tail. (small)

4. The shark has _____ hearing than many other creatures do. (sensitive)

5. The _____ kind of shark weighs 15 tons. (large)

6. Some people say that sharks are the _____ of all fish. (dangerous)

7. Sharks really do very _____ harm to people. (little)

8. _____ people are killed by cars than by sharks. (many)

9. Sharks swim at a _____ speed than some boats. (fast)

10. Any _____ movements may attract nearby sharks. (quick)

11. Sharks have _____ hearing. (keen)

12. The _____ evidence of sharks can be found in teeth, spines, and scales that appeared millions of years ago. (early)

12 Words That Describe or Explain Verbs

An **adverb** is a word that *describes* a *verb* in a sentence. Adverbs are used with both action and state of being verbs. Most adverbs answer the questions *when? where?* and *how?* the action of the sentence takes place.

Adverbs are often found next to the verbs they describe, but sometimes there are other words separating them. All root words ending with the suffix *-ly* are adverbs.

Examples: I will answer the phone *later.* (Adverb *later* answers the question *when?* about the verb *will answer.*)

Here are your missing glasses. (Adverb *here* answers the question *where?* to describe the verb *are.*)

Phillipe *bravely* extinguished the trash fire. (Adverb *bravely* answers the question *how?* about the verb *extinguished.*)

Adverbs can also be used to *modify* (add new meaning to or change the meaning of) verbs, adjectives, or other adverbs. They also answer the question *to what degree?*

Examples: He has *yet* to come. (Adverb *yet* slightly changes the meaning of the verb *to come.*)

Your display was *very* pretty. (Adverb *very* answers the question *to what degree?* about the adverb *tired.*)

    yet   so   again   even   really   very

Adverbs can also be used with verbs to *show comparison.* Like adjectives, they change their form to show different comparisons. The rules for changing adverb forms to show comparison are similar to the rules for changing adjective forms to show comparison. There are two rules for using adverbs to compare:

- **•Rule 1** Some adverbs add *-r* or *-er* to compare two things and *-est* to compare three or more (*late, later, latest; soon, sooner, soonest*).
- **•Rule 2** Most adverbs use *more* or *most* with the adverb to show comparison (*nearly, more nearly, most nearly; reluctantly, more reluctantly, most reluctantly*).
  Note: Some words can be used as both adjectives and adverbs, for example, *great, slow, aware, lonely, friendly,* etc.

WORKPLACE APPLICATION

Alan saw this ad in the newspaper.

Help Wanted: Must be hardly worker.

Do you think this ad says what it means? Why or why not?

_____

_____

_____

Rewrite the ad correctly.

_____

_____

_____

Now write your own ad for a childcare helper.

_____

_____

_____

EXERCISE 102

What Is an Adverb?

Adverbs describe or explain verbs. They answer the questions *how? when?* and *where?* an action takes place. Most adverbs are found next to the verb. Sometimes there will be other words between the verb and the adverb.

A. Circle the verb described by each underlined adverb. Write *how? when?* or *where?* in the space provided to show how the underlined word describes the verb.

Example: Fitness instructors (work) hard to ensure their clients' safety during exercise.   *how?*

1. Instructors <u>carefully</u> explain each exercise. _____

2. They demonstrate each exercise to the clients <u>first</u>. _____

3. Then they <u>closely</u> watch as the clients perform the exercise. _____

4. The instructors <u>gently</u> guide their clients through the steps required to learn a routine. _____

5. A full aerobic routine is <u>slowly</u> learned. _____

6. Clients can then master the proper form <u>first</u>. _____

7. Stretching is done ever so <u>slowly</u>. _____

8. Cautions about not bouncing or jerking are taken <u>seriously</u>. _____

B. Underline the adverb and circle the verb it describes. Then write *how? when?* or *where?* in the blank to show how the adverb describes the verb.

Example: The temperature (reached) 100 degrees <u>yesterday</u>.   *when?*

1. Ali sold ice cream outside from a cart. _____

2. He waited patiently for customers. _____

3. The temperature rose quickly. _____

4. He soon shaded his stand with an umbrella. _____

5. Ali then noticed a crowd at the nearby bus stop. _____

6. The people stood uncomfortably in the hot sun. _____

7. Ali immediately moved his stand. _____

8. His business improved there. _____

EXERCISE 103

Identifying Other Adverbs

Adverbs describe verbs. They answer the questions *when? where?* and *how?* an action happens.

A. Circle the descriptive word in each sentence. Underline the verb it describes.

Example: Sara Janski <u>worked</u> (continually) during the sale.

1. She answered questions politely.
2. She definitely had a good crowd.
3. Sara sat outside with the cash box.
4. Her business improved steadily.
5. She started it alone.
6. Now she has many workers.
7. She always deals in American handicrafts.
8. She holds sales frequently.
9. Word of the sales spreads rapidly.
10. She is quite successful.

B. Add an adverb or adverbs to each sentence.

Example: The sale began _____ *early* _____ .

1. People lined up _____.
2. Customers _____ liked the jewelry.
3. Many people bought placemats _____.
4. The goods were displayed _____ in the store.
5. Bowls were arranged _____ on tables.
6. Sales continued _____.
7. Vases were put on shelves _____.
8. Sara and her employees worked _____.
9. The sale closed _____.
10. The customers left the store _____.

EXERCISE 104

Using Adverbs

Some adverbs describe verbs by answering the questions *when? where?* and *how?* Others answer the question *to what degree?*

A. Use a word from the word list to complete each sentence.

Example: _____ *Recently* _____ I had an interesting experience.

Word List	
yet	clumsily
cautiously	again
yesterday	down
so	near
fearfully	later
suddenly	swiftly
quickly	always
recently	very
carefully	clearly

1. _____ I saw a ball of feathers by the road.

2. I went _____ toward it to see what it was.

3. It hopped and ran _____ toward the grass.

4. Its beak showed _____ that it was a hawk.

5. It had not learned to fly _____ well.

6. _____ that day, I saw a swooping bird.

7. It was _____ close that I could see its eyes.

8. It dropped _____ into the grass nearby.

9. The large bird rose _____.

10. The bird flew _____ away.

B. Underline the adverb that tells *when? where?* or *how?* Then write the verb that the adverb describes.

Example: A small bird peeped <u>loudly</u>.   _____ *peeped* _____

1. I walked quietly toward the grass.   _____

2. Soon I saw a baby hawk.   _____

3. It hopped clumsily.   _____

4. I moved slowly.   _____

5. As I came near, the hawk stared.   _____

6. I stopped suddenly.   _____

7. I watched hopefully.   _____

8. I knew that people occasionally care for wild animals.   _____

9. I silently watched the hawk.   _____

10. After a while it hopped away.   _____

More Practice Using Adverbs

Adverbs describe verbs *when? where?* and *how?* Others answer the question *to what degree?*

A. Circle the adverb in each sentence that answers the questions *when? where? how?* and *to what degree?*

Example: We could (finally) afford to take the family on vacation.

1. Eagerly we headed for Mammoth Cave in Kentucky.
2. We peered inside and gasped.
3. Extremely large stalactites hung from above.
4. They were very impressive to see.
5. Then we saw the stalagmites rising from the floor.
6. These stone formations looked quite pretty.
7. We walked carefully through the gigantic cave.
8. Soon we came to a special tourist attraction.
9. We looked silently at a 2400-year-old mummy.
10. How did it get here?

B. Circle each adverb that answers the questions *when? where? how?* or *to what degree?*

Example: We waited (impatiently) for the others.

1. Those cars are manufactured here.
2. The motorcycle skidded on very loose gravel.
3. Ralph spoke excitedly of his new job.
4. "We'll eat later," Mitch remarked.
5. "But I'm hungry now," his date wailed.
6. Tell the children to play outside.
7. My boss is being too strict about the dress code in this heat.
8. A gray bat fluttered overhead.
9. The rookie pitcher was extremely nervous.
10. They were rather irritated by the sound of the dripping faucet.

EXERCISE 106

Comparisons of Actions

Adverbs change form to compare two or more actions.

A. Complete the chart below by writing the correct adverb forms. The first one has been done for you.

Adverb	Comparing Two Actions	Comparing Three or More Actions
cheerfully	more cheerfully	most cheerfully
hard		
	faster	
		most gently
		most firmly
	more excitedly	
		most eagerly
		most politely
likely		

B. Underline the correct form of the adverb in parentheses in each sentence.

Example: The clerk answered the telephone (<u>rudely</u>, more rudely).

1. He spoke as (quickly, most quickly) as he could.

2. "Ben's Pizza," he said. "We deliver (faster, fastest) than our competitors."

3. "Please speak (more slowly, most slowly)," said the caller.

4. "Okay," said Ben. "This is Ben's Pizza. Do you want to order (sooner, soonest) or later? I'm waiting."

5. "I don't think I want to order at all," said the caller. She hung up the phone (angrily, more angrily).

6. Ben should have spoken (more politely, most politely).

7. His rudeness (more likely, most likely) cost him a sale.

8. Customers expect to be greeted (more respectfully, most respectfully).

9. Many customers can (more easily, most easily) be lost through rudeness than through any other method.

10. Clerks who are (most eager, more eager) than Ben for business will not treat customers rudely.

EXERCISE 107

Additional Comparisons of Actions

Adverbs change form to compare two or more actions.

A. Complete the chart by writing the correct adverb form. The first one has been done for you.

Adverb	Comparing Two Actions	Comparing Three or More Actions
1. late	later	latest
2.	more happily	
3.		earliest
4. carefully		
5.	sooner	
6. easily		
7. high		
8.		most loudly
9. fast		
10. clearly		

B. Write the correct adverb form in parentheses in the space provided.

Example: I wake up (early) than anyone in my family.   _____earlier_____

1. Of all the bus routes, this one comes (near) to
   my house.   _____

2. Spring will arrive (soon) than you expect.   _____

3. I watched the game (closely) than Scott.   _____

4. Our train arrived (late) of all.   _____

5. Lou runs (fast) in track shoes than in sneakers.   _____

6. Of the entire chorus, Mr. Jacobs sings (loudly).   _____

7. Our dog can jump (high) than the fence.   _____

8. Jake has the (fast) pitch in the league.   _____

9. Pat finished the research (slow) than her secretary.   _____

10. I work (efficiently) than she did.   _____

13 Using Descriptive Words Correctly

Adjectives and adverbs are important words in sentences. They add to or describe the two most important elements in a sentence—the subject and the verb. Adjectives and adverbs can be either single words, or they can be adjective or adverb phrases.

Examples: This is a *new* house. (Adjective *new* describes the subject, *house.*)

This is the *newest* house *on the hill*. (Adjective *newest* and adjective phrase *on the hill* both describe the subject, *house.*)

The meeting went *well*. (Adverb *well* describes the verb, *went.*)

We hurried *as quickly as we could out the door*. (Adverb phrases *as quickly as we could* and *out the door* both describe the verb, *hurried.*)

Adjectives and adverbs are often formed from the same principal part, or simplest form, of a word. Both adjectives and adverbs sometimes add *-er* and *-est* to the principal part to make adjective or adverb forms. Both sometimes use *more* or *most* with the principal part to make adjective or adverb forms.

Only adverbs sometimes add *-ly* to a principal part to create adverb forms. Knowing this can help you to choose the correct adjective or adverb to make sentences.

Examples: The day is *warm*. (description of subject, so choose adjective, *warm*)

The staff greeted us *warmly*. (description of verb, so use adverb, *warmly*)

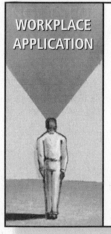

WORKPLACE APPLICATION

John called his boss to report that he was "under the weather." Can you think of two other ways John could describe his condition to his boss?

_____

_____

_____

_____

Some adjectives and adverbs are easily confused. *Good, well, bad,* and *badly* are examples. *Good* and *bad* are adjectives. They describe the *condition* of nouns and subjects. When *good* and *bad*, in all their forms, are used with linking verbs such as *is, was, feel, look, seem, get,* or *become,* they almost seem like adverbs, but they are not.

Examples: I feel *good.* I feel *bad.*

The report looks *good.* The timing feels *bad.*

Badly and *well* are adverbs. Use them to describe verbs or verb phrases.

Examples: I tested *badly.*

She will do *well* in her new job.

Exception: The word *well* can be an adjective or an adverb. When *well* refers to health, it is an adjective. Otherwise, it is an adverb.

Examples: I feel *well.* (describes the health of the subject—adjective)

I hit the ball *well.* (describes the verb—adverb)

EXERCISE 108

Sentences With Descriptive Details

The subject and verb in a sentence often contain other words that describe or add to the meaning.

A. Circle the simple subject in each sentence. Underline the words or phrases that describe the subject.

Example: The new (racket) on the bench is mine.

1. Many people of various ages sat beside the tennis court.
2. Fuzzy, yellow balls flew over the net during the match.
3. The fans in the stands cheered noisily.
4. A skillful woman hit the ball across the net.
5. Her young, eager opponent hit the ball weakly.
6. Her wooden racket returned the ball smoothly.
7. The weary player on the other side changed his stroke.
8. A brisk wind helped the ball cross the net.
9. The great speed of the ball did not dazzle his opponent.
10. A firm backhand won the match for the woman.
11. The younger player jumped over the net to shake her hand.
12. The proud winner of the tennis match smiled.

B. Underline the verb in each sentence. Circle each word or phrase that describes the verb.

Example: The woman (occasionally) hit a poor serve.

1. She played courageously in the hot summer sun.
2. She served well at the beginning of the match.
3. The athlete sharply returned the tricky serves.
4. The ball quickly crossed the net.
5. The two players soon were playing their best.
6. They both really enjoyed the match.
7. The players greatly improved their skills.
8. They began cautiously but performed beautifully.

Using Descriptive Words With Subjects or Verbs

To decide what kind of descriptive word to use in a sentence, determine what the word will describe. Will it describe the subject or the action of the sentence? Most of the time action descriptions end in *-ly.* If the descriptive word ends with *-y,* usually the *-y* is changed to *-i* before *-ly* is added.

A. Add *-ly* to form adverbs.

Example: warm _____*warmly*_____

1. nice   _____
2. dainty   _____
3. sudden   _____
4. hearty   _____

5. dutiful   _____
6. slow   _____
7. odd   _____
8. kind   _____

B. In each sentence circle the correct word in parentheses. Underline the word or words it describes. The word may be a noun or a verb.

Example: Lil <u>was sleeping</u> (dreamy, (dreamily)) on the couch.

1. Her boss was sitting in a (quiet, quietly) corner.
2. The phone rang (noisy, noisily).
3. Madge spoke (cheerful, cheerfully).
4. Her (soft, softly) voice came over the line.
5. "Could you please speak more (loud, loudly)?" asked Lil.
6. Madge was (excited, excitedly) as she said something.
7. "That's great news!" cried Lil (happy, happily).

C. Use each descriptive word to write a sentence with a workplace subject.

Example: soft   *The cafeteria gave us soft vegetables.*

1. softly   _____
2. rough   _____
3. gently   _____
4. simple   _____

EXERCISE 110

More Practice Using Descriptive Words

Adjectives describe nouns and pronouns. Adverbs describe verbs or other descriptive words.

A. Underline the word in parentheses that completes each sentence correctly. Notice whether the word is describing a noun or a verb.

Example: The director felt (<u>good</u>, well) about the television show.

1. The stage crew worked (steady, steadily) to prepare the props.
2. We were able to get (real, really) good seats in the audience.
3. The rehearsals seemed to go (good, well) for everyone.
4. The female lead was (quick, quickly) to memorize her lines.
5. The producer seemed quite (nervous, nervously).
6. The cast waited (anxious, anxiously) for the start of the show.
7. Their makeup had been (careful, carefully) applied.
8. The director was (sure, surely) everything would be fine.
9. The entire audience watched the performance (close, closely).
10. Each scene led (gradual, gradually) to the thrilling climax.
11. The applause was (really, real) loud.

B. Write the word *sure, surely, real,* or *really* in the space provided.

Example: Did the movie _____*really*_____ get better after the first half hour?

1. The lead spoke his lines _____ well.
2. One supporting actor was _____ good too.
3. He _____ will be nominated for an Oscar.
4. The detective in the movie was very _____ of herself.
5. The actress was _____ right for the part.
6. The detective was _____ the butler did it.
7. The audience _____ was quiet.
8. The whereabouts of the butler was a _____ mystery.
9. The ending was a _____ surprise to everyone.

Review of Descriptive Words

Adjectives describe nouns and pronouns. Adverbs describe verbs or other descriptive words.

A. Write the word in parentheses that completes the sentence correctly.

Example: Goldenrod, a wild flower, grows _____*freely*_____ along roads.   (free, freely)

1. The _____ flowers bloom in spring and autumn.
   (beautiful, beautifully)

2. People fear that goldenrod will _____ make them sneeze.
   (sure, surely)

3. Allergies to goldenrod are _____ rare, however.   (real, really)

4. Thomas Edison studied goldenrod _____.   (careful, carefully)

5. He was _____ to learn more about it.   (eager, eagerly)

6. He decided goldenrod could be _____ as a source of rubber.
   (useful, usefully)

7. Goldenrod grows _____ in many places.   (abundant, abundantly)

8. Edison was _____ to point this out.   (quick, quickly)

9. Others found that it makes a _____ tea.   (delightful, delightfully)

B. Rewrite the incorrect sentences correctly.

Example: People weren't surely that Edison was correct.
         People weren't sure that Edison was correct. _____

1. Edison successful extracted the rubber from goldenrod. _____
   _____

2. Today scientists think high of his results. _____
   _____

3. They are sure Edison was rightly. _____

4. Goldenrod is a very usefully plant. _____

5. It can be harvested easy. _____

6. Its small yellow flowers smell fragrantly. _____
   _____

EXERCISE 112

Good, Bad, Well, and *Badly*

Use *good, bad, well,* and *badly* correctly. *Good* and *bad* describe nouns or pronouns.

A. Choose the correct word in parentheses, and write it in the space provided.

Example: Our team played (good, well) in the tournament.   *well*

1. Gil and I work (good, well) together.   _____
2. I write (bad, badly) with my opposite hand.   _____
3. Tony writes (good, well) with either hand.   _____
4. That rusty old car backfires (bad, badly).   _____
5. Believe it or not, that engine still runs (good, well).   _____
6. One of these radiators leaks (bad, badly).   _____
7. Robert bowls (good, well) only with his own ball.   _____
8. Tom gave a (good, well) presentation to the group.   _____
9. I did (good, well) on my evaluation.   _____
10. The forecaster predicted a (bad, badly) thunderstorm.   _____
11. Our lawn needs the rain (bad, badly).   _____
12. The entry of the deserted old building creaked (bad, badly). _____

B. Rewrite each sentence, using the correct form of the descriptive word.

Example: My sore throat feels worser this morning.
         My sore throat feels worse this morning.

1. Marnie restocks more better than Lois.

   _____

2. The assembly plant's roof is leaking worstest of all.

   _____

3. I like spring betterer than fall.

   _____

4. Have you ever seen worser weather than this?

   _____

EXERCISE 113

More Practice Using *Good, Bad, Well,* and *Badly*

Good and ***bad*** **describe nouns or pronouns.** ***Well*** **and** ***badly*** **describe verbs.**

A. Underline the descriptive word in each sentence. Write whether the word describes a noun or a verb.

Example: Carmen plays the keyboard <u>well</u>.   *verb*

1. She is a good member of the team.   _____
2. The other members think well of her.   _____
3. Carmen does not make bad mistakes.   _____
4. She has a good sense of timing.   _____
5. She reads instructions well.   _____
6. Every day she has a good record.   _____
7. Carmen treats her customers well.   _____
8. She has a good attitude.   _____
9. Carmen's boyfriend does not file badly.   _____
10. He had a bad practice session today.   _____

B. Underline the correct word in parentheses.

Example: He is the (better, <u>best</u>) drummer I've heard.

1. I think that he plays (better, best) than Buddy Rich did.
2. I play (bad, badly).
3. That man plays the drums even (worse, worst) than I do.
4. In fact, he plays (worser, worst) of all.
5. Mario plays the saxophone (well, better).
6. He has a (better, more better) tone than Eric does.
7. Who is the (better, best) sax player in the world?
8. I feel (bad, badly) about the delay.
9. The dress looks (good, well) on you.
10. This fabric feels (better, best) than that one.

EXERCISE 114

Review of *Good, Bad, Well,* and *Badly*

Good and **bad** describe nouns or pronouns. **Well** and **badly** describe verbs.

A. Circle the correct descriptive word in parentheses, and underline the word it describes.

Example: The buyer at this store <u>buys</u> (good, (well)).

1. The shoes go (bad, badly) with that outfit.
2. I want that dress (bad, badly).
3. I like it (good, well) enough to buy it now.
4. My husband shops (good, well) for clothes.
5. That woman dresses (bad, badly) for a dressmaker.
6. Do you think that fabric will wear (good, well)?
7. It looks (bad, badly) without some kind of belt.
8. Would it go (good, well) with high boots?
9. How (bad, badly) do you want that suit?
10. That skirt should fit (good, well).

B. Write *good, bad, well,* or *badly* in the space provided to complete each sentence correctly.

Example: The fabric is _____*badly*_____ damaged.

1. I feel _____ about the skirt that didn't fit.
2. Would it make you feel _____ to wear that sweater?
3. I'm glad we decided to dress so _____.
4. I think that tie looks _____ with that shirt.
5. The combination of blue and brown is not _____.
6. I don't do so _____ with clothes.
7. Can you manage _____ without that dress?
8. I can do pretty _____ at home.
9. That sweater would look _____ on you.
10. You wouldn't look so _____ yourself.
11. It feels so _____ to go window-shopping!
12. Some customers behave _____ in stores.

14   Capitalization

Capitalization involves using capital letters. Capital letters are used for the first letter of all proper names, including names of most business places.

Examples: John Smith   We may travel to Japan on business.

Abbott Company   Mayor Brint gave us the key to the city.

Claremont College

Adjectives formed from proper names are also capitalized.

Examples: The workers from the Japanese company are looking forward to our visit.

Cuban cigars are a specialty item.

Initials, or *single letters that represent proper nouns,* are also capitalized.

Examples: R. C. Chambers (*R. C.* stands for "Robert Charles.")

M.A.D.D. (*M.A.D.D.* stands for "Mothers Against Drunk Drivers.")

Proper names can include names of special places or things. The first letters of these words are capitalized, too.

Examples: Indian Lake

Revolutionary War

Titles of people should be capitalized.

Examples: Is the Senator home?

He is the President of the United States.

Titles of books, songs, movies, magazines, and other similar works are capitalized. Use capital letters for all main words but not the connecting words—unless the connecting word is the first or last word in the name.

Examples: Gone With the Wind (book)   Restaurant Cooking (magazine)

Fog (poem)   The Daily Tribune (newspaper)

Candle in the Wind (song)

An **abbreviation** is *a shortened form of a word*. Many abbreviations start with capital letters. Some use a period at the end.

Examples: Mr. Robert Long   (*Mr.* stands for *mister.*)

Feb. 14   (*Feb.* is short for *February.*)

Dr. Hansen   (*Dr.* is short for *doctor.*)

Mrs. (Ms.) Sue Rowe   (*Mrs.* stands for *mistress; Ms.* is a generic term that stands for *mistress* [married] or *miss* [unmarried].)

1200 Coon Rd. (Dr., Ave.) (*Rd.* stands for *road, Dr.* stands for *drive, Ave.* stands for *avenue.*)

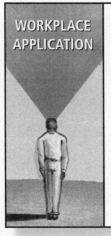

WORKPLACE APPLICATION

Circle the missing capitalization and write in the correct punctuation for this office e-mail message.

brenda sue:

I received your request dated jan 5. It will be fine for you to use a vacation day to visit your family in boston. If you can, visit the red lion inn. They have great chowder. Have fun.

bob

Capitalizing Names and Descriptive Words

Capitalize all proper names and all descriptive words formed from those names.

A. In the sentences below, underline all the words that should be capitalized.

Example: <u>I</u> plan to visit <u>new</u> <u>zealand</u> and <u>australia</u> soon.

1. there are many places that I want to visit during my life.

2. first I want to visit california, utah, and new mexico.

3. some spring, i want to see england's ancient castles.

4. I want to take uncle phil to mt. rushmore.

5. I would like to see the u.s. senate in washington, d.c.

6. I would like to learn japanese while visiting tokyo.

7. the cultures of japan and china fascinate me.

8. australia will be the start of my trip in september.

9. i will spend the fall on another continent.

B. Rewrite the sentences. Capitalize all the names, initials, and descriptive words that should be capitalized.

Example: dr. chi, a chinese professor, can speak six languages.

Dr. Chi, a Chinese professor, can speak six languages.

1. Many people in north america speak the english language.

2. Many people in canada speak french as well as english.

3. The official language of mexico is spanish.

4. sarita a. ramirez, from mexico city, can speak english.

5. She will tour the united states in August.

6. sarita's tour is sponsored by the latino foundation.

More Practice Capitalizing Names and Descriptive Words

Proper names and descriptive words formed from proper names are always capitalized.

A. Circle all the names that should be capitalized.

Example: Dina studies computers at (wilford) (academy.)

1. At the airport we saw karl waetzel, the austrian skier.

2. Did you read that article about president clinton?

3. Last spring my uncle opened his own business, martin's video arcade.

4. People travel to vancouver, british columbia, for the beautiful scenery.

5. The sale was so well received that it ran from may to july.

6. One man from kenya, another from west germany, and a woman from china all work in the central office.

7. I saw that new comic on the *tonight show* last night.

8. The high note musical agency had a party at the restaurant.

9. That is the agency on st. olaf's avenue that lee talks about.

10. When exactly were the middle ages?

11. My wife likes the food of southeast asia.

12. I prefer the cooking of spain.

B. Each numbered pair below contains a two-word name and a descriptive word before a common noun. Capitalize each item correctly.

Example: **a.** swiss cheese   **b.** swiss guards
                Swiss cheese   _Swiss Guards_

1. **a.** mediterranean sea   **b.** mediterranean country

    _____

2. **a.** atlantic ocean   **b.** atlantic coastline

    _____

3. **a.** russian dressing   **b.** russian revolution

    _____

EXERCISE 117

Capitalizing Titles

Capitalize the first word, the last word, and every important word in the titles of books, movies, songs, and other works.

A. Capitalize the following titles correctly. Underline those titles that are considered to be full-length works and use quotation marks around shorter works or portions of larger works.

Example: no bad dogs   (book)   <u>No Bad Dogs</u>

1. it's a wonderful life   (movie)   _____

2. new york times   (newspaper)   _____

3. the way we were   (song)   _____

4. the old gumbie cat   (poem)   _____

5. auto shop owners   (magazine)   _____

6. what color is your parachute?   (book)   _____

7. working smarter, not harder   (article)   _____

8. the monkey's paw   (story)   _____

9. a fistful of dollars   (movie)   _____

10. down in the valley   (song)   _____

B. Write a title for each of the items below and write it correctly in the space provided. Underline those titles that should be underlined, and use quotation marks around those that take quotation marks.

Example: song   <u>"Blue Suede Shoes"</u>

1. book _____

2. movie _____

3. song _____

4. newspaper _____

5. play _____

6. magazine _____

7. article _____

8. poem _____

EXERCISE 118

More Practice Capitalizing Titles

Capitalize the first and last words and every important word in a title.

A. Capitalize the following titles and the names of people and rewrite them in the space provided. You will capitalize 28 words. Remember to underline italicized titles.

Example: *all the president's men* <u>All the President's Men</u>

1. *beauty and the beast* _____
2. "tree at my window" _____
3. *till we meet again* _____
4. mayor tom bradley _____
5. "the noise of waters" _____
6. queen elizabeth _____
7. *the milwaukee journal* _____
8. "the city in the sea" _____
9. general george patton _____
10. *reader's digest* _____

B. Underline the words that should be capitalized in the following sentences.

Example: Sara subscribes to *sports illustrated* and *time*.

1. The author of *the natural* was Bernard Malamud.
2. Isak Dinesen's life was told in *out of africa*.
3. Jeffrey saw *star wars*, *the empire strikes back*, and *return of the jedi* on the same day.
4. Did Willie Nelson write the song "on the road again"?
5. *the san francisco chronicle* is a famous newspaper.
6. Who wrote "the battle hymn of the republic"?
7. We saw Grant Wood's painting, *american gothic*, yesterday.
8. The television series *this old house* won an award.
9. James Agee wrote the story "a mother's tale."
10. Steven saw the Broadway play *death of a salesman*.

EXERCISE 119

Review of Capitalizing Titles

Capitalize the first word, the last word, and all important words in a title.

A. Rewrite these titles, capitalizing them correctly. You will capitalize 37 letters. Remember to underline italicized titles.

Example: "puppet on a chain"   *"Puppet on a Chain"* _____

1. *the old man and the sea* _____
2. member of the wedding _____
3. "bridge over troubled water" _____
4. *the last emperor* _____
5. "casey at the bat" _____
6. "the legend of sleepy hollow" _____
7. "the midnight ride of paul revere" _____
8. *in search of excellence* _____
9. *the joy of cooking* _____
10. "yesterday" _____
11. *u.s. news and world report* _____
12. *national geographic* _____

B. Underline the titles of people that should be capitalized in each sentence. You will underline 13 words.

Example: "Is <u>president</u> Alt waiting?" he asked.

1. "We must leave now, senator," said the aide.
2. "Is the president at the White House?" asked senator Murdge.
3. "Yes, and congressman Filbert is there too," said mrs. Banks.
4. The secretary of state may visit queen Elizabeth.
5. Last month dr. and mrs. Truesdale saw prime minister Atlee.
6. Someday I would like to meet mrs. Clinton.
7. Right now they are interviewing ambassador Solin.
8. The lawyer spoke to judge Roberts yesterday.
9. Well, here we are, right behind princess Margaret.

EXERCISE 120

Using Abbreviations

An abbreviation is a shortened form of a word. An abbreviation sometimes begins with a capital letter and ends with a period.

A. Circle each letter that should be capitalized and add punctuation where needed.

Example: mr. j. thomas mason

1. june 9 1999
2. miss jennifer macy
3. 684 mararoneck ave
4. dr francis a tooley
5. thurs nov 21

6. gen raymond madison
7. mon jan 5
8. 1701 meeting house rd
9. ms hannah k eberhardt
10. mr and mrs jules chavitz

B. Write an abbreviation for each underlined word.

Example: Follow <u>Route</u> 4 to Clarksburg   _____*Rte.*_____

1. Turn left at Tottenham <u>Drive</u>.   _____
2. Continue past Henderson <u>Boulevard</u>.   _____
3. Look for Canterbury <u>Street</u>.   _____
4. The gatekeeper is Arlo Hines, <u>Junior</u>.   _____
5. Ask for Enid <u>Lilia</u> Brown.   _____
6. She will take you to <u>Doctor</u> Donomora.   _____
7. Here are the dates that I saw the doctor: _____
   a. <u>October</u> 18   _____
   b. <u>November</u> 25   _____
   c. <u>Wednesday</u>, May 20   _____
   d. <u>Friday</u>, June 19   _____
8. <u>Professor</u> McCoy taught the class.   _____
9. Do you know <u>Colonel</u> Smith?   _____
10. She lives on Fifth <u>Avenue</u>.   _____

EXERCISE 121

More Practice Using Abbreviations

An abbreviation is a shortened form of a word.

A. The items below are for an appointment book. Rewrite each item by abbreviating the underlined words.

Appointments

Example: Sunday—Debbie Williams   Sun.—D. Williams

1. Monday—December party   _____
2. Tuesday—Doctor Juanita López   _____
3. Wednesday—go to Post Office   _____
4. Thursday—January report   _____
5. Friday—Elm Street fair   _____
6. Saturday—Illinois taxes due   _____

B. Rewrite each address using abbreviations for the underlined words. Use postal abbreviations for the state names.

Example: Major James Peter Hannah   Maj. J. P. Hannah

1125 Accord Road   1125 Accord Rd.

Smithtown, New York 11787   Smithtown, NY 11787

1. Sergeant Elizabeth Ann Nichols   _____
   Rural Route 3   _____
   Danville, Virginia 24541   _____
2. Doctor Sidney David Morris   _____
   58 Pinetree Drive   _____
   Dallas, Texas 75252   _____
3. Marjorie Susan Hull   _____
   2 Ocean Road, Apartment 5   _____
   San Jose, California 95122   _____
4. Reverend Joseph Jones   _____
   Post Office Box 200   _____
   Kingsport, Tennessee 37664   _____

15 Punctuation

Punctuation directs the flow of thoughts in sentences. There are several kinds of *punctuation marks* for different jobs in sentences.

A **comma** is a punctuation mark. Commas indicate when a *pause* is intended. Sometimes commas *separate words or phrases*, such as names used in the direct address of another person.

Examples: Jim, did you receive those documents?

Did you receive those documents, Jim?

Yes, Jim, I did send you the documents.

Commas are also used to *set off* other introductory words or phrases.

Examples: Sorry, but I cannot find them.

Well, please look again.

If you wish, I'll start looking now.

Commas also set off the parts of dates and addresses.

Examples: Sunday, July 4, 1999

2203 Riverdale Rd.

Las Vegas, Nevada

Commas are used to separate independent thoughts, items in a series, noun phrases, or interrupting words or phrases in sentences.

Examples: I work in retail, and I sometimes work in payroll. (Comma separates two independent thoughts.)

Nelda bought nail polish, hair spray, and lipstick for the salon. (Commas separate items in a series.)

The secretary ordered more paper, the heaviest weight possible. (Comma separates noun phrase *the heaviest weight possible*.)

On the way in, by the way, I saw Anna. (Commas separate interrupting phrase *by the way*.)

Other punctuation marks include *periods*, *question marks*, and *exclamation points* used at the ends of sentences.

Periods are used at the ends of *statement or command* sentences.

Examples: I see the first snow falling**.** (statement)

Look out the window**.** (command)

Question marks punctuate the ends of question sentences.

Example: Are you sure you saw it**?** (question)

Exclamation points punctuate the ends of *exclamation* sentences.

Example: Yes, of course, I'm sure**!** (exclamation)

The **colon** is a punctuation mark that indicates a *long pause*. It sometimes means "as follows." Colons are often used to introduce a long series, which may be written as a list.

Example: These are our concerns today**:** time cards, personal phone calls, personal E-mail, and tardiness.

Colons can also be used to *indicate time* or *to punctuate the greeting of business correspondence.*

Examples: 10**:**45

12**:**00

Dear Sir**:**

Semicolons are somewhere between commas and colons. They indicate a *pause that is longer than a comma, but shorter than a colon*. Semicolons are most often used to separate independent thoughts that are *not* separated by a connecting word. However, semicolons may be used to separate independent thoughts that begin with certain connecting words or word phrases. The most common of these are *therefore, however, consequently, thus, in fact, so, in addition to*, and *meanwhile*.

Examples: I know I'm late**;** I apologize.   *or*   I know I'm late**;** therefore, I apologize.

Often we stay late**;** today we're leaving early.   *or*   Often we stay late**;** however, today we're leaving early.

Quotation marks enclose words that are *directly spoken or quoted*. The actual dialogue is enclosed within the quotation marks. Punctuation that is part of the dialogue goes inside the quotation marks as well. Often, commas separate the dialogue from the rest of the sentence.

Examples: "Can I help you?" asked the clerk.

"No, I'm just looking," said the customer.

"OK," said the clerk, "feel free to take your time."

(Note: In the first sentence, the question mark is part of the dialogue, so the question mark goes inside the quotation marks.)

Quotation marks can also enclose certain *titles*, such as magazine articles or songs.

Examples: "Are You Ready for Today's Jobs?" (magazine article title)

"Sweet Surrender"   (song title)

Dashes are punctuation marks that indicate a *sudden or unexpected interruption* in the flow of a thought in a sentence.

Example: They told me—imagine this—I'm overqualified.

Dashes also indicate thoughts that *explain*, or thoughts that are added as an *afterthought*.

Examples: Interviewing—especially the first time—is anxiety-provoking.

I came across poorly—or so I believed at the time.

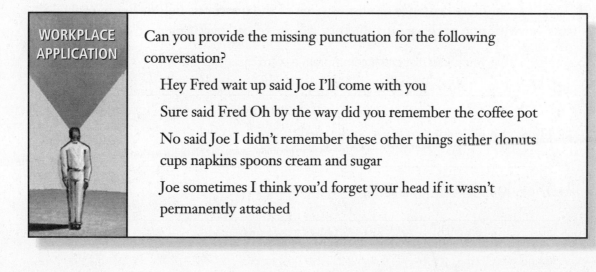

WORKPLACE APPLICATION

Can you provide the missing punctuation for the following conversation?

Hey Fred wait up said Joe I'll come with you

Sure said Fred Oh by the way did you remember the coffee pot

No said Joe I didn't remember these other things either donuts cups napkins spoons cream and sugar

Joe sometimes I think you'd forget your head if it wasn't permanently attached

EXERCISE 122

Using Commas

Use commas to set off names in addresses, and use them after introductory words or phrases. Names can be set off anywhere in a sentence. Introductory words or phrases come at the beginning of a sentence.

A. Add commas where they are needed in each sentence.

Example: Wake her up Vicki!

Wake her up, Vicki!

1. Today is moving day Jeb.
2. Mr. Evans are you ready to unload the truck?
3. Sal and John will lend you a hand Donna.
4. Be careful Wayne of the heavy furniture.
5. Put those pictures in the bedroom Sal.
6. Did you remember Vicki to mark the boxes?
7. Do you think Mr. Evans that we'll ever finish?
8. Donna this is going to be a great apartment!

B. Write a complete sentence to answer each of the questions below. Begin each answer with one of these introductory words: *yes, no, well,* or *oh.*

Example: Did you know that *credit* comes from a word meaning "I trust"?

No, I didn't realize that.

1. Have you ever applied for a credit card?

_____

2. Why do you think some people misuse credit?

_____

3. Have you ever been denied credit?

_____

4. Do you know what collateral is?

_____

5. How could I learn more about credit?

_____

EXERCISE 123

Commas in Dates and Addresses

Commas are used to set off the parts of a date or an address.

A. Add commas where they are needed in the sentences below. Some sentences may need more than one comma.

Example: I am going to Williamsburg Virginia.

I am going to Williamsburg, Virginia.

1. I will be leaving on Monday August 8.
2. I will return on Thursday August 11.
3. Along the way I will stop in Harrisburg Pennsylvania.
4. I will also go through Parkton Maryland on my way south.
5. My destination is XYZ Company 62 Putnam Street Williamsburg Virginia
6. On August 10 1999 I will deliver my report there

B. Add commas where they are needed in the letter below.

126 Mulhaven Road
Lancaster Pennsylvania 17062
July 5 1999

Mr Tom Snyder Sales Manager
XYZ Company
62 Putnam Street
Williamsburg Virginia 23185

Dear Mr. Smith:

I received your letter dated Tuesday July 3. I am preparing copies of my report for your staff. They will be ready by Friday August 5. I can have them sent to you on August 5 or I can bring them with me on August 11. I will look forward to our lunch at the Traveller's Stop Restaurant 1171 Brandywine Boulevard Williamsburg. I have confirmed its location. It is right near the expressway. I will meet you there at noon August 11.

Sincerely,

Ms. Adrienne Taft
Sales Manager

EXERCISE 124

Using Commas Correctly in Sentences

Use commas to separate independent thoughts. Use them to separate items in a series, noun phrases, and interrupting words.

Copy each sentence, adding commas where needed.

Example: I work by the way for a small local newspaper.

I work, by the way, for a small local newspaper.

1. Nora Jim and Paco are in charge of the news.

   _____

2. I handle the editorials and Len draws the cartoon.

   _____

3. Ben the best writer on the staff is the editor.

   _____

4. Jo our photographer takes pictures of special events assemblies and sports.

   _____

   _____

5. Phil lays out the copy and Ellen proofreads.

   _____

6. A newspaper requires hard work but we enjoy it.

   _____

7. Sam interviews people takes notes and writes stories.

   _____

8. He interviewed Ed Flynn the police chief.

   _____

9. Mr. Flynn by the way has led a very interesting life.

   _____

10. He explores caves but he also enjoys gourmet cooking.

    _____

11. I eat franks and beans macaroni and cheese or pizza.

    _____

EXERCISE 125

More Practice Using Commas Correctly in Sentences

Use a comma to indicate a short pause or separation in a sentence.

A. Add commas where necessary in the following paragraphs. Underline each comma. There are 16 commas to add.

Example: Miners ranchers and pioneers helped to establish towns.
Miners, ranchers, and pioneers helped to establish towns.

(1) You may think that the California Gold Rush ended about 1900 but you are mistaken. (2) A new type of miner one eager to get rich quickly has started to mine the California mountains. (3) The towns in these mountains once thriving communities are now considered ghost towns. (4) These towns however are the places where modern miners are returning in search of more gold.
(5) Tourists hikers and serious prospectors are searching the streams of Sierra County.

(6) Many amateur miners people who are not concerned about real profit use the traditional mining pan. (7) Of course as any miner knows a metal pan has to be held over a fire to blacken it. (8) Otherwise the miners can't see the yellow gleam that is gold. (9) These days however plastic pans are used by most miners.

B. Rewrite each sentence, inserting commas where they are needed.

Example: Tim Karl and Michael traveled to California.
Tim, Karl, and Michael traveled to California.

1. Well I washed all the dirt out of the pan Karl.

   _____

2. Although this looks like gold it may be only pyrite.

   _____

3. If you wait I'll get my magnifying glass.

   _____

4. Would you carry the tweezers the jar and my old hat?

   _____

EXERCISE 126

Review of Commas in Sentences

Use commas to set off certain words, phrases, and thoughts.

A. Insert commas in each sentence as needed.

Example: Susan had a suggestion for Emily her sister-in-law.

Susan had a suggestion for Emily, her sister-in-law.

1. Let's take a walk Emily.
2. We'll walk to Seventh Avenue along Thirty-fifth Street and up Sixth Avenue.
3. It sounds interesting but isn't that a lot of walking?
4. Yes but I think you'll have a good time.
5. One area the garment district is famous.
6. After I put on some comfortable shoes we'll get started.
7. Elton maybe you would like to join us.
8. Unfortunately I already have plans for this afternoon.
9. Then Emily and I will go but we'll miss you.
10. Be sure to bring a camera sunglasses and a sweater.

B. Insert commas in the paragraph as needed.

Example: Walking briskly they began their tour.

Walking briskly, they began their tour.

(1) Hurrying along workers wheel racks of clothes across the streets. (2) Did you know Emily that dresses are made in batches of one thousand? (3) Here is Fashion Avenue another name for Seventh Avenue. (4) Each store makes a certain kind of garment Emily. (5) There is bridal wear men's wear sportswear and much more. (6) We'll never see everything in one visit but it's fun to try. (7) Historically this has always been an area for immigrants. (8) The garment district a busy place employs thousands of workers. (9) Although it's noisy now it is quiet at night. (10) The Fashion Institute a school is nearby. (11) You can take courses in design fabric and color. (12) Incidentally don't the coats fall off the racks? (13) Where may I ask are the people who do the sewing?

EXERCISE 127

Punctuating the Ends of Sentences

The punctuation mark used at the end of a sentence depends on the kind of sentence. Punctuation marks can be periods (.), question marks (?), or exclamation points (!).

A. Rewrite each sentence below, adding the appropriate punctuation mark for each kind of sentence.

Example: I have never seen a live buffalo   (statement)

I have never seen a live buffalo.

1. Once there were millions of them   (exclamation)

2. Imagine what a sight they were   (command)

3. Are there many buffalo herds today   (question)

4. There are still herds in some areas   (statement)

5. They are protected by the federal government   (statement)

B. Rewrite each sentence below with the correct end punctuation. Then write whether each sentence is a statement, question, exclamation, or command.

Example: I was late for work today

I was late for work today.   statement

1. Didn't you set your alarm

2. Well, of course I did

3. Why didn't you get up

4. I didn't hear the alarm

EXERCISE 128

Colons

A colon indicates a long pause. It can mean "as follows" when it is used to introduce a list. Colons are also used to indicate time and to punctuate greetings in business correspondence.

A. Add colons to the sentences below to mean "as follows."

Example: Bring me these items from the supply room staples, paper clips, and pencils.

Bring me these items from the supply room: staples, paper clips, and pencils.

1. Some examples of jobs for the future might include data bank coordinator, personal coach, computer nurse, personal shopper, and caterer.

2. If you start a home secretarial business, you might need new equipment computer, desk, phone, fax, modem, and answering machine.

3. A word processing business might provide typing for various businesses newsletters, bulletins, handbooks, pamphlets, and flyers.

4. There are several advantages to home businesses flexibility, freedom, creativity, and personal responsibility.

5. There are also a few disadvantages no escape from work, undependable income, and limited social environment.

6. Some of the products we sell are toys, games, and recreational equipment.

B. Add colons to the following to indicate time.

Example: 2 00   2:00

1. 5 00   **2.** 1 30   **3.** 3 45   **4.** 11 56   **5.** 3 29

C. Add colons to the following business greetings.

Example: Dear Sir   Dear Sir:

1. To Whom It May Concern   3. Dear Editor
2. Dear Mr. Abbott   4. Gentlemen

EXERCISE 129

Semicolons

A semicolon is used to separate parts of a sentence. A semicolon (;) creates a pause that is shorter than a colon (:), but longer than a comma (,). Use a semicolon to separate independent thoughts that are not separated by a comma or a connecting word.

A. Read the two sentences for each item. Then combine them with a semicolon.

Example: Some people go fishing. Others watch whales.

Some people go fishing; others watch whales.

1. Whales are not fish. They are mammals.

   _____

2. Mammals breathe air. Therefore, whales breathe air.

   _____

3. Some people draw the whales. Others photograph them.

   _____

4. The West Coast is whale country. Whale watching is best there.

   _____

B. Add colons or semicolons to the letter below.

(1) Dear Sir

(2) Thank you for your interest in chartering one of our whale-watching boats. **(3)** Let me tell you how people watch whales in these three states Washington, Oregon, and northern California. **(4)** Fishermen here are not busy in winter therefore, they take people whale watching. **(5)** The trip takes all day some trips are longer. **(6)** For instance, there are journeys beginning at 1000 A.M. on a Monday and ending at 1000 A.M. the next Monday. **(7)** Some of the boats are 60 feet long they can hold 60 passengers. **(8)** Whales are attracted to boats they swim close to them. **(9)** Diving whales make circles these are called footprints. **(10)** Whale watchers stay alert they look for footprints.

Yours truly,

Maria Fonseca

EXERCISE 130

Quotation Marks

Quotation marks enclose a speaker's exact words. Quotation marks also enclose certain titles, such as songs and magazine articles.

A. Write quotation marks where needed in these sentences.

Example: Charles, I asked, have you read this?

          "Charles," I asked, "have you read this?"

1. I told Charles about an article called Dreams Do Come True.

2. Was it good? asked Charles.

3. Yes, Charles, I answered, it was taken from a book.

4. The book is quite good, I said.

5. It sounds interesting, commented Charles.

6. I like books on business advice, he added.

7. Would you like to borrow this book? I asked.

8. Charles nodded and said, That would be great.

9. He turned to the chapter called A Good Start.

10. I think you'll like it, I said, because it is so helpful.

B. Rewrite each sentence, enclosing the direct quotations in quotation marks. If the sentence is correct, write *correct*.

Example: This is a nice vacation, I said.

          "This is a nice vacation," I said.

1. I think I'll take a walk, said Mike.

    _____

2. I'll stay here and read, I replied.

    _____

3. When Mike returned, he told me that the man next door was in the Navy.

    _____

4. That's interesting, I said, because his wife is in the Air Force.

    _____

5. He asked me how I had learned that by reading a book.

    _____

Dashes

A dash is a punctuation mark that indicates a long pause for an explanation or afterthought.

A. Add dashes to the following sentences to indicate an explanation.

Example: At 20 below 0 a record low temperature class was canceled.

At 20 below — a record low temperature — class was canceled.

1. Work, eat, and sleep these are all I do.

_____

2. Wine, women, and song now that is a phrase whose time is past.

_____

3. Take down the ladder it's right behind you.

_____

4. I will go if I can get ready in time.

_____

5. This job my first is a challenge.

_____

6. That sign the red and white one shows our logo.

_____

B. Rewrite the following sentences, using dashes to separate the afterthoughts from the rest of the sentence.

Example: I think that's everything well, maybe not.

I think that's everything—well, maybe not.

1. I wish I could never mind I changed my mind.

_____

2. I agree I think with your basic point.

_____

3. This should go no, wait that's not right.

_____

4. John won't like this but he'll never know.

_____

16   Using Correct Vocabulary and Spelling

It is important to use correct word choice and spelling in sentences. Knowledge of words and word parts will help you to use correct vocabulary and spelling in your workplace writing.

Prefixes and **suffixes** are parts of word *beginnings* and word *endings*, respectively. A *prefix* is a part added to the *beginning* of a word. A *suffix* is a part added to the *end* of a word. Both prefixes and suffixes change the meaning of the original word.

Here are some common prefixes and suffixes and their meanings:

Prefixes	**Suffixes**
re- (means "again")	*-ful* (means "full of")
un- (means "not")	*-ment* (means "an act or state")
im- (means "not")	*-er* (means "someone who does something")
in- (means "not")	

Examples: I will *rewrite* my résumé. (*Rewrite* means "to write again.")

This plan is *unsatisfactory.* (*Unsatisfactory* means "not satisfactory.")

You are so *impatient!* (*Impatient* means "not patient.")

These reports are *inaccurate.* (*Inaccurate* means "not accurate.")

Be *careful* with that equipment. (*Careful* means "full of care.")

Milk provides *nourishment.* (*Nourishment* means "in the state of being nourished.")

John is a *hiker.* (*Hiker* means "someone who hikes.")

Synonyms, antonyms, and **homonyms:** *Synonyms* are words that mean the *same,* or about the same, thing but they are spelled differently. *Antonyms* are words with the *opposite,* or almost the opposite, meanings. They are spelled differently. *Homonyms* are words that are pronounced the *same* but have different meanings. They may also be spelled differently.

Examples: **Synonyms:** Her desk was *untidy.* Her desk was *messy.* (*Untidy* and *messy* mean almost the same thing.)

Antonyms: This was a *good* day. This was a *bad* day. (*Good* and *bad* have opposite meanings.)

Homonyms: I *threw* the paper away. I went *through* the door. (*Threw* and *through* sound the same but have different meanings and different spellings.)

Negative words that mean *no* or *not* are often used incorrectly. Use only one negative word in a sentence to mean *no* or *not*.

Examples: Say: There was *no one* here.   Don't say: There *wasn't no* one here.

Say: I *never* saw her.   Don't say: I *didn't never* see her.

Say: I *can't* do anything about it.   Don't say: I *can't* do *nothing* about it.

Other words that mean *no* or *not* include *neither, nowhere,* and *hardly.*

Examples: Say: She *isn't* here *either.*   Don't say: She *isn't* here *neither.*

Say: It is *hardly* worth it.   Don't say: It *isn't hardly* worth it.

Say: I couldn't find it *anywhere.*   Don't say: I *couldn't* find it *nowhere.*

Spelling rules help you to remember how to spell difficult or unusual words.

- **•Rule 1**   Use *-i* before *-e*, except after *-c*.

  Examples: s*ie*ve   rel*ie*ve   rece*i*ve   perce*i*ve

  bel*ie*ve   retr*ie*ve   conce*i*ve   dece*i*ve

- **•Rule 2**   *Q* is always followed by *u*.

  Examples: *qu*ick   *qu*aint   e*qu*al   e*qu*ator

- **•Rule 3**   Some letters are *silent*. They appear for spelling, but they are not pronounced. These silent letters may include the second vowel letter in a vowel pair (*ea, ai, ay,* etc.) or silent first letters (*h*).

  Examples: l*ea*se   pl*ai*n   pl*ay*   *h*onor

- **•Rule 4**   Some letters are pronounced differently than they are spelled (*-ph* is often pronounced as *-f*).

  Examples: *ph*ase   *ph*obia   *ph*ysical   *ph*one

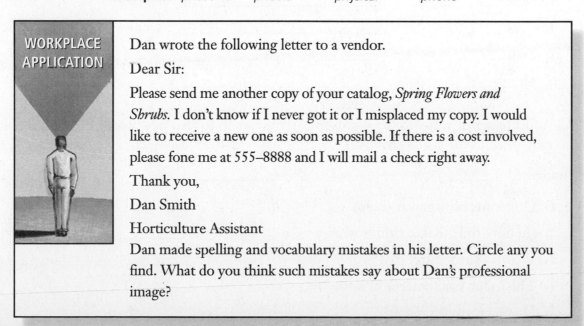

WORKPLACE APPLICATION

Dan wrote the following letter to a vendor.

Dear Sir:

Please send me another copy of your catalog, *Spring Flowers and Shrubs.* I don't know if I never got it or I misplaced my copy. I would like to receive a new one as soon as possible. If there is a cost involved, please fone me at 555–8888 and I will mail a check right away.

Thank you,

Dan Smith

Horticulture Assistant

Dan made spelling and vocabulary mistakes in his letter. Circle any you find. What do you think such mistakes say about Dan's professional image?

EXERCISE 132

Prefixes and Suffixes

A prefix is a group of letters added to the beginning of a word. A suffix is a group of letters added to the end of a word. Both prefixes and suffixes change the meaning of a word.

A. Add the correct prefixes to the following words to make new words. Choose from *re-*, *un-*, *in-*, and *im-*.

Example: ___*re*___write   *rewrite* _____

1. _____ new   _____
2. _____ able   _____
3. _____ humane   _____
4. _____ possible   _____
5. _____ do   _____
6. _____ land   _____

B. Add the correct suffixes to the following words to make new words. Choose from *-ful*, *-ment*, and *-er*.

Example: health_____   _____ *healthful* _____

1. agree _____   _____
2. test _____   _____
3. pain _____   _____
4. treat _____   _____
5. excite _____   _____
6. plumb _____   _____

C. Add a prefix or suffix to the words in parentheses to form a new word. Write the new word in the space provided.

Example: ___*un*___likely   _____ *unlikely* _____

1. Our conversation was (help).   _____
2. (Action) only makes things worse.   _____
3. We may (negotiate) that deal.   _____
4. This video has (entertain) value.   _____
5 Do you (call) his name?   _____
6. The mistakes were (plenty)   _____

EXERCISE 133

Synonyms

Synonyms are different words that mean the same or almost the same thing.

A. Write a synonym for each word below. Write your answers in the space provided.

Example: kind _____*gentle*_____

1. colleague _____

2. cafeteria _____

3. building _____

4. entry _____

5. seminar _____

6. keyboard _____

B. Circle the two words in each set that are synonyms.

Example: (clock)   bracelet   (watch)

1. condo   apartment   office

2. career   hobby   job

3. tired   angry   mad

4. boss   employee   supervisor

C. Write the synonym you choose in Exercise A for each of the following words. Then use both the word and its synonym in a sentence. The two sentences should have similar meanings.

Example: kind _____*gentle*_____   *Mary was a kind person.*
                                                    Mary was a gentle person.

1. colleague _____

_____

_____

2. cafeteria _____

_____

_____

3. building _____

_____

Antonyms

An antonym is a word that means the opposite, or almost the opposite, of another word.

A. Write an antonym for each word below.

Example: work   _play_

1. dependable   _____

2. habitual   _____

3. misfortune   _____

4. perfect   _____

5. shy   _____

6. early   _____

B. Circle the two words that are antonyms.

Example: (always)   seldom   (never)

1. timely   common   unusual

2. tardy   ready   punctual

3. promptly   delayed   arrived

4. exit   enter   stop

C. Write the antonym you chose in Exercise A for each of the following words. Then use both the word and its antonym in a sentence. The two sentences should have opposite meanings.

Example: work   _____play_____   _I'm going to work now._
                                                         I'm going to play now.

1. dependable   _____

_____

_____

2. habitual   _____

_____

_____

3. misfortune   _____

_____

EXERCISE 135

Homonyms

Homonyms are words that are pronounced the same and may be spelled the same but have different meanings.

A. Choose the correct spellings of the homonyms below to match the meanings of the sentences. Use the space provided to write your answers.

Example: The farmer (bread, bred) his sheep.   _____*bred*_____

1. Marlita, come (meat, meet) my new friend Sue.   _____
2. Our office team played in the hockey (meat, meet).   _____
3. We serve only prime (meat, meet) in our restaurant.   _____
4. These plants will (die, dye) if you don't water them.   _____
5. This (die, dye) is the perfect color to use on that cloth.   _____
6. (There, Their) go our last customers.   _____
7. (There, Their) purchase was quite large.   _____
8. (Their, They're) not going to be back for a while.   _____

B. Write sentences using the following homonyms in the space provided.

Example: heal, heel
      How long did it take for your elbow to heal?
      The heel of my right foot is sore from these shoes.

1. blue, blew _____

_____

2. pair, pear _____

_____

3. peek, peak _____

_____

4. rode, road _____

_____

5. plain, plane _____

_____

6. patience, patients _____

Negative Words

Negative words indicate "no" or "not." Only one negative word should be used in a single sentence. Remember that "-n't" also means "not."

A. Underline the correct word in parentheses to complete each sentence.

Example: I didn't (ever, never) know I could play basketball.

1. There wasn't (nobody, anybody) to teach me.
2. There wasn't a court (anywhere, nowhere) nearby.
3. I didn't know (nothing, anything) about the game.
4. There wasn't (no, any) sense in studying the game.
5. Isn't there (anyone, no one) who could teach me?
6. I (never, ever) knew the park district taught basketball.
7. There weren't (no, any) classes near my home.
8. I didn't think (nobody, anybody) could teach me to play.

B. Rewrite each sentence correctly in the space provided. Avoid using two negatives in one sentence. You may have to omit or change words.

Example: There isn't nothing like a good game.

There is nothing like a good game.

1. I'm not never a bad sport.

_____

2. It isn't none of my business, but some people are bad sports.

_____

3. They never give no congratulations when you do well.

_____

4. I didn't have no idea free throws would be so difficult.

_____

5. There isn't nothing better than sinking a jump shot.

_____

6. I didn't know nothing could be such fun.

_____

Using Negative Words Correctly

Use only one negative word when you mean "no."

A. Choose the correct word from the pair in parentheses, and write it in the space provided.

Example: Tim hasn't sold (any, no) tickets.   *any*

1. We couldn't find (anything, nothing) for our boss's birthday. _____

2. I (can, can't) hardly work in this light. _____

3. There wasn't (anyone, no one) in the store. _____

4. Sue doesn't have a time card (either, neither). _____

5. We didn't go (anywhere, nowhere) last night. _____

6. Vic (was, wasn't) never out of the store. _____

7. I haven't told (anybody, nobody) about the sale. _____

8. (Almost, Hardly) nothing escapes my boss's notice. _____

9. There (were, weren't) no seats left in the meeting room. _____

10. Our boss hasn't (any, no) idea about the surprise party. _____

B. Rewrite each sentence in two ways to correct the negative word mistake.

Example: My son's hamsters weren't nowhere in his room.

    My son's hamsters weren't anywhere in his room.

    My son's hamsters were nowhere in his room.

1. I couldn't find neither of them upstairs.

_____

_____

2. They haven't never escaped before.

_____

_____

3. There are hardly no places left to look.

_____

_____

EXERCISE 138

I Before *E* Spelling Rule

Use *i* before *e*, except after *c*.

A. In each word pair below, circle the word that is spelled correctly.

Example: (relieve)   releive

1. seive   sieve
2. concieve   conceive
3. receive   recieve
4. beleive   believe
5. retrieve   retreive
6. deceive   decieve
7. perceive   percieve

B. Write the correctly spelled word in the space provided. Choose words from the list
    in Exercise A.

Example: I used a _____*sieve*_____ to make the flour finer.

1. I did _____ my paycheck this afternoon.
2. Can you _____ how much of our paychecks go to taxes?
3. It's impossible to _____ why this should be.
4. Perhaps if I lived in another country, I would not _____
   this way.

C. Write four sentences of your own using any of the *-i* before *-e* words.

Example: *I had my dog retrieve the tennis balls.*

1. _____

   _____

2. _____

   _____

3. _____

   _____

4. _____

   _____

Other Useful Spelling Rules

Q is always followed by *u*, for example, *quit*.

A. Write *q*, *u*, or *qu* in the space provided.

Example: Come ____ick! Look at this! _____*qu*_____

1. The q__ality supervisor talked to the inspectors. _____
2. The Amish painting has a ____uaint look. _____
3. I need a q__arter. I'm low on change. _____
4. The stacks look like their numbers are e__al. _____
5. The imaginary line around the center of the earth is
   called the e__ator. _____

B. Write *p*, *h*, or *ph* in the space provided. Some letters have sounds that do not match their spellings; for example, *ph* sounds like *f*.

Example: Let me take your ____oto with my new camera. _____*ph*_____

1. He's going through a ____hase. _____
2. ____ysical exercise can help reduce stress. _____
3. Don't get a p__obia about meeting the boss. _____
4. E.T., ____one home! _____
5. ____illipe, where are your team members? _____

C. Some words have a silent letter; for example, *wr* sounds like *r*. Write *r* or *wr* in the space provided.

Example: Please ____ite your name more clearly. _____*wr*_____

1. May I have a ____ide to your house? _____
2. I sprained my ____ist recently. _____
3. How many of your answers were ____ong? _____
4. How many of your answers were ____ight? _____
5. Are you going to ____ap his gift? _____

More Useful Spelling Rules

Some letters are silent. They are used to write the word, but they are not pronounced.

A. Circle the silent letters in the underlined words.

Example: Do you ⓚnow the correct answer?

1. Please find me some <u>plain</u> paper.
2. Maria can <u>play</u> that computer game quite well.
3. <u>Honor</u> is its own reward.
4. You really <u>failed</u> your examination?
5. Our staff is operating at <u>peak</u> capacity.
6. Please be <u>honest</u> with me.
7. This may be a <u>breach</u> of promise.
8. Must I <u>stay</u> late again today?
9. I will <u>write</u> the letter today.
10. Steve likes to <u>sail</u> on the weekends.

B. Choose the word from each pair that is spelled correctly. Write the correct word in the space provided.

Example: What subject does he (tech, teach)?   *teach*

1. Please turn down the (het, heat).   _____
2. We closed shop when the water (man, main) broke. _____
3. The waiter dropped the (tray, tra) of soup.   _____
4. (Honestly, Onestly), you are slow!   _____
5. He (claims, clams) to be somebody he's not.   _____
6. (Eat, Eet) your lunch before the rush.   _____
7. I (pra, pray) that it will be a slow day.   _____
8. Is that meat (tanted, tainted)?   _____

17   Combining Sentence Parts

Sometimes sentences have two or more singular nouns used as subjects. When a sentence has multiple singular subjects, a plural verb is used.

Examples: A pen and a pad <u>are</u> on the table.

<u>Do</u> Joan, Cliff, and Yolanda still work here?

Multiple subjects can be joined with connecting words or phrases (*and; both . . . and;* etc.). Sometimes two sentences with different subjects but the same verb are combined to make one sentence with a multiple subject. Then the verb in the sentence is changed from singular to plural.

Example: The <u>letter</u> <u>has</u> arrived. The <u>package</u> <u>has</u> arrived.

Change to: The <u>letter</u> <u>and</u> the <u>package</u> <u>have</u> arrived.

Or: <u>Both</u> the <u>letter</u> <u>and</u> the <u>package</u> <u>have</u> arrived.

Multiple Subjects that are singular and joined by or, either . . . or, neither . . . nor, or not only . . . but also, need a singular verb.

Examples: Either May or June is a good time for my vacation.

Neither his son nor his daughter has the key.

Not only the bridge but also the road is flooded.

Subjects that are plural and joined by or, either . . . or, neither . . . nor, or not only . . . but also, need a plural verb.

Examples: Neither the boys not the girls have the missing key.

Not only the chairs but also the tables are ruined.

Subjects that are both singular and plural joined by or, either . . . or, neither . . . nor, or not only . . . but also, need a verb that agrees with the closer subject.

Examples: Either Ms. Varca or her students have copies of the book.

Not only my friends but I am voting for her.

Sometimes two sentences have the same subject but two different verbs. The two sentences can be combined to make one sentence with multiple verbs. A connecting word (*and, but, if, when,* etc.) joins the two sentences into one.

Example: The <u>pump</u> <u>leaked</u>. The <u>pump</u> <u>poured</u> water onto the floor.

Change to: The <u>pump</u> <u>leaked</u> <u>and</u> <u>poured</u> water onto the floor.

Sometimes two sentences have two separate and independent thoughts. You can combine two sentences with two independent thoughts into one sentence by using a comma and a connecting word, or a semicolon and a connecting word.

Example: I left the showroom for a moment. A customer came in.

Change to: I left the showroom for a moment, <u>and</u> a customer came in.

Example: I brought my lunch. I ate in the cafeteria with Brenda.

Change to: I brought my lunch; <u>but</u> I ate in the cafeteria with Brenda.

Example: The store is closed. Finally we can leave.

Change to: The store is closed, <u>so</u> finally we can leave.

Combining sentences can show *how* ideas are related. You can combine subjects, verbs, or whole sentences to indicate a relationship between two separate sentences. You may have to change the verb number or omit some unnecessary words.

Example: Waitresses work in restaurants. Cooks work there, too.

Change to: <u>Both</u> <u>waitresses</u> <u>and</u> <u>cooks</u> work in restaurants.

When two or more *similar* or *related ideas* are used in the same sentence, the ideas are said to be **parallel.** Always express parallel ideas in a parallel sentence structure. Use either all single words, all phrases, or all independent thoughts, but not a combination of these.

Example: Say: Please bring <u>paper</u>, <u>pencil</u>, and <u>pens</u>.

Don't say: Please bring <u>paper</u>, <u>pencils</u>, and <u>bring some pens</u>.

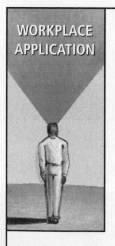

WORKPLACE APPLICATION

Tom said, "I need to stay home from work today. I need to rest. I am sick. I will call my boss. I will tell my boss that I will not be at work."

Can you rewrite what Tom said in two sentences? How would you change the sentence structure? Which words would you add, omit, or change? Rewrite Tom's conversation to show the changes you would make.

_____

_____

_____

EXERCISE 141

Combining Subjects

A verb must agree in number with its subject. Multiple subjects call for a plural verb.

A. Circle the verb in parentheses that completes each sentence correctly.

Example: Both managers and workers (is, (are)) coming to the picnic.

1. Judy Towne and Sue Herbst (is, are) bringing sandwiches.
2. Tony and Heather from the office (are, is) bringing fruit.
3. Company picnics and other events (is, are) good for morale.
4. Volleyball and softball (is, are) two games we will play.
5. My boss and I (is, are) helping with the games.
6. We (need, needs) all the help we can get.
7. Jerry Katz and Andrew McNeil (has, have) agreed to bring bats.
8. Both Margaret and Ed Ori (enjoy, enjoys) volleyball.
9. Most people (want, wants) to play softball first.
10. Both management and staff (hopes, hope) it won't rain.

B. Rewrite each pair of sentences by combining the subjects. Use *and* or *both . . . and* to help form the sentence. You may need to change the form of the verb.

Example: Linn has new job duties. Kate has new job duties.

Linn and Kate have new job duties.

1. Linn is taking a night course. Kate is taking a night course.

   _____

2. My supervisor comes in at 6 A.M. The plant manager comes in at 6 A.M.

   _____

3. The time clock runs late. The wall clock runs late.

   _____

4. Our bowling league wins many games. Their bowling league wins many games.

   _____

EXERCISE 142

More Practice Combining Subjects

When you combine sentences to make one sentence with a pair of subjects, make sure the subjects and verb agree.

A. Choose the correct form of the verb in parentheses, and write it in the space provided.

Example: Tara and I (study, studies) the classified ads.   _study_

1. A heading and a picture (appear, appears) on this group of ads. _____

2. Both the words and the pictures (help, helps) readers
   find the information.   _____

3. Either our store or our competitors (is, are) planning a sale.   _____

4. Neither my colleagues nor my friend (like, likes) sales as
   much as Tara and I.   _____

5. Either the date or the address (was, were) wrong.   _____

B. Using the words in parentheses, combine the pairs of sentences to make one sentence with a pair of subjects. If necessary, change the form of the verb so it agrees with the subject.

Example: A sale was advertised. A special discount was advertised.   (Both . . . and)
   Both a sale and a special discount were advertised.

1. Don wants a business someday. I want a business someday.   (Both . . . and)

   _____

2. My friends are calling tonight. Don is calling tonight.   (Either . . . or)

   _____

3. Don has enough money now. I have enough money now.   (Neither . . . nor)

   _____

4. An independent business costs money. A franchise costs money.   (Both . . . and)

   _____

5. These buildings rent offices. That building rents offices.   (Either . . . or)

   _____

6. My boyfriend likes country music. I like country music.   (Not only . . . but also)

   _____

EXERCISE 143

Combining Verbs

When two sentences have the same subject, they can sometimes be combined to form one sentence. The new sentence "shares" the one subject. The subject in the second sentence is dropped; then *and* combines the two sentences.

A. Combine the verbs in each pair of sentences. Write the new sentence in the space provided.

Example: Ben Ritchie woke up late. Ben jumped out of bed.

Ben Ritchie woke up late and jumped out of bed.

1. He jumped into his clothes. He rushed down the stairs.

   _____

2. Ben's wife smiled at him. Ben's wife offered him some orange juice.

   _____

3. Ben gulped down the juice. Ben ate rapidly.

   _____

4. Ben's wife told him to slow down. Ben's wife reminded him it was Saturday.

   _____

5. Ben had thought it was a work day. Ben was relieved.

   _____

B. Underline the complete verb in each sentence. Then circle the main verbs.

Example: I closed the drapes and turned on the lights in the conference room.

1. During my lunch, I opened the newspaper and began to read.
2. Don leaned back in his chair and closed his eyes.
3. The boss walked outside and enjoyed the sun.
4. We all relaxed and appreciated the lunch break.
5. The baby clapped his hands and laughed merrily.
6. The clown danced and sang for the children.
7. I read the book last night and took it back to the library today.

EXERCISE 144

Combining Subjects and Verbs

Two sentences with the same verb or the same subject can often be combined into one sentence.

A. Combine each pair of sentences to make one sentence with a pair of subjects.

Example: Jackals are wild dogs. Coyotes are wild dogs.

Jackals and coyotes are wild dogs.

1. Wolves are also members of the dog family. Foxes are also members of the dog family.

2. Raccoon dogs come from Asia. Dholes come from Asia.

3. Huskies like very cold climates. Malamutes like very cold climates.

4. My boyfriend likes all different breeds of dogs. I like all different breeds of dogs.

B. Combine each pair of sentences to make one sentence with a pair of verbs.

Example: Collies herd sheep. Collies watch out for predators.

Collies herd sheep and watch out for predators.

1. Dalmatians lived as mascots in firehouses. Dalmatians ran beside the engines to fires.

2. Newfoundlands have thick coats. Newfoundlands make good retrievers.

3. Most breeds enjoy the water. Most breeds can swim well.

EXERCISE 145

Combining Sentences

You can combine two independent thoughts (sentences) by using a comma and a connecting word.

Example: Many people love to travel. I do too.   (and)

Many people love to travel, and I do too.

1. Travel by ship appeals to me. Travel by plane would also be enjoyable.   (and)

   _____

   _____

2. Once sea journeys were on sailing ships. Now most sea passengers travel by ocean liner.   (but)

   _____

   _____

3. Would you like to sail around the world? Would you rather fly?   (or)

   _____

   _____

B. Write whether each sentence has one independent thought or two.

Example: Travel is both educational and enjoyable.   *one*

1. England has many wonderful old homes, and its cathedrals are well worth visiting.   _____

2. The vineyards of France are beautiful, and tourists also enjoy the sunny beaches in the south.   _____

3. I want to see the Taj Mahal in India and the Great Wall of China.   _____

4. I dream of visiting the famous cities of Europe and of Asia.   _____

5. These are dreams now, but someday my travels will be a reality.   _____

More Practice Combining Sentences

You can combine two related sentences by joining them with a comma and a connecting word.

Use a comma and the connecting word in parentheses to combine each pair of sentences.

Example: Sandy was going camping. His car didn't work.   (but)

Sandy was going camping, but his car didn't work.

1. He considered a borrowed one. His friend favored a used one instead.   (but)

   _____

   _____

2. A truck would do. A van might be a possibility.   (or)

   _____

   _____

3. The van would be more comfortable. He could also use it as a camper.   (and)

   _____

   _____

4. A hot dog truck was for sale. It gave him a new idea.   (and)

   _____

   _____

5. The windows and awning looked funny. He liked them anyway.   (but)

   _____

   _____

6. His friend suggested rebuilding the interior. Sandy could just use it to sell
   hot dogs.   (or)

   _____

   _____

7. They laughed at the truck. Sandy bought it anyway.   (but)

   _____

   _____

Review of Combining Sentences

Sometimes two sentences with related ideas can be combined into one sentence.

A. Combine each pair of related sentences. Use a comma and the connecting word *and*, *but*, or *or* as indicated.

Example: Amelia Earhart was born in 1898. She grew up in Kansas.   (and)

Amelia Earhart was born in 1898, and she grew up in Kansas.

1. Amelia Earhart flew airplanes. She flew with great skill.   (and) _____

2. She flew across the United States alone. She crossed the ocean alone.   (and)

3. People admired Amelia. They thought she was crazy.   (or) _____

4. She crossed the ocean. She did not realize her dream.   (but) _____

5. She tried to fly around the world. She disappeared.   (but) _____

B. Study the four sets of sentences below. Combine the two sets that are related. If a set should not be combined, write the words *do not combine*.

Example: Jacqueline Cochran was a pilot. She became famous.

Jacqueline Cochran was a pilot, and she became famous.

1. Jacqueline was an expert pilot. She set many records. _____

2. Jacqueline grew up in a foster home. She flew many planes. _____

3. She flew a fighter plane in 1936. She was married. _____

4. She often flew alone. Sometimes she flew with a partner. _____

Combining Subjects, Verbs, and Sentences

Combine subjects, verbs, and sentences to show how ideas are related.

A. Rewrite the sentence pairs by combining subjects, verbs, or whole sentences. Change the verb number if needed.

Example: Winter brings cold weather. Winter causes icy problems.

Winter brings cold weather and causes icy problems.

1. In Maine, rivers freeze. Lakes freeze too.

   _____

2. Cars cross the Kennebec River on a drawbridge. Trucks and buses cross too.

   _____

   _____

3. Winter weather prevents river traffic. Winter weather causes delays.

   _____

4. In spring, ice blocks the river waters. Ice rams the bridge.

   _____

5. Huge boats hit the ice at full power. They break it up.

   _____

B. Rewrite the following paragraph. Combine subjects, verbs, or whole sentences to make longer, smoother sentences.

   The *Snohomish* is an icebreaker. The *Yankton* is one too. These are large boats. They are powerful. They work together. They are a team. The work is dangerous. It requires skill. These boats are fitted with sharp blades. The blades are in the front. The blades cut the ice. The blades break the ice.

   _____

   _____

   _____

   _____

   _____

   _____

   _____

EXERCISE 149

Keeping Sentences in Parallel Form

Parallel ideas should always be written in parallel form.

A. Circle the letter of the sentences with parallel form.

Example: (a) Being a waitress requires stamina, energy, and you have to be able to laugh at things.

(b) Being a waitress requires stamina, energy, and a sense of humor.

1. (a) Concerns about computers include access, computer viruses, and issues about keeping important information private.

   (b) Concerns about computers include access, computer viruses, and privacy issues.

2. (a) Some see technology as oppressive, dehumanizing, and catering to people who like to sell things.

   (b) Some see technology as oppressive, dehumanizing, and commercial.

3. (a) Aside from their problems, computers link people, products, and ideas.

   (b) Aside from their problems, computers link people, products, and the thoughts of different people.

4. (a) Other issues, like drug screening, result in more job dismissal, job transfer, or even denial of employment.

   (b) Other issues, like drug screening, result in more job dismissal, job transfer, or even being denied a job in the first place.

5. (a) We hope the situation will be better for our children and their children.

   (b) We hope the situation will be better for our children and the children that they have.

B. Using parallel form, write four sentences that include the word groupings below.

1. coffee break	lunch	quitting time
2. visual	attention-getting	persuasive
3. insurance	flextime	maternity leave
4. phones	faxes	photocopy machines

_____

_____

_____

LESSON

18   Independent and Dependent Thoughts

As you recall from Lesson 17, some sentences contain one or more whole ideas, or **independent thoughts.** Other sentences contain phrases that have a subject and a verb but do not make sense by themselves. These are called **dependent thoughts.** They are dependent because they need a subject and a verb to complete an idea.

Example: I am a hard worker, so I'm sure I can do this job. (two independent thoughts)

   If I work hard, I can do this job. (one dependent thought—*if I work hard;* and one independent thought—*I can do this job.*)

Dependent thoughts are combined with independent thoughts in sentences by connecting words. You have already learned some connecting words. Here is another list of connecting words that are often used to connect dependent thoughts with independent thoughts to make sentences. Notice that there are several connecting phrases as well.

Connecting Words and Phrases

if	which	when	before
who	since	while	because
although	whenever	however	which means that
as soon as	whereas	that	

Two sentences with two independent thoughts can also be combined to make one sentence with one independent and one dependent thought. The longer single sentence often helps ideas to flow better.

Example: Frances gave the report. Frances is from the accounting department.

Change to: Frances, from the accounting department, gave the report. (The phrase, *from the accounting department,* is a dependent thought in this sentence.)

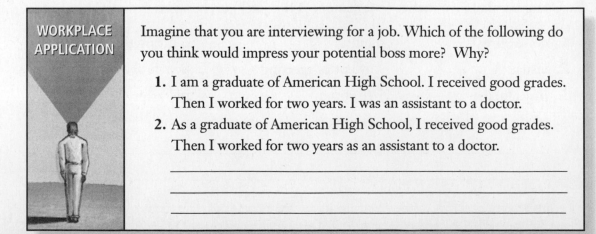

WORKPLACE APPLICATION

Imagine that you are interviewing for a job. Which of the following do you think would impress your potential boss more? Why?

1. I am a graduate of American High School. I received good grades. Then I worked for two years. I was an assistant to a doctor.
2. As a graduate of American High School, I received good grades. Then I worked for two years as an assistant to a doctor.

_____

_____

_____

EXERCISE 150

What Are Independent Thoughts?

An independent thought has a complete subject and a complete verb. Some sentences have two or more subjects, verbs, or independent thoughts.

A. Each independent thought below has a pair of subjects or a pair of verbs. Place *S* above each subject and *V* above each verb.

Example: Wolfgang Amadeus Mozart was born and raised near Salzburg, Austria.

1. Myths and legends surround Mozart's life.
2. Mozart wrote and performed many songs.
3. Mozart and his sister were talented young people.
4. Many kings and queens heard young Mozart's music.
5. The violin and piano were popular instruments during Mozart's lifetime.
6. Mozart and his family traveled throughout Europe.
7. The emperor and empress of Austria met Mozart.
8. Mozart's operas and concerts entertain many people even today.
9. His music is played and sung by famous artists.
10. My girlfriend and I saw a movie about Mozart.

B. Write whether each sentence has *one* or *two* independent thoughts.

Example: Mozart studied violin and piano.   _____one_____

1. Mozart and his sister showed great talent at an early age.   _____
2. His sister was very skilled, but Mozart was a musical genius.   _____
3. His father taught music, and Mozart learned quickly.   _____
4. He composed and produced an operetta at the age of 12.   _____
5. Mozart met the Austrian emperor, and he performed for him.   _____
6. Most people loved his music, but some were puzzled by it.   _____
7. Mozart received many gifts for playing, but he was not rich.   _____
8. Mozart had a sense of humor, and he enjoyed puns.   _____
9. Mozart studied and wrote music for most of his life.   _____
10. His music is still loved and appreciated.   _____

Identifying Independent Thoughts

An independent thought has a complete subject and a complete verb. Some sentences have two or more subjects, verbs, or independent thoughts.

A. Underline each subject once and each verb twice in the independent thoughts below.

Example: <u>Tourists</u> and <u>students</u> <u><u>flock</u></u> to Rome each year.

1. They enjoy the city and visit its historic sites.
2. The catacombs attract and inspire many people.
3. These underground paths and tombs date to Roman times.
4. Funerals and memorial services were held in them.
5. San Callisto and San Sebastiano are famous catacombs.
6. The builders cut and dug the tombs out of rock.
7. In the sixth century, invaders uncovered and destroyed many tombs.
8. Historians investigate and study these catacombs.
9. Ancient writings and paintings decorate these tunnels.
10. Wall pictures show ancient people and tell about events.

B. Write whether each sentence has *one* or *two* independent thoughts.

Example: Each year thousands of people visit the catacombs.   _____*one*_____

1. Some people say the tunnels are long, but they are not. _____
2. The catacombs stretch 100 miles at most.   _____
3. Five catacombs are open, but the rest remain closed.   _____
4. Visitors to the catacombs once used candles, but now there is electricity.   _____
5. Fresco paintings decorate the walls.   _____
6. Some paintings show scenes, and others show figures.   _____
7. Inscriptions describe and identify people in the tombs.   _____
8. Some of the graves are sealed with bricks.   _____
9. There are catacombs in places other than Rome.   _____

EXERCISE 152

Review of Independent Thoughts

The part of a sentence that has a subject and a verb and makes sense by itself is an independent thought.

A. Underline each independent thought in the sentence once. Underline the comma and connecting word twice.

Example: The pony express began in 1860, but it lasted only a year.

1. The pony express did not last long, but it was important.
2. The telegraph system reached Missouri, but it stopped there.
3. Mail was carried by ships, or it was sent by wagon train.
4. These methods were slow, and better service was needed.
5. Riders rode 2000 miles, and each trip took 10 days.
6. The horses had to be quick, or the riders did not use them.
7. The riders rode in relays, but each horse went 15 miles.
8. Most riders rode 75 miles, but some rode farther.
9. The mail was picked up in Missouri, and it was taken rapidly to California.
10. Early trips took 10 days, but later the trips were shorter.

B. Write an *S* above each subject and a *V* above each verb. Place a comma before each connecting word that joins independent thoughts.

Example: The routes were dangerous but the riders were brave.

$$\overset{S}{}\quad \overset{V}{}\quad \overset{S}{}\quad \overset{V}{}$$
            The routes were dangerous, but the riders were brave.

1. Life in the pony express was hard and it was lonely.
2. The West was a wilderness and stations were miles apart.
3. The riders changed horses quickly and then they rode off.
4. They rode under any conditions and their bags held the mail.
5. Workers packed the mail and it usually arrived safely.
6. The company tested many riders but it chose only the best.
7. A few riders became famous and legends began about some.
8. Delivery of the mail was fast but mail was lost once.
9. The telegraph started and the pony express ended.
10. Mail service continued but people still remember the pony express.

EXERCISE 153

What Are Dependent Thoughts?

A dependent thought has a subject and a verb but does not make sense by itself.

A. Write *S* if the group of words below is a sentence, or an independent thought.
Write *D* if the group of words is a dependent thought.

Example: Bullets are a writing tool that can help your reading get noticed.   _____*S*_____

1. A bullet—that little black circle or square.   _____

2. Get your message across to the reader quickly and concisely.   _____

3. Encouraging the reader to scan the information if time is short.   _____

4. Keeping attention of readers more easily.   _____

5. Bullets help you organize important information.   _____

6. Chose only the most important points.   _____

7. Setting them down in a logical order.   _____

8. Require no "lead in" or "summary."   _____

9. Bullets allow you to "hit and run" with your message.   _____

10. Instead of saying, "Accept responsibility, find out what needs to be   _____
    done, and get it done right away," say

11. • Accept responsibility.   _____

12. • Find out what needs to be done.   _____

13. • Get it done right away.   _____

B. Write *D* if the underlined part of each sentence is a dependent thought.
Write *I* if it is independent.

Example: A workplace communications newsletter surveyed its readers,   _____*D*_____
    and it came up with the following findings.

1. Eighty-four percent of the readers said interpersonal communication
   skills were among the top three most important job skills.   _____

2. Seventy-nine percent said the ability to write well is important.   _____

3. Sixty-nine percent wanted employees who could speak well.   _____

4. Only 40 percent of those who answered the survey rated
   education or work experience in the top three categories.   _____

5. Personal appearance placed last, as only 18 percent of
   readers rated it in the top three.   _____

Practice Using Dependent Thoughts

Some sentences have an independent thought combined with one or more dependent thoughts.

A. Underline the dependent thought in each sentence. The dependent thought can be at the beginning, in the middle, or at the end of the sentence.

Example: <u>If you want to learn to fly</u>, you must take lessons.

1. Some airplanes, when they are full, carry over 450 passengers.
2. More efficient jets were built since fuel became expensive.
3. Jet aircraft fly at over 500 mph as long as they are cruising.
4. Aircraft that fly long distances carry fuel in their wings.
5. When a jet takes off, fuel may be one-third of its weight.
6. Helicopters, which climb vertically, usually fly forward.
7. Motorless gliders can climb if the currents are suitable.

B. Rewrite each independent thought as a longer sentence by adding a dependent thought. Begin each dependent thought with the word in parentheses.

Example: I crawled out of my bed   (as soon as)   _____

   I crawled out of my bed   (as soon as)   *my alarm rang.*

1. I gulped down breakfast   (since) _____

   _____

2. I dried my shirt,   (which) _____

   _____

3. It was time to move   (when) _____

   _____

4. I took the train   (that) _____

   _____

5. Sometimes I get blisters   (because) _____

   _____

6. The sun came out   (after) _____

   _____

EXERCISE 155

Identifying Independent and Dependent Thoughts

Sometimes a sentence has one independent thought and one or more dependent thoughts.

A. Write a new sentence by adding a dependent thought to each independent thought below. Use the words in parentheses to introduce the dependent thoughts.

Example: Chloe had to get to the store   (before)   _____*it closed.*_____

1. She wanted to rent a tape   (that) _____

   _____

2. She had to hurry   (because) _____

   _____

3. Her friend Anita stopped her   (while) _____

   _____

4. Together they crossed the street   (when) _____

   _____

5. They sprinted through the door   (as) _____

   _____

6. Chloe quickly found the tape   (that) _____

   _____

B. Read each sentence below. If the sentence has a dependent thought, underline it.

Example: Computers do many things <u>that are hard for people to do</u>.

1. Because computers seldom make errors, people have come to rely on them to do important work.
2. Some animated motion pictures are made with computers, which make most of the detailed drawings.
3. Scientists, who require precise calculators, have been using computers for many years.
4. Many new automobiles contain small computers that control the engine and the instrument panel.
5. Computers have become more powerful in recent years, but they are less expensive.

Review of Independent and Dependent Thoughts

Some sentences have one independent thought and one or more dependent thoughts. When the dependent thought begins the sentence, a comma separates the thought from the independent thought.

A. Rewrite each sentence by adding a dependent thought to the independent thought. Use the word in parentheses to introduce the dependent thought.

Example: The tournament had started.   (although)

The tournament had started although it was raining hard.

1. The company's tax refund was late.   (because) _____

_____

2. The furniture in the office was covered.   (while) _____

_____

3. City streets become slippery.   (when) _____

_____

4. You know it is dangerous.   (if) _____

_____

5. I remained at work.   (until) _____

_____

6. The meeting began again.   (when) _____

_____

B. Underline the dependent thought in the sentences below. Do not mark sentences with no dependent thoughts.

Example: Tennis is a game <u>that requires great strength and speed</u>.

1. When four people play tennis, the game is called doubles.
2. If only two play, the game is called singles.
3. Tennis began about 800 years ago.
4. Since players had no rackets then, they hit the ball with their palms.
5. Because they hit the ball this way, it was called the game of the palm.
6. Today, players use rackets, and the game is much faster.
7. Early rackets were wooden, but now many are made of metal.

EXERCISE 157

Combining Sentences Using Dependent Thoughts

You can use dependent thoughts to combine sentence pairs. Sometimes a comma or commas separate the dependent thought from the rest of the sentence.

A. Combine each sentence pair by making one a dependent thought. Begin the dependent thought with the word or words in parentheses.

Example: A business letter is more formal than a personal letter.
It does not have to be stuffy.   (although)

Although a business letter is more formal than a personal letter, it does not have to be stuffy.

1. You want to avoid stilted writing. It sounds impersonal and may turn off a potential customer.   (that) _____

    _____

2. Practice speaking what you write. You can see if your writing sounds conversational.   (so that) _____

    _____

3. Being too casual can also be a problem. It may make your customer feel unimportant.   (since) _____

    _____

B. Combine the sentences by making one a dependent thought. Begin the dependent thought with the word or words in parentheses.

Example: "Bloated" writing means using unnecessary words.
Some people do this when trying to sound important. (which)

"Bloated" writing means using unnecessary words, which some people do when trying to sound important.

1. Management has recently taken the request under advisement.
    They will be able to deliver their response in the near future.   (whereas)

    _____

    _____

2. Reading your writing out loud can help make it sound more conversational. It also helps you spot mistakes, such as bloating or grammar errors.   (while)

    _____

    _____

19 Using Descriptive Details in Sentences

As you may recall from Lessons 11 through 13, adjectives and adverbs are words used to describe nouns, pronouns, and verbs. By combining sentences that contain descriptive details, you can make longer, more interesting sentences.

Some words may have to be omitted or changed when you rewrite the single sentence using the descriptive details. Some words may change position in the sentence.

Example: The photocopies were too light. They were not readable.

Change to: The photocopies were so light, they were unreadable.

Or: The photocopies were too light to be readable.

Example: The seminar was long. It was boring. It was useless.

Change to: The seminar was long, boring, and useless.

Sometimes a verb form can be used to show descriptive details. The verb form may be used alone or with other words in a descriptive phrase. This verb form is called a **verbal.** It is often used to add detail to nouns and pronouns.

Examples: The *anticipated* sale has begun. (*Anticipated* is a verbal made from the verb *anticipate;* it describes *sale.*)

Those customers *waiting in line* appear to be anxious. (*Waiting in line* is a verbal phrase; it describes *customers.*)

Adding a new cashier, the manager solved the problem. (*Adding a new cashier* is a verbal phrase; it describes *manager.*)

Verbal phrases should always be placed as close as possible to the word they describe in a sentence. This makes sentences clearer and avoids confusion.

Example: Say: Stopping for coffee, I missed the bus.

Don't say: I missed the bus, stopping for coffee. (Was the *bus* stopping for coffee?)

Example: Say: Showing improvement in job performance, I got a good evaluation.

Don't say: I got a good evaluation showing improvement in job performance.

(Did the *evaluation* improve its job performance?)

Sometimes a noun or noun phrase follows another noun to help identify or explain it. Use commas to separate the descriptive noun or noun phrase.

Examples: The meeting, <u>a sales update,</u> was held at 3 P.M.

Dealers, <u>especially those in the South,</u> surpassed their quotas.

The largest sale was made by Arnold, <u>a dealer from Atlanta.</u>

Sometimes a noun or noun phrase can be used to combine two sentences. A noun or noun phrase can replace a second short, or choppy, sentence to create one longer, smoother sentence.

Example: Marilyn and Patrice are friends. They do everything together.

Change to: Marilyn and Patrice, <u>friends,</u> do everything together.

Example: I work at Sam's Automotive. It is a car repair shop.

Change to: I work at Sam's Automotive, <u>a car repair shop.</u>

Example: Let's take these jackets to Mr. Arnold for repair. He is the tailor.

Change to: Let's take these jackets to Mr. Arnold, <u>the tailor ,</u> for repair.

WORKPLACE APPLICATION

Natasha received this E-mail on her computer:

> Natasha:
> Meet me and we will go for coffee in the lobby.
> Sue

Natasha went to Sue's desk but was unable to find her friend. Could there have been a miscommunication in this E-mail message? Rewrite Natasha's E-mail to read more clearly.

_____

_____

_____

Placement of Descriptive Details

Place details as close as possible to the words they describe.

A. Rewrite each sentence and place the descriptive detail close to the word it describes or explains.

Example: The juice in the sink that was too hard to drink was thawed.

The juice that was too hard to drink was thawed in the sink.

1. Oozing across the floor, Samantha watched the ketchup. _____

   _____

2. He removed a fish from the freezer that was 16 inches long. _____

   _____

3. The customer wore a felt hat on her head that was much too large. _____

   _____

4. Pulling off the highway at the exit, we saw the tour bus. _____

   _____

B. Rewrite each sentence in two ways. Write the word in parentheses in two different positions in each sentence to show how sentence meaning changes.

Example: Some people watched the finish.   (only)

Some people watched only the finish.

Some people only watched the finish.

1. Each crew knows how to handle its machine.   (just)

   _____

   _____

2. One vehicle can travel 180 miles per hour.   (only)

   _____

   _____

3. Some vehicles are built from a few materials.   (only)

   _____

   _____

4. Five vehicles completed 50 laps.   (just)

   _____

   _____

EXERCISE 159

Combining Sentences With Details

Short sentences that have descriptive words and phrases can sometimes be combined into a single, more interesting sentence.

A. Combine the multiple sentences below into one simpler, more interesting sentence. Omit any unnecessary words.

Example: Bus drivers take people to work, even on rainy days. They take people to work, even on gloomy days. They take people to work, even on snowy days.

Bus drivers take people to work even on rainy,
gloomy, or snowy days.

1. Bus drivers carry all kinds of passengers. Some are young. Some are old. Some are rich. Some are poor. _____

_____

2. Bus drivers are responsible for the safety of their passengers. They are responsible for the comfort of their passengers. _____

_____

3. Many bus drivers work part-time. They may put in only 20 to 30 hours per week. They may put in even less time. _____

_____

4. Some bus drivers work split shifts. They drive for several hours in the morning. They drive for several hours in the evening. _____

_____

B. The long, green bus pulled up to the curb. It squealed to a stop. The front door opened. It made a whooshing sound. Three passengers got off. One was a tall, red-headed student. He wore a black cap. One was an elderly gentleman with a cane. One was a young businesswoman. Then two passengers boarded. The bus pulled away again.

_____

_____

_____

_____

_____

EXERCISE 160

More Practice Combining Sentences With Details

Combine sentences with descriptive words and phrases to make smoother, more readable sentences.

Write one sentence for each numbered item below. Combine the descriptive words and phrases.

Example: The trips were long. They were difficult. They were sometimes dull.

The trips were long, difficult, and sometimes dull.

1. In the 1840s many women were courageous. They were adventurous.

2. Wives of whaling-ship captains waited patiently. They waited bravely.

3. The families of the sea captains sometimes sailed with them. They sailed for years at a time.

4. The women wrote in their diaries daily. They wrote thoughtfully. They wrote faithfully.

5. They told of strange sights. They told of adventures. They told of tragedies.

6. The people aboard the ship had adventures on the ocean. They had adventures in foreign ports.

7. Sometimes storms raged fiercely. They raged destructively.

EXERCISE 161

Verbals as Descriptive Details

Sometimes a verb form, or verbal, can be used to show descriptive details. The verbal may be used alone or with other words in a descriptive phrase. Verbals are often used to add detail to nouns and pronouns.

A. Underline each verbal in the sentences below. If the verbal is part of a descriptive phrase, put the phrase in parentheses.

Example: People waiting in the lobby are eager to hear the concert.

People (waiting in the lobby) are eager to hear the concert.

1. Walking down the aisles, ushers show people to their seats.
2. Some of the musicians practicing on stage tune their instruments.
3. The conductor dressed in a tuxedo directs the orchestra.
4. He stands on a raised platform.
5. Waving his baton, he signals the orchestra to play loudly.
6. The gleaming brass trumpets blare.
7. The booming drums sound like thunder.
8. The crashing cymbals sound like lightning.
9. The music filling the auditorium is powerful.
10. Clapping their hands, people in the audience appreciate the performance.
11. Facing the audience, the conductor bows.

B. Underline the verbal phrase in each sentence. Then draw two lines under the noun or pronoun that the phrase describes.

Example: Hippocrates, known as the "Father of Medicine," lived in ancient Greece.

Hippocrates, known as the "Father of Medicine," lived in ancient Greece.

1. He was a brilliant doctor dedicated to his profession.
2. He treated patients suffering from illnesses.
3. Using scientific approaches, he tried to understand diseases.
4. He wrote books describing his medical procedures.

EXERCISE 162

Placement of Verbal Phrases

A verbal phrase should be placed as close as possible to the word that it describes so that the meaning of the sentence is clear.

A. Underline the sentence in each pair that places the verbal phrase correctly.

Example: Boiling in the pot, the cook stirred the soup.

<u>The cook stirred the soup boiling in the pot.</u>

1. The photographer took a picture focusing his camera lens.
   Focusing his camera lens, the photographer took a picture.
2. The circus featured lions jumping through fiery hoops.
   Jumping through fiery hoops, the circus featured lions.
3. Racing toward the finish line, the fans applauded the runners.
   The fans applauded the runners racing toward the finish line.
4. Injured in the game, the doctor bandaged the athlete's leg.
   The doctor bandaged the athlete's leg injured in the game.
5. My husband washed his car parked in the driveway.
   Parked in the driveway, my husband washed his car.

B. Rewrite each sentence to correct the position of the misplaced verbal phrase.

Example: Borrowed from the office, I couldn't find my notepad.

I couldn't find my notepad borrowed from the office.

1. The manager found a mistake looking over the report.

   _____

2. The dispatcher called the dock supervisor using the intercom.

   _____

3. Written in a foreign language, she couldn't read the fax.

   _____

4. I almost missed the bus running down the street.

   _____

5. Advertised in the newspaper, I applied for the job.

   _____

6. Lying on the floor, the mechanic found the socket.

   _____

Using Nouns as Descriptive Details

Sometimes a noun or noun phrase follows another noun to identify or explain it. Use commas to separate nouns and noun phrases that provide descriptive details.

A. Add commas to set off each descriptive noun detail.

Example: We watched a television show about Kashgar a city in China.

   We watched a television show about Kashgar, a city in China.

1. The guide Mr. Yakub showed the American television crew around.

2. The bazaar a kind of open market was exciting.

3. Many animals mostly sheep and goats are sold here.

4. Camels the ships of the desert are traded too.

5. The buyers nomadic herdsmen look for bargains.

6. The merchants clever sellers look for business.

7. Kashgar an oasis city is in the Takla Makan Desert.

8. Long ago Kashgar was on an important trade route the Silk Road.

9. A famous traveler Marco Polo once stopped here.

10. The people of Kashgar are Uighers descendants of a Turkish group.

B. Circle the descriptive noun or noun phrase in each sentence. Underline the noun it describes.

Example: Some Uighers live in <u>yurts</u>, (cloth tents.)

1. Tall mountains, the Pamirs, are on one side of Kashgar.

2. People use wooden carts, popular means of transportation.

3. Donkeys, traditional beasts of burden, pull the carts.

4. Poplars, graceful trees, line the dusty roads to Kashgar.

5. Many farmers sell fruit, melons and oranges, at the bazaar.

6. In turn they buy needed goods, oil and meat.

7. Camel bells, desert necessities, are traded here also.

8. Lively bargaining, a favorite pastime, fills the bazaar.

EXERCISE 164

Using Nouns as Descriptive Details to Combine Sentences

A noun or noun phrase sometimes follows a noun and identifies or explains it. Such descriptive noun details may be used to combine short, choppy sentences.

A. Write the descriptive noun detail and the noun or noun phrase that it explains or identifies on the line below.

Example: Government jobs—where a local, state, or national agency or body is the employer—employ millions of workers.

Where a local, state, or national agency or body is the employer—government jobs.

1. Governments, systems for creating and keeping control over group activities, come in many different sizes. _____

_____

2. Most state or local governments fall into one of five groups—county, municipality, township, school district, or special district. _____

_____

B. Combine each pair of sentences into a single sentence with a descriptive noun phrase. Set the phrase off correctly, using one or more commas or dashes.

Example: An increase in the U.S. population resulted in a greater need for government jobs. The increase was from about 150,000,000 in 1950 to about 250,000,000 in 1990.

An increase in the U.S. population, from about 150,000,000 in 1950 to about 250,000,000 in 1990, resulted in a greater need for government jobs.

1. Benefits are often generous in government jobs. Benefits include such extras as paid vacations, sick leave, medical insurance, and retirement plans.

_____

_____

2. Tuition assistance is often a benefit in state government jobs. Tuition assistance provides help with the cost of higher education.

_____

_____

More Nouns as Descriptive Details to Combine Sentences

Sometimes a noun or noun phrase follows a noun and identifies or explains it. Such noun details can be used to combine sentences.

A. Draw one line under the descriptive noun phrase in each sentence below. Draw two lines under the noun that the phrase explains or identifies.

Example: Ernest Hemingway, a fiction writer, was born in 1899.

Ernest Hemingway, a fiction writer, was born in 1899.

1. He grew up in Oak Park, a suburb of Chicago.

2. His father, a doctor, took him on trips to northern Michigan.

3. In high school, Hemingway excelled in two sports, boxing and football.

4. After graduation, he worked as a reporter for the *Star*, a newspaper in Kansas City.

5. *In Our Time*, a collection of his short stories, was published in 1924.

6. He wrote two war novels, *A Farewell to Arms* and *For Whom the Bell Tolls*.

B. Combine each pair of sentences into a single sentence with a noun phrase set off with a comma or commas.

Example: An old fisherman lived in Cabanas. Cabanas is a village in Cuba.
An old fisherman lived in Cabanas, a village in Cuba.

1. Alone in a rowboat, he caught a giant fish. The giant fish was a marlin.

_____

_____

2. Sharks attacked and devoured the marlin. Sharks are a menace to fishermen.

_____

_____

3. Ernest Hemingway wrote a short novel based on this true story. The novel is *The Old Man and the Sea.* _____

_____

_____

20 Improving Sentence Structure

A **sentence fragment** is a group of words that may look like a sentence, but it is not a complete thought. A sentence fragment may be missing a subject, a verb, or both. Sentence fragments can be corrected by joining two fragments to make one sentence. Capitalization and punctuation may need to be changed, and a connecting word may need to be added.

Example: Our work hours. From 8 A.M. to 4:30 P.M.

Change to: Our work <u>hours are from</u> 8 A.M. to 4:30 P.M.

Example: Sometimes I miss lunch. Get hungry by 2 P.M.

Change to: Sometimes I miss <u>lunch and get</u> hungry by 2 P.M.

Run-on sentences are two sentences written together as one sentence without the correct punctuation and capitalization. To provide clarity, you need to separate most run-on sentences. Change capitalization and punctuation as needed to fit the two new sentences. Sometimes run-on sentences can be combined instead of separated. Use a semi-colon or a comma and a connecting word to combine related run-on sentences.

Example: There never seems to be enough time in a day I always have too much to do.

Change to: There never seems to be enough time in a <u>day. I</u> always have too much to do.

Or: There never seems to be enough time in a <u>day; I</u> always have too much to do.

Example: Sometimes I wish I could be two people I could get more done.

Change to: Sometimes I wish I could be two <u>people; I</u> could get more done.

Or: Sometimes I wish I could be two <u>people, so</u> I could get more done.

As you can see from the examples above, sentences are not always more interesting just because they are longer. However, sometimes you can expand sentences and make them better. Adding details like descriptive words, verbals, and noun phrases adds interest to simple sentences.

Example: I was late for the meeting.

Change to: I was late for the meeting <u>in room 2B</u>. (Add descriptive details.)

Or: I was late for the meeting, <u>a monthly performance review</u>. (Add noun phrase.)

Or: <u>Rushing</u>, I was late for the meeting. (Add verbal.)

On the other hand, sentences can also be improved by condensing them to make them clear and concise. Eliminate any unnecessary words (especially *and*, *so*, etc.) or words that have the same or similar meanings. As you learned in Lessons 17 through 19, sentences can be improved by helping words and phrases in parallel structure and details close to the word they describe.

Example: The meeting was called to order and the secretary read the agenda so everyone now knew what to expect, which was that a suitable, workable manager had been chosen, finally, at last.

Change to: The meeting was called to order. After the secretary read the agenda, everyone knew what to expect. Finally, a suitable manager had been chosen. (Omitted words and phrases: *and, so, now, which was that, at last, workable*; descriptive word moved: *finally*)

Sentences can also be improved by *varying sentence types* and *changing sentence beginnings*. You can sometimes vary and condense sentences by *summarizing facts* from one sentence and adding them to the beginning of another sentence.

Example: We went to Cincinnati. This took place after our visit to Dayton.

Change to: After our visit to Dayton, we went to Cincinnati. (Summarize second sentence; change beginning of first sentence to include summary.)

WORKPLACE APPLICATION

Can you improve this newsletter article's opening paragraph? (Clue: You might expand or combine sentences, eliminate wordiness, or change sentence structure and word placement.)

Company Merger Creates New Opportunities

Our company, Bradley Plastics, is merging with another company this company is called Smith Manufacturing. This merger will allow us to create new products, sell more products, and we can also start to sell our products overseas. All of us workers who work here at Bradley Plastics can look forward in the future to more and better things to come.

_____

_____

_____

_____

_____

EXERCISE 166

What Are Sentence Fragments?

A group of words punctuated like a sentence but not expressing a complete thought is called a sentence fragment. A sentence fragment may be missing a subject, a verb, or both.

A. Write *sentence* if the group of words is a complete sentence. Write *fragment* if the group of words is not a complete sentence.

Example: Interested in a new job.   _____*fragment*_____

1. I looked in the paper for ideas.   _____
2. Took the bus to the community college.   _____
3. Several interesting classes for people like me. _____
4. I enrolled in a real estate course.   _____
5. Meets Tuesday and Thursday evenings.   _____

B. Join each fragment and sentence to make a complete sentence.

Example: The Internet, sometimes called the information superhighway. Provides a new
                place. To search for jobs.

                The Internet, sometimes called the information superhighway, provides a new
                place to search for jobs.

1. Job-related computer bulletin boards are good places to read about jobs. Or to post a résumé. _____

   _____

2. Many computer bulletin boards cater to local communities. So jobs listed would likely be local jobs. _____

   _____

3. Commercial (fee-based) information services. Provide another alternative for job seekers. _____

   _____

4. Most libraries provide free access to the Internet. Along with assistance or training in Internet use. _____

   _____

Correcting Sentence Fragments and Run-On Sentences

A group of words punctuated like a sentence but not expressing a complete thought is called a sentence fragment. A run-on is two or more sentences without proper punctuation between them.

A. Correct each fragment by joining it to the sentence from which it was separated. Add punctuation as needed.

Example: You can study a history. Of shoes.

You can study a history of shoes.

1. In prehistoric times. People tied skins around their feet.

2. An early shoe. The sandal was worn in Egypt, Greece, and Rome.

3. Sandals were made. From hard leather or plant fibers.

4. When people wanted warmth. They wore soft leather shoes.

5. Boots were originally used. For hunting.

B. Rewrite each run-on sentence below with a connecting word and, if necessary, a comma.

Example: Shoes are useful they protect your feet.

Shoes are useful, and they protect your feet.

1. Moccasins were made of animal skins they were comfortable.

2. Heeled shoes originated in the 1400s they were wooden.

3. Heels were helpful they kept feet from mud and water.

4. Some shoes had pointed toes others had platforms.

More Practice Correcting Sentence Fragments

A group of words punctuated like a sentence but not expressing a complete thought is called a sentence fragment.

A. All the groups of words are sentence fragments except one. Add words as needed to make the others complete, and then rewrite the new sentences in the blanks. Write *correct* for the group of words that is already a sentence.

Example: Asked for directions.

A man in a jeep asked for directions.

1. That beautiful autumn day.

2. Arrived at the doctor's office.

3. Took a bus downtown.

4. I could hardly believe my eyes!

5. My brother and his family.

B. Each item below contains two sentences and a fragment. Correct each fragment by attaching it to the sentence to which it belongs. Write the new sentence in the blank.

Example: The restless class cheered. When the instructor arrived. Now the training
                could begin.

The restless class cheered when the instructor arrived.

1. Please forgive Sam. He isn't awake yet. Because his alarm wasn't set.

2. I enjoy work. That takes me outside. I work as a telephone repair person.

What Are Run-On Sentences?

Run-on sentences are two sentences written together, without the correct capitalization and punctuation between them.

A. Some of the sentences below are run-ons. Write *correct* in the space below if the sentence is not a run-on. If the sentence is a run-on, correct it by separating it into two sentences, changing capitalization and punctuation as necessary.

Example: A bulldozer is a big machine it can do the work of many people with shovels.

A bulldozer is a big machine. It can do the work of many people with shovels.

1. Some workers lost their jobs. They had to look for other jobs.

2. Many people work in service jobs some are waiters, waitresses, clerks, and food service providers.

3. Some jobs were lost when computers began to be used others were created.

4. People must sometimes retrain for new jobs sometimes they must return to school.

B. Correct the run-ons with a semicolon or a comma and a connecting word.

Example: I bought the produce yesterday it is already spoiled.

I bought the produce yesterday, but it is already spoiled.

1. We need to deal with change be flexible.

2. Change is a part of life everything changes over time.

3. Change can be fun we have the right attitude.

4. By accepting change, we make it our ally it can no longer threaten us.

EXERCISE 170

Correcting Run-On Sentences

Write a separate sentence for each complete thought. Begin each sentence with a capital letter, and end it with a period.

A. Correct any run-on sentence. If a sentence is correct, write *correct*.

Example: India is a large country its population is dense.

India is a large country. Its population is dense.

1. The monsoon season brings heavy rains and flooding.

2. Farms are small most farmers are very poor.

3. The people of India speak many indigenous languages most educated Indians also speak English.

B. Rewrite the paragraph. Correct any run-on sentences.

    Canada is a huge country it lies to the north of the United States. Canada has English-speaking people and French-speaking people. It also has many immigrants from Asia, Africa, and Europe. To many U.S. natives, Canada is a vacationland the country is also our most important trading partner.

More Practice With Run-On Sentences

It is best to write a separate sentence for each complete thought so you do not run your sentences together, but you can combine related ideas.

Rewrite the run-on sentences. Separate those that are two complete thoughts with a period. Combine those that have related thoughts with a comma and a connecting word.

Example: Our cooking class meets on Tuesdays we prepare a variety of foods.   (separate)

Our cooking class meets on Tuesdays. We prepare a variety
of foods.

1. Our first project was vegetable soup chopping all those vegetables was a lot of work.   (separate)

   _____

   _____

2. The next lesson was chili I cut back on the amount of hot peppers.   (combine)

   _____

   _____

3. Spaghetti can be made with tomato sauce you can substitute tomato paste and water.   (combine)

   _____

   _____

4. Soon we will learn to bake I just love the smell of fresh bread!   (separate)

   _____

   _____

5. There are never any leftovers the students in our class always eat up their projects.   (separate)

   _____

   _____

6. Someday I will be a chef people from all over will flock to my restaurant.   (combine)

   _____

   _____

Review of Run-On Sentences

A run-on sentence contains two or more sentences written together without the correct punctuation between them.

Correct each run-on. Punctuate with a semicolon or a comma and a connecting word, or separate the run-on into two sentences.

Example: Conflicts arise at work as well as at home we should try to reduce or avoid conflicts in both places.

Conflicts arise at work, as well as at home. We

should try to reduce or avoid conflicts in both places.

1. Conflicts at work can result in more than hurt feelings they may involve job loss as well. _____

   _____

2. Most conflicts can be worked out you won't always be able to solve every problem, but you can find ways to compromise. _____

   _____

3. Believe it or not, conflicts can be useful they can help build relationships.

   _____

   _____

4. Negative reactions can be discussed they can lead to better understanding.

   _____

   _____

5. Conflict gives you a reason to think about your behavior when you do, you may see some things you want to change. _____

   _____

6. Perhaps your communication skills could be improved you could use some training in that area. _____

   _____

7. You could attend a seminar or class one that deals with both communication and conflict would be a good choice. _____

   _____

Expanding Sentences

Your sentences can become more interesting and exact when they are expanded with details: descriptive words, verbals, and noun phrases.

Expand each sentence below by adding a descriptive word or phrase. Write your new sentence in the space provided.

Example: The fire alarm rang.

The fire alarm rang in the station house.

1. The firefighters prepared.

_____

2. The fire chief gave orders.

_____

3. The fire truck raced.

_____

4. The firefighters turned on hoses.

_____

5. The building smoked.

_____

6. A crowd gathered.

_____

7. One person was injured.

_____

8. An ambulance arrived.

_____

9. The firefighters looked exhausted.

_____

10. A firefighter climbed.

_____

11. Police patrolled the crowd.

_____

12. A newspaper reporter took pictures.

_____

EXERCISE 174

Making Sentences Clear and Concise

To write better sentences, do not overuse *and* or *so*. Avoid unnecessary words. Position descriptive words close to the words they describe.

A. In the sentences below, cross out any unnecessary *and* or *so*. Add the correct punctuation.

Example: In 1923 Charles Lindbergh bought his own plane. ~~and~~ H̶e borrowed $500 to

pay for it. ~~and~~ I̶t was the first time he flew alone.

1. As time passed, he became an experienced pilot so he wanted to be the first person to fly nonstop across the Atlantic Ocean and he planned the flight for months.

2. Lindbergh accomplished what he set out to do and he broke the world record for a nonstop airplane flight so many honored Lindbergh for his achievement.

B. Rewrite each sentence omitting any unnecessary words.

Example: Lindbergh was a brave and courageous flyer.
     Lindbergh was a brave flyer.

1. He did not have enough supplies and they were inadequate.

2. He made a successful nonstop flight without any stops.

C. Find the misplaced descriptive details. Write the sentences correctly.

Example: He was out of fuel when he nearly landed.
     He was nearly out of fuel when he landed.

1. People cheered and applauded on the ground.

2. When he landed, Lindbergh was very tired in France.

More Practice Making Sentences Clear and Concise

Make sentences clear and concise by using phrases that are similar in form (parallel), eliminating wordiness, and positioning details close to the word they describe.

Improve each sentence by making the underlined words parallel, eliminating wordiness, or moving misplaced details.

Example: I have many maps in my room <u>hanging on the wall</u>.

I have many maps hanging on the wall in my room.

1. I like looking at maps and <u>to draw them</u>.

   _____

   _____

2. My cousin has a map of Europe, <u>and it is a road map of that continent</u>.

   _____

   _____

3. <u>One day</u> she likes to plan the car trip that she hopes to take.

   _____

   _____

4. It's fun comparing old and recent maps of the same place and <u>to see the differences</u>.

   _____

   _____

5. I imagine <u>in my mind</u> traveling to all the places on the map.

   _____

   _____

6. <u>On the old maps</u> you can hardly recognize the shapes of the continents.

   _____

   _____

7. Mapmakers <u>from satellites</u> get highly accurate pictures of the earth.

   _____

   _____

8. Cartographers make our maps and <u>are the people who study them</u>.

   _____

   _____

EXERCISE 176

More Practice Improving Sentences

Write better and communicate more clearly by making your sentences clear, smooth, and concise.

Improve the sentences below by changing the underlined words, eliminating wordiness, or moving misplaced details.

Example: Comets can be <u>really extremely</u> spectacular sights.

Comets can be spectacular sights.

1. Most comets are faint, fuzzy, and <u>it is difficult to recognize them</u>.

2. Comets are <u>large, huge,</u> gigantic clouds of gas and dust.

3. The only solid part is the comet's nucleus—a lump of <u>cold</u> ice, <u>dusty</u> dirt, and stones.

4. The brightest comets can sprout enormous tails, <u>the length of which can be tens of millions of miles long</u>.

5. The ancient Chinese thought comets brought famine, sickness, and <u>could cause war</u>.

6. Comets <u>clearly</u> cannot be seen if it is cloudy.

7. Halley's Comet appears <u>and is seen</u> every 76 years.

8. My grandmother saw Halley's Comet when she was young <u>through a telescope</u>.

9. Halley's Comet will appear around the year 2061 <u>next</u>.

Review of Improving Sentences

Make your sentences clear and concise.

Rewrite the following sentences by correcting misplaced details, making words or phrases parallel, or eliminating wordiness.

Example: The poet Emily Dickinson was sensitive, intelligent, and a creative person.

The poet Emily Dickinson was sensitive, intelligent, and creative.

1. Emily Dickinson wrote poetry during her lifetime that was never published.

2. She lived in Amherst, which is a city in the state of Massachusetts.

3. She carefully observed nature and watched it closely.

4. In her poetry she described a snake, a bird, and how a storm looks.

5. She wrote poems about life and death on scraps of paper.

6. She had an original way of rhyming words, punctuating lines, and the use of capitalization.

7. Her poem is very imaginative about the month of March.

8. Admirers of Emily Dickinson enjoy reading the story of her life in biographies.

9. Her father was a successful lawyer and a member of Congress and treated her sternly.

EXERCISE 178

Varying Sentence Structure

Writing can be made interesting by varying the length and kind of sentences.

Guideline 1:   Combine sentences with similar meanings.

Example: Elizabeth Blackwell graduated from an American medical school. She graduated in 1847.

Elizabeth Blackwell graduated from an American medical school in 1847.

Guideline 2:   Combine two simple sentences with a connecting word.

Example: Elizabeth faced resentment. Today most people respect women doctors.

Elizabeth faced resentment, but today most people respect women doctors.

Guideline 3:   Vary sentence beginnings. Summarize the information from one sentence in a phrase, and put it at the start of another sentence.

Example: She founded the country's first school of nursing. This event happened after the Civil War.

After the Civil War, she founded the country's first school of nursing.

Guideline 4:   Change a statement into a question, command, or exclamation.

Example: Elizabeth Blackwell was a pioneer in the medical profession.

Why was Elizabeth Blackwell a pioneer in the medical profession?

Rewrite the sentence using the guideline in parentheses.

1. The medical profession is opening up.   (4) _____

_____

2. In the past, most doctors were men. Now women are in medical school.   (2)

_____

3. More young black people are studying to be doctors. More young Hispanics are too.   (1) _____

4. Many of these students will be dedicated doctors. This will happen in the future.   (3) _____

21   Identifying Main Ideas

A **paragraph** is a group of sentences about one idea. That idea is the main idea. A sentence that states the main idea is called the **topic sentence.**

Example: A job interview tests our ability to stand up under pressure. It requires us to be at our best in a new environment, among strangers. Not only that, it requires us to think clearly and speak intelligently while experiencing anxiety. *(This paragraph is about the pressures of a job interview. The underlined sentence is the topic sentence.)*

A topic sentence states the main idea of the paragraph. The rest of the paragraph expands on the main idea, adding other **supporting details.**

Example: Vacations are fun and relaxing.   *(topic sentence)*
Some sentences that might be added to support and expand this main idea include:
- We don't have to get up early if we don't want to.
- We can set our own schedule.
- We can see and do things that we don't normally get to see and do.

When you are writing paragraphs, it is important to limit the ideas to the topic sentence. Make sure that your supporting sentences help explain, or add to, your main topic. Do not include sentences or details about unrelated topics.

Examples: To the topic sentence, *Friday is my favorite day,* you might add supporting sentences and details that include the following:
- It is the final workday before the weekend.
- Everyone in the office is in a better mood on Fridays.

You would *not* add sentences such as these, which are not related:

I am going to visit my sister over vacation.
My boss asked me to work late today.

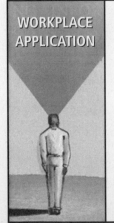

WORKPLACE APPLICATION

Write some supporting sentences and details that you might add to the following topic sentence: The length of the traditional workweek should be cut from 40 hours to 35 hours. Compare your sentences with those of others.

_____

_____

_____

_____

_____

EXERCISE 179

Main Idea in a Paragraph

A paragraph is a group of sentences about one idea. That idea is called the main idea.

A. Read each paragraph below. Circle the letter of the phrase that states the topic of the paragraph.

1. Last week we inspected an old building slowly falling down near Greenfield. The wood was rotting. The windows were broken, and the front door was missing. One man said the building "sank to its knees in slow motion."

   a. the job of the building inspector

   b. an old building slowly falling down

   c. a man fixing the holes in a roof

2. An exhibit of sculptures by Isamu Noguchi opened last night at the Tisbury Museum. Noguchi was there. The exhibit features his works in stone, metal, and wood.

   a. sculptures at a museum

   b. a very popular exhibit

   c. opening of an exhibit featuring the works of Isamu Noguchi

B. Write the main idea of each paragraph below.

1. A smoke alarm is an important safety device. To inform the public, a film about smoke alarms will be shown at Fisk Hall at eight o'clock tonight. The admission is $1.50. Captain Reed of the fire department will lead a discussion after the film. The proceeds will go to the Firehouse Fund.

   _____

   _____

2. Rosa was up to bat. She was nervous because she always struck out. There were already two outs. The bases were loaded. It was the bottom of the ninth, and the score was tied. The ball hitting the bat made a cracking sound in Rosa's ears. The ball sailed toward center field and over the bleachers. The score was 10 to 6. Rosa's company team had won!

   _____

   _____

Topic Sentences

A sentence that states the main idea of a paragraph is called a topic sentence.

The topic sentence has been omitted from each of the following paragraphs. Read the paragraphs and the topic sentences that follow them. Then underline the best topic sentence for each paragraph.

Statistics tell us that only about 30 percent of all phone calls are completed on the first try. Voice mail allows us to spend less time calling back and more time getting our message across. Many businesses use voice mail today to allow customers to place orders over the phone. Voice mail is also used as an "audio bulletin board." Supervisors can leave messages about meetings or give instructions to employees. However, not all voice mail is used for businesses. Voice mail has become popular in homes, too. Family members can keep in touch through individual messages. The ability to retrieve a message from a remote phone makes voice mail even more convenient.

1. Voice mail is a tool to help businesses grow.

2. Voice mail is a very efficient way to leave messages.

3. Voice mail will probably not be used in the future.

The best voice-mail messages are short messages. Remember, busy people may have dozens of messages to listen to. It is never a good idea to leave a complaining, negative message. Such comments are better suited for live conversations. Likewise, no confidential information should ever be left on voice mail. At times others, such as secretaries or family members, may listen to voice mail for a receiver. It is also considered rude to send a voice message from a very noisy place, such as a restaurant. Wait until you can find a quiet place to make your call. Finally, don't rely solely on voice mail. Messages do get lost. Leave important messages with a secretary or another person, as well as on voice mail.

1. Voice mail can sometimes get into the wrong hands.

2. Don't ever leave rude messages on voice mail.

3. There are standard rules of etiquette for using voice mail.

Identifying Topic Sentences and Supporting Details

A topic sentence states the main idea of a paragraph. Other sentences add details to support the topic.

A. Each item below has a topic sentence and two sentences that contain supporting details. Circle the letter of the topic sentence.

Example: **a.** Don't make excuses or try to shift the blame.

(b.) When you make a mistake, admit it.

c. Excuses will not help you; they will just make things worse.

1. a. A straightforward, sincere apology is best.

   b. A lengthy explanation with your apology is not necessary.

   c. It may sound more like an excuse than an apology.

2. a. Offering no excuses, your apology sounds more sincere and believable.

   b. If you are quick to acknowledge your mistake, others usually are quick to forgive.

   c. Most employers are usually willing to forgive an honest mistake, if it is admitted right away.

3. a. Ask, "What can I do to make this up to you?"

   b. Assure those involved that the mistake will not happen again.

   c. If possible, try to make amends.

B. Read the details listed below. Write a topic sentence for each set.

Example: colleague, superior, customer

If a colleague, superior, or customer offends you in some way, do not attack him or her in front of others.

1. poised, restraint, class

_____

_____

2. withhold criticisms, speak privately, change behavior

_____

_____

EXERCISE 182

Review of Topic Sentences and Supporting Details

A topic sentence is a statement of the main idea of a paragraph.

A. Read each group of sentences below. Then underline the topic sentence.

Example: People from other countries often vacation in the United States.

Europeans enjoy visiting Chicago as well as Boston.

South Americans often come to Los Angeles and Houston.

1. Many American swimmers have won world fame.

   Florence Chadwick was the first woman to swim the English Channel in both directions.

   Johnny Weismuller broke many world records.

   Mark Spitz won seven Olympic gold medals.

2. The Sears Tower is in Chicago, Illinois.

   New York has the World Trade Center.

   The United States has many famous skyscrapers.

3. The official language of Brazil is Portuguese.

   Brazil and Portugal had a close relationship.

   Brazil was a Portuguese colony until 1822.

4. Night owls may get only a few hours of sleep before their alarms ring.

   People who are night owls may go to bed way past midnight.

   Night owls stay up late.

B. Choose and write one of the topic sentences below. Then write four supporting details in sentence form.

Newspaper stories are often inaccurate. Working alone is better than working on a team. A company should offer health insurance. Even a bad job is often better than no job.

1. Topic sentence

   _____

2. Details

   a. _____

   b. _____

   c. _____

   d. _____

EXERCISE 183

Keeping Supporting Sentences on the Topic

When you write a paragraph, make sure your supporting sentences help explain your main idea. Do not include other topics in the same paragraph.

A. Read the paragraph below. Then rewrite it by starting with the topic sentence and omitting the unnecessary sentence.

> I attended my grandmother's eightieth birthday party. Children and adults at a young/old day care center are going to art classes, storytelling, cooking sessions, and games. Each child and adult has a special "buddy" that he or she spends time with. A new program is enriching the lives of senior and young citizens. This program promises to give young and old a lot of hugs and to provide them with lasting friendships.

_____

_____

_____

_____

_____

_____

_____

_____

_____

_____

B. Read each topic sentence below. Then write two detail sentences that keep to the main idea of the topic sentence.

1. Supervised training is a good idea for every new employee.

_____

_____

2. You should exercise three or four times a week.

_____

_____

More Practice in Keeping Supporting Sentences on the Topic

Each sentence in a paragraph should support the main idea expressed in the topic sentence.

Identify the main idea of the paragraph. Then write the paragraph, leaving out any sentence that does not relate to the main idea. Do not copy the numbers. The paragraph should have eight sentences.

(1) I remember the first time I saw the ocean at dawn. (2) I like to get up early in the morning. (3) Frothy breakers crashed on the deserted beach. (4) Driftwood bleached as white as bone littered the cool, damp sand. (5) My sister likes to collect driftwood for her garden. (6) The sea's distant surface shone like a mirror. (7) At first, the sun was only a tiny, red lump piercing the blue-black sky. (8) As it rose, it began to look like a molten lead coin. (9) It got very hot later in the day. (10) I'm glad I brought plenty of suntan lotion. (11) A breeze as faint as a sleeping baby's breath rustled the dune grass behind me. (12) The day had just begun.

_____

_____

_____

_____

_____

_____

_____

_____

_____

_____

_____

_____

_____

_____

_____

_____

LESSON

22   Writing to Tell a Story

When you write to tell a story, you must first be sure that your reader can understand what you are saying. Writing correct sentences helps you do that. Second, you must move your reader from idea to idea smoothly and logically. Third, you must be sure that your reader can follow the order of events within your story.

Transition words and **phrases** are used to show the order of events, as well as the relationships between ideas.

Example: In the following paragraph, note how the underlined transition words and phrases show both the sequence of events and the relationship between one idea and the next.

> I went to a job interview today. (1) <u>At first</u> I was so nervous, I did not think I could speak. I waited in the waiting area, and (2) <u>soon</u> the manager called me in. (3) <u>Instead</u> of making me nervous, she was very kind, and I began to relax a little. (4) <u>After a while,</u> I was speaking freely and confidently. (5) <u>Tomorrow</u> I start a new job. (6) <u>Finally,</u> I can fully relax.

Transition Words and Phrases

after	at first	now	finally	later
next	soon	then	far	inside
behind	beyond	outside	inside	just as
instead of	in addition	for instance		

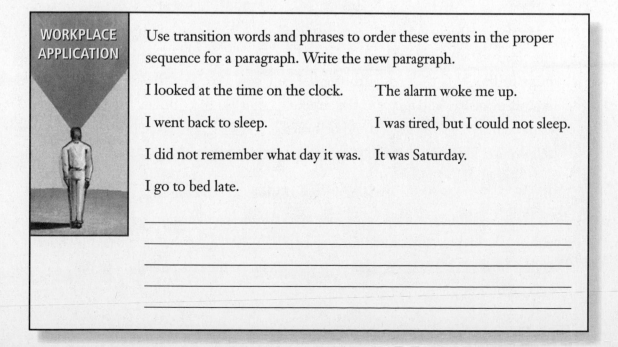

WORKPLACE APPLICATION

Use transition words and phrases to order these events in the proper sequence for a paragraph. Write the new paragraph.

I looked at the time on the clock.   The alarm woke me up.

I went back to sleep.   I was tired, but I could not sleep.

I did not remember what day it was.   It was Saturday.

I go to bed late.

_____

_____

_____

_____

_____

Transitions in Paragraphs

Transitions are words and phrases that help sentences flow in a paragraph. They make the move from idea to idea, and from sentence to sentence.

A. Underline all the transition words and phrases in the paragraph below.

> I have never realized how busy this city really is. After I left the apartment building today, I noticed many different activities. For example, meter readers were busy checking gas and electric meters. Just as I was about to board the bus, an ambulance sped down the street. Above me, a window washer cleaned the windows of an office building. Then I noticed a pair of joggers on their way to the park.

B. Fill in the blanks in the following paragraphs with one of the transition words or phrases above each paragraph.

1. In addition   For instance   Just as

    Every GED student should have a method. _____, a student should have a quiet study area. _____ to being quiet, the area should be well lighted and properly equipped. _____ a carpenter needs the proper tools to do the job, so should a student have the proper tools for studying—paper, pens, pencils, and a dictionary.

2. Outside   Behind   Inside   Beyond   Far

    Hank sat quietly in an old rocking chair. _____ him, the heat from the fireplace warmed his back. _____, the wind blew the snow into huge drifts, _____ the yard. Hank could see that the snow was blocking his driveway and much of the street. _____ down the road, the faint sound of a snowplow could be heard. _____ the house, Hank felt secure, knowing that the plow was on its way to clear the street.

3. Before   Finally   Then   While   Behind

    _____ Allison went to school she ate breakfast. _____ riding on the bus she studied for a test. _____ she gave back the book to the boy _____ her. _____ the bus pulled up to the school building.

What Is a Narrative Paragraph?

A narrative paragraph relates an event or series of events that happened over time. When you write a narrative paragraph, state the events in the order in which they happened.

A. Read the sentences below first. Number the lines on the left to show the order in which the sentences would appear in paragraph form.

_____ **1.** Through a friend, Janet learned about a job opening at Big K Dude Ranch in Wyoming.

_____ **2.** Janet, who loved horses, wanted to work at a dude ranch but did not know where to look for a job.

_____ **3.** Then two weeks later, Janet made a follow-up call to Big K Dude Ranch, but the ranch manager was not in.

_____ **4.** Nervous and excited, Janet arrived at Big K for her interview.

_____ **5.** After a successful interview, Janet was hired as a ranch hand.

_____ **6.** Later that day, the ranch manager called Janet back and arranged to interview her the following week.

_____ **7.** Janet first mailed her résumé to Big K, mentioning her friend as a reference.

_____ **8.** Janet left a polite voice-mail message for the ranch manager, including times when she could be reached by phone.

B. Write a narrative paragraph about being a ranch hand. Use clue words to help you tell the events in sequence.

wake up before sunrise   put bridles and saddles on horses

evenings play guitar and sing   a big breakfast
   around the fire   late afternoon come back tired and

take tourists on riding tours   sore, but happy

_____

_____

_____

_____

_____

_____

Using Transition Words

In narrative writing, use transition words to make the sequence of events clear and easy to follow.

A. Read the following paragraph. Write the transition word or phrase from each numbered sentence in the space provided.

   Melissa, a salesperson, wanted to change jobs. **(1)** First, Melissa thought about the other kinds of jobs she might like to do. **(2)** Then she wrote out a list, starting with her top choices. **(3)** Next Melissa listed her skills, starting with her best skills. **(4)** After that Melissa matched her skills with her desired jobs. **(5)** Melissa soon found that she both liked, and had the job skills to be, a trainer. **(6)** Now Melissa could begin to work toward changing her career.

1. _____   3. _____   5. _____

2. _____   4. _____   6. _____

B. Read the paragraph below. Complete each sentence by writing an appropriate transition word in the space provided.

   (1) _____ Melissa went to the library to get books about careers in the training field. **(2)** _____ Melissa read all she could about becoming a trainer. **(3)** _____ Melissa talked to friends and coworkers about the training sessions they attended. **(4)** _____ Melissa felt she had all the information she needed to get started.

C. Write a narrative paragraph about how you could change jobs or seek a promotion. Use transition words.

_____

_____

_____

_____

_____

_____

_____

_____

_____

EXERCISE 188

Writing a Narrative Paragraph

When you write narrative paragraphs, use clue words and phrases to help sequence events.

A. Fill in each blank with a clue word or phrase that helps make the sequence clearer.

_____ I decided to quit smoking. _____
I threw out all my cigarettes and matches. _____ I
went to the store for vegetables and gum to have on hand.
_____ I went to the park _____ jogged a
bit to get my mind off smoking. _____ I was beginning to feel a little tense. _____ that day I almost
bought a pack. But so far I still haven't smoked a cigarette.

Clue Words
and
today
yesterday
first
next
last
now
then
at first
before
after a while
soon
later
finally
last night

B. Write a narrative paragraph that tells about one event. Choose a
topic of your own or one from the suggestions below. Sequence
the details from first to last by using clue words and phrases from
the box. Then edit your paragraph for correct grammar and punctuation.

An Embarrassing Moment on My Job That I Would Like to Forget

A Time I Was in Charge of Something at Work

The Best Day at My Job

An Employee Achievement I Am Proud Of

_____

_____

_____

_____

_____

_____

_____

_____

_____

_____

_____

_____

More Practice Writing Narrative Paragraphs

Write a narrative paragraph when you want to tell a story about events that have happened over a period of time.

A. In the narrative paragraph below, fill in each blank with a transition word or phrase that makes the sequence of events clear. Choose words from the list below.

> At the beginning of the year, Elena was hurt very badly in an automobile accident. _____ her life was very difficult. _____ she remembers very little of that time. When Elena was finally released from the hospital, she continued to spend most of her time sleeping. _____ she was able to do some reading or drawing. _____ came the big event, when Elena was allowed to get out of bed for a short time each day. _____ , Elena began seeing a physical therapist who worked out a complete program of exercise for her. It took much hard work and almost the entire year, but Elena was _____ able to return to work.

Transition Words and Phrases
- - - - - - - - - - -
after
at first
eventually
finally
later
meanwhile
next
now
soon
then

B. Rearrange the sentences below in time order by renumbering them. Begin with the sentence that states the main idea. Use the transition words and other clues to help you. Finally, write the sentences as a narrative paragraph.

1. _____ On Thursday, she would jog one mile.

2. _____ After that, she would ride her bike.

3. _____ Elena devised a summer exercise program for herself.

4. _____ Finally, on the weekend, she would lift weights.

5. _____ First, on Mondays, she would swim in the park pool.

6. _____ Late Friday afternoon she played tennis.

7. _____ On Wednesday evening Elena's bowling team meets.

23   Describing People, Places, and Things

Paragraphs are made up of sentences that all deal with one main topic or idea. Sentences in a paragraph should explain their ideas completely, yet concisely. They should also use **details** that are *vivid* and that allow the reader to "see" the events of the story in his or her mind. *Specific, vivid details* using all the reader's five senses can "paint a picture with words." Details about feelings can help the reader to "be there" in the story. Details about **spatial order** *show location or position.* Both help the reader to "see" an event.

Example: The following paragraph can be rewritten in more detail to create a vivid story that appeals to the senses.

The new cafeteria was about to open. People waited outside. They could smell food cooking. They could see new equipment and furnishings. They were eager to enter.

Change to: The **(1)** *long-awaited* opening of the new cafeteria was finally at hand. People waited **(3)** *outside* crowded into the **(2)** *corner* of the lobby. **(3)** *Directly ahead,* the doors were still closed. But smells of **(1)** *pungent* barbecued spareribs and **(1)** *yeasty* baked breads filled the air. Glimpses of **(1)** *shiny chrome* silverware on **(1)** *bright green and red plaid* tablecloths could be seen. People began to move **(3)** *forward,* and someone pushed a barrier cone to **(2)** *the right* of the entrance. The crowd could wait no longer to go inside.

Added words create **(1)** vivid sensory details, **(2)** a sense of specific spatial position, and **(3)** a sense of spatial relationship.

Another way to use description is to *compare* and *contrast* people, places, or things. **Comparison** shows the ways in which things are the *same.* **Contrast** shows how things are *different.* A compare/contrast example chart follows that can help you identify details to write about.

Comparing Part-Time and Full-Time Jobs

Comparisons	Contrasts
1. Both provide income.	1. Part-time usually provides less income than full-time.
2. Both usually require time away from home.	2. Usually, part-time requires less time away from home.
3. Both leave less time for self and family.	3. Part-time usually leaves more time for self and family.
4. Both provide training and job skill development.	4. Full-time may allow for more training and job skill development.

Comparisons and contrasts can be used to add details to sentences and paragraphs.

Example: A full-time job may provide you with more income than a part-time job. However, a full-time job may require you to give up more. You may have less time for your family and for yourself, as well.

Facts and **examples** are used to show "how-to." They are also used to tell about things and ideas. Transition words and phrases connect facts and ideas.

Examples: In this paragraph, items numbered **(1)** show facts or ideas, items numbered **(2)** are examples that support the facts or ideas, and items numbered **(3)** are connecting words.

To get the right job for you, **(3)** *first* **(1)** you can think about what it is that you like to do. **(3)** *For instance,* **(2)** you may decide that you like to work with people. **(3)** *Next* **(1)** you can think about the kinds of things you do well. The **(3)** *final* step **(1)** would be to determine how much money you need. **(2)** You may need more or less money than others.

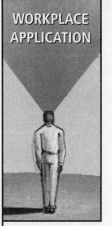

WORKPLACE APPLICATION

Compare and contrast your job status with its opposite. If you are employed, what are the advantages and disadvantages? What are the advantages and disadvantages of being unemployed?

_____

_____

_____

_____

_____

_____

EXERCISE 190

Writing a Descriptive Paragraph

A descriptive paragraph creates a vivid image of a person, place, or thing. Specific details are important in descriptive paragraphs.

A. List five details that describe your favorite possession. If possible, include some details that are not visual. For example, you might use the sense of touch to describe the coarseness or the smoothness of the object.

1. _____

2. _____

3. _____

4. _____

5. _____

B. List ten details about one of the subjects below. Some details should show your feelings about the subject, and others should show the physical appearance of the person, place, or thing.

your first job	an interesting person you met through work
your favorite person at work	your favorite lunch
the most special surprise you've ever had	your favorite vacation spot
the best job you've ever had	a good boss
an unusual thing you've done at work	the best way to enjoy your job

1. _____

2. _____

3. _____

4. _____

5. _____

6. _____

7. _____

8. _____

9. _____

10. _____

EXERCISE 191

More Practice Writing Descriptive Paragraphs

A descriptive paragraph paints a picture in words.

A. Choose one of the subjects below. List five details to describe it. Each detail should appeal to one of the five senses.

your workplace   your favorite restaurant

a pond   a job interview

an outdoor barbeque   a factory

1. _____

2. _____

3. _____

4. _____

5. _____

B. Write a short descriptive paragraph about the subject you chose in Exercise A. Begin your paragraph with a topic sentence that identifies what you are describing. Use at least four of the details you listed in Exercise A.

_____

_____

_____

_____

_____

_____

_____

_____

_____

_____

_____

_____

_____

_____

_____

EXERCISE 192

Review of Writing Descriptive Paragraphs

A descriptive paragraph creates a vivid image of a person, place, or thing.

A. Read the descriptive paragraph below. List five details in the paragraph that help you visualize the scene.

    The woof, woof, arf, arf of barking dogs filled the air. This sound was accented occasionally by the squawk of a bird. The air smelled strongly of pet urine and old sawdust. Kennel worker Chen Woo stepped softly into the room. "Quiet down guys," he whispered. "Shh. . . ." Chen calmly moved from cage to cage, gently speaking to each animal in patient, hushed tones. Soon the din of animal sounds dropped to a slightly lower level. Chen touched the soft, fluffy fur of a Siamese cat and got an appreciative purr in return. He drew several pails of fresh, cool water and poured them into the nearly empty containers of four large dogs. One bulky, brown and black German Shepherd mix licked Chen's hand before slurping up the fresh water. Chen moved to another cage and began cleaning out the night's mess. A half-dozen white mice scurried into the opposite corner as Chen cleared away the debris. Chen then brought in fresh sawdust and sprinkled it over the bottom of the cage. His day as a kennel worker was getting off to a typical start.

1. _____

2. _____

3. _____

4. _____

5. _____

B. Write a descriptive paragraph about a coworker or a place where you have worked. Use specific details and precise, descriptive words.

_____

_____

_____

_____

_____

_____

_____

Using Spatial Order to Arrange Supporting Details

You can use words or phrases that describe spatial order to help readers visualize details about position and movement.

A. Read the following paragraph and write answers to the questions following it.

A sign to the left of the door reads: "Danger. Moving Machinery. Authorized Personnel Only." Peeking through the doorway, one can see several large, dark green metal presses heavily soiled with a black, oily film. Men in light blue shirts with a company logo stand ready to press buttons to load and unload the next sheet of metal to be stamped. Walking through the door, one can see the largest of the machines directly ahead. A giant monster, it towers overhead, almost reaching the ceiling. A conveyor belt brings a piece of metal toward the mouth of the waiting monster. To the right, a ten-foot-tall rack awaits the finished product, a side panel for someone's new automobile.

1. What words or phrases indicating spacial order are used in this paragraph?

   _____

2. What words of spatial details—left to right, near to far, or top to bottom—are used? _____

   _____

3. What word in the sentence describing the conveyor belt is used to indicate that the conveyor belt is moving forward, not backward?

   _____

B. Write a paragraph about what you see when you look around your work area. Describe objects and people as you see them and use some spatial-order words that you have learned.

   _____

   _____

   _____

   _____

   _____

   _____

   _____

   _____

Practice Arranging Details in Spatial Order

You can use spatial order to help organize supporting details clearly.

A. Read the paragraph below. Then underline the words or phrases used to indicate spatial order.

> In downtown Chicago, the buildings are close together, and it is easy to get from one to another quickly. On your lunch hour you can walk outside and enter a world of choices for places to go and things to do. You can run across the street and catch a quick cup of coffee and a sandwich. Then you might go to the corner, turn right, and be at your favorite department store. Here you can pick up a pair of earrings or perhaps a new tie. You might want to drop your clothes off at the cleaner's next door. In front of you, you might see a street vendor with some lovely jewelry to sell. Behind you might be a street musician offering soothing sounds for busy shoppers. All too soon, your lunch break will be over. You'll walk back down the street to your office building, pleased with all you've done in just an hour.

B. Write a letter to a friend describing a new skill you have acquired. Arrange the details in spatial order—for example, left to right, top to bottom, or near to far. Use words or phrases that indicate spatial relationships.

EXERCISE 195

Writing a Descriptive Paragraph Using Spatial Order

Use sensory details, descriptive words, and spatial order to write clear, vivid descriptive paragraphs.

Write a paragraph using spatial order to describe a place. You may wish to describe your favorite spot to relax or the place where you work. If you have trouble visualizing a subject, use a photo of a scene instead.

1. Name the place you plan to describe. _____
   _____

2. What type of spatial order will your description follow—top to bottom, near to far, or left to right? _____
   _____

3. List some vivid, sensory details you will use. _____
   _____
   _____

4. Write your topic sentence. It should tell what place you are describing.
   _____
   _____

Now write your paragraph on the lines below.

_____
_____
_____
_____
_____
_____
_____
_____
_____
_____
_____
_____

EXERCISE 196

Comparing and Contrasting

To compare means to identify likenesses among things. To contrast means to identify differences.

A. Choose two people to compare and contrast. The chart below will help you categorize the points to compare and contrast. Fill out the chart by adding descriptive details under each heading. Try to choose two persons who are different in physical appearance and interests.

Person's Name	Physical Appearance	Interests
_____	_____	_____
	_____	_____
	_____	_____
	_____	_____
_____	_____	_____
	_____	_____
	_____	_____
	_____	_____

B. For each pair of words below, write one descriptive sentence that compares the words and one sentence that contrasts them. Use words and phrases, such as *both*, *however*, or *on the contrary*, that signal comparisons and contrasts.

1. computer, typewriter _____

_____

_____

_____

2. bus, car _____

_____

_____

_____

3. boss, employee _____

_____

_____

_____

Writing a Comparison/Contrast Description

A paragraph of comparison and contrast explains how two things are alike and how they are different.

A. Each phrase below describes either an automobile or a motorcycle. Write the word *automobile* or *motorcycle* after each phrase to indicate which it describes. Write *both* if the description fits both vehicles.

1. comfortable in bad weather _____

2. fits in narrow places _____

3. lets you see passing scenery _____

4. uses small amount of fuel _____

5. can have mechanical problems _____

6. has trunk for large items _____

7. holds several passengers _____

8. provides transportation _____

9. moves fast _____

B. Choose one of the following pairs—or a pair of your own—to compare and contrast. List as many similarities and/or differences between the two as you can.

men and women   working at home and working from a business location

spring and fall   first day on the job and last day on the job

_____

_____

_____

_____

_____

_____

_____

_____

_____

_____

More Practice Comparing and Contrasting

Use comparison and contrast to show how people, places, or things are alike or different.

Pair up the facts under the chart to show comparisons and contrasts. Write them in the chart where they belong. One contrast has been done for you.

	Typewriter	Computer
Comparisons	1. _____ 2. _____ 3. _____ 4. _____	1. _____ 2. _____ 3. _____ 4. _____
Contrasts	1. Used in business since the late 1800s 2. _____ 3. _____ 4. _____ 5. _____	1. Used in business since the mid-1900s 2. _____ 3. _____ 4. _____ 5. _____

Facts About the Typewriter

1. Has been used since the late 1800s
2. Has letter and number keys
3. Uses only ribbons for printing
4. Prints paper right in machine
5. Can print only one type style
6. Has space bar and return bar
7. Uses no silicon chips
8. Can create letters and other documents

Facts About the Computer

1. Has been used since the mid-1900s
2. Can create letters and other documents
3. Uses silicon chips to store information
4. May use dry ink cartridges
5. Has letter and number keys, among others
6. Printed pages go through separate machine (printer)
7. Has space bar and return bar
8. Can print any number of different typefaces (fonts)

Review of Comparing and Contrasting

To compare means to identify similarities among things. To contrast means to identify differences.

A. Read the information. Then fill in all the blank boxes in the chart.

flute: a small, slender, pipelike musical instrument of high pitch belonging to the woodwind family, played by blowing across a hole near one end

tuba: a large wind instrument of the brass family, of low pitch, played by blowing into a mouthpiece

Name of Instrument	Type of Instrument	Tone	How It Is Played	Size
flute	woodwind			
		low pitch	by blowing into a mouthpiece	

B. For each pair of items below, write one sentence that compares them and one sentence that contrasts them.

Example: automobile, bicycle

Both automobiles and bicycles have wheels and brakes. However, automobiles have four wheels and bicycles have only two.

1. book, magazine _____

_____

_____

2. table, desk _____

_____

_____

3. memo, letter _____

_____

_____

4. nail, screw _____

_____

_____

EXERCISE 200

Using Comparing and Contrasting to Write Explanatory Paragraphs

Explanatory paragraphs of comparison and contrast tell how things are alike and how they are different.

Write a comparison paragraph or a contrast paragraph using information from the chart about migration. Use comparison or contrast clue words to make your writing clear. Make sure that your paragraph has a topic sentence.

	Monarch Butterflies	Birds
Comparison	• Migrate south for winter • Travel up to 2000 miles • Make their winter homes in trees • Return north in spring	• Fly south for winter • Some fly thousands of miles • Nest in trees • Migrate north in spring
Contrast	• Begin winter migration during summer • Individual monarchs migrate separately • Thousands hang from branches of pines • Remain inactive most of winter • Feed only on milkweed	• Migrate in fall for winter • Migrate in flocks • Nest separately in trees • Are active through winter months • Eat insects, grubs, or fruit

_____

_____

_____

_____

_____

_____

_____

_____

_____

Writing Other Types of Explanatory Paragraphs

An explanatory paragraph uses facts to explain something.

A. Read the following explanatory paragraph. Then list four transition words and phrases used in the paragraph.

Giving directions to get to a certain place sounds very simple, but it is one of the most difficult things in the world to do well. If you follow these steps, you should be able to help someone get to wherever he or she wants to go. First, think through the entire route before you start giving directions. Then, find out how familiar the person is with the area. If the person knows the area well, you could include a few details that a stranger wouldn't know. On the whole, you should tell the person only the essential details of the directions. Finally, include only landmarks that are easy to see. Who knows? The next time you're in a strange place, you may meet someone who's as good at giving directions as you are!

1. _____   3. _____

2. _____   4. _____

B. Complete the following activities as you would if you were preparing to write an explanatory paragraph.

1. Choose one of these suggested topics: how to shop for a car, how to prepare for an interview, how to make a successful speech, what a VCR is, why computers are popular, or use a topic of your own.

   Topic: _____

2. Write a topic sentence for your paragraph.

   _____

3. List the details you will include in your explanation.

   _____

   _____

   _____

   _____

4. List transition words and phrases that you could use.

   _____

5. Write your paragraph on a separate sheet of paper.

EXERCISE 202

Keeping on the Topic When Writing Explanatory Paragraphs

One kind of explanatory paragraph develops a topic by giving examples. This kind of explanatory paragraph should begin with the topic sentence. All examples that follow should relate to the main topic and be arranged in proper sequence.

A. Number the following sentences in the order they would appear in an explanatory paragraph. The topic sentence should be first. Cross out any sentence that does not keep to the main idea.

_____ 1. The boss may say that she (he) welcomes your input, yet become annoyed when you give it.

_____ 2. A boss often has many ideas of his (her) own.

_____ 3. She (he) may be threatened by your good idea.

_____ 4. The boss may feel you're trying to take over his (her) job.

_____ 5. Making a suggestion or presenting a new idea to a boss can be tricky.

_____ 6. Be careful with surprises! They may not be a good idea.

B. Now write an explanatory paragraph of your own. Write your topic sentence first. Make sure your supporting sentences relate to the main idea. Plan your paragraph on another sheet of paper, and write your final draft here.

24   Writing to Influence Others

Persuasive paragraphs are written to *convince* someone of something. Persuasive paragraphs start with an *opinion*. Then the opinion is backed up and supported by additional details.

These **supporting details** should be strong enough to convince. They should be relevant to the opinion and not off the topic. You should use only those facts, opinions, and supporting details that relate directly to your topic.

Example:

Opinion:	It is a good idea to take your lunch to work.
Relevant facts, examples:	It can be less expensive.
	You can make sure you get foods you like.
	It can be easier to monitor nutrition.
Off the topic or weak examples:	Yesterday you ate at your mom's. (off topic)
	Maria brings her lunch. (weak reason)

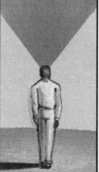

WORKPLACE APPLICATION

Joe wrote the following report to share his opinion about why he should be team leader.

I think I would make a good team leader because I really like people. I am easy to get along with. Everyone tells me I am a good friend. I am organized, hard-working, and disciplined. I believe I have influence over others. If not, I can usually get my way by arguing the best. I really want to be team leader. My wife would like it, too.

Do you agree or disagree with Joe's opinion that he would make a good team leader? Why or why not? Which facts and examples shaped your opinion?

_____

_____

_____

_____

_____

EXERCISE 203

Writing a Persuasive Paragraph

A persuasive paragraph tries to convince the reader that an opinion is sound by giving strong reasons to support that opinion.

A. Read the topics listed below and choose five about which you have an opinion. Write a topic sentence that expresses your opinion for each.

Watching television	Raising the minimum wage
Taking a year off	Completing high school
Discount bus fares	Day care for employees' children
Destroying the wilderness	Exploring outer space
Filling out a time sheet	Using a computer

Example: Discount bus fares help people who are on fixed incomes.

1. _____

2. _____

3. _____

4. _____

5. _____

B. Choose three topic sentences from those you wrote above. List three reasons that support your opinion in order from least convincing to most convincing.

1. _____

   a. _____

   b. _____

   c. _____

2. _____

   a. _____

   b. _____

   c. _____

3. _____

   a. _____

   b. _____

   c. _____

EXERCISE 204

Practice Writing a Persuasive Paragraph

In a persuasive paragraph, the writer tries to convince the reader that an opinion is valid by giving strong reasons to support it.

A. Choose five topics from the list below. For each, write a sentence that states an opinion, explains a problem to be considered, or urges some action concerning the topic.

women's sports	television advertising	charities	computers	jogging
workplace equipment	workplace relationships	inflation	voting	dieting

1. Topic: _____   Sentence: _____
   _____

2. Topic: _____   Sentence: _____
   _____

3. Topic: _____   Sentence: _____
   _____

4. Topic: _____   Sentence: _____
   _____

5. Topic: _____   Sentence: _____
   _____

B. Choose one of the topic sentences you wrote above. Then develop a list of supporting details relevant to your opinion.

Topic sentence from above: _____
_____

Supporting details: _____
_____
_____
_____
_____
_____
_____
_____
_____

Using Relevant Information in Persuasive Paragraphs

Use relevant information to support your position. All facts should refer to the main topic and be important to the topic.

A. Read the paragraph. Circle the sentence that states the position. Cross out any statements that are irrelevant to the position. Then copy what is left on the lines below.

> A good mentoring relationship should involve a seasoned employee taking a new or younger employee under his or her wing. Mentors should usually be older employees with experience. They should like to help young people who show potential. A mentor should help an employee learn the "ropes" of a job— the values, established procedures, etc. A mentor should also give advice about paths to success and warn of pitfalls. A good mentor will often "go to bat" for his or her employee and help secure raises or promotions. I had a mentor once myself.

_____

_____

_____

_____

_____

_____

_____

B. Read the position sentence that follows. Then write two or more sentences that support the position with relevant facts.

> People being mentored need to do their part to learn about the realities of their business or trade.

_____

_____

_____

_____

_____

_____

_____

✓ Final Checkup

Choose the correct form for the noun, pronoun, or proper noun in parentheses. Write your answer in the space provided.

1. (Mr. Smith, mr. smith) is my manager.   _____

2. Mr. Smith is my (managers, manager).   _____

3. (He, Him) has an office down the hall.   _____

4. Tomorrow we will travel to (dayton, Dayton).   _____

Choose the correct word to complete the sentences below. Write your answer in the space provided.

5. (Your, You're) going to have a problem with that.   _____

6. The (mentor's, mentors) help was appreciated.   _____

7. (It's, Its) getting late.   _____

8. (They're, Their) going to meet us after work.   _____

Choose the correct verb or verb phrase in parentheses. Write your answer in the space provided.

9. (Shall, Will) you help me?   _____

10. I (feel, feels) a headache coming on.   _____

11. It (was, were) gone for a while, but now it's back.   _____

12. Let's both (look, looks) for my lost aspirin bottle.   _____

Choose the correct form of the following verbs or verb phrases. Write your answer in the space provided.

13. The supervisor (has gave, has given) us the day off.   _____

14 He (told, tells) us to go home.   _____

15. I will need to (teach, learn) new job skills to   _____

become an apprentice.

16. The manager (let, leave) me take a class in welding.   _____

Identify the following sentences as a statement **(S)**, command **(C)**, question **(Q)**, or exclamation **(E)**. Write your answer in the space provided.

17. Are you leaving? _____

18. Yes, I am. _____

19. Then tell me why. _____

20. No, I can't! _____

Complete the following sentences by adding appropriate connecting words. Write your answer in the space provided.

21. I could use a word processor _____ a computer   _____

for this task.

22. Marie wants to stay, _____ I don't.   _____

23. _____ I leave now, she'll have to find a ride home.   _____

24. I guess I'll stay _____ wait for Marie.   _____

Identify the objects of the underlined verbs or connecting words in the following sentences and write your answer in the space provided.

25. Tony <u>read</u> his report. _____

26. He <u>identified</u> several problem areas. _____

27. The manager <u>asked</u> Tony a question. _____

28. Tony wrote <u>in</u> his notebook. _____

In the following sentences, underline the complete subject once and the complete verb twice.

29. Employee complaints are taken seriously.

30. More women work here than men.

31. Female employees make up 60 percent of our workforce.

32. Some women receive less pay than men do for the same work.

Choose the correct subject, object, or possessive form for the pronouns in the sentences below. Write your answer in the space provided.

33. Let (we, us) help you with that. _____

34. Sarah asked (him, he) to perform the task. _____

35. They locked (theirselves, themselves) out of   _____

the office.

36. Rhonda and (me, I) found the key. _____

Match the correct subject with the correct verb in the following sentences. Write your answers in the space provided.

37. Justin, Luis, and he (are, is) in the meeting. _____

38. The work (was, were) extremely difficult. _____

39. (Success, Successes) did not always come easily. _____

40. Several (experience, experiences) paid off in the end. _____

Choose the correct form of the indefinite pronoun to complete each sentence below. Write your answer in the space provided.

41. (All, Each) of them is a customer of ours. _____

42. Are (no one, none) our competitor's customers? _____

43. (Few, No one) shop there any more. _____

44. (Either, Neither) they do or they don't; we'll soon _____
    find out.

Choose the correct pronoun to complete each sentence below. Write your answer in the space provided.

45. Workshops on different topics are offered: (they, it) _____
    start at 3 P.M.

46. (These, That) seats are open. _____

47. Can you move (this, these) chair? _____

48. (These, This) was a good experience. _____

Choose the proper adjectives or adverb in parentheses. Write your answer in the space provided.

49. The (delayed, delaying) response finally came. _____

50. Wait (patient, patiently) and you will get an answer. _____

51. I (really, real) hope you are right. _____

52. The showroom looks (good, well). _____

Choose the correct article for the sentences below. Write your answer in the space provided.

53. (A, An) arrangement was made to save the merger. _____

54. Place (the, a) folders on the desk. _____

55. I think she is (a, an) honest person. _____

56. This day was (a, an) especially difficult one. _____

Choose the correct word to show comparison in the sentences below. Write your answer in the space provided.

57. The meeting was (longer, longest) than I thought. _____

58. The supervisor was (friendlier, friendliest) than _____
usual.

59. Please wait on (this, these) customer. _____

60. I felt (bad, badly), but I came to work anyway. _____

Circle the letters that should be capitalized.

61. I work at a store called bob's bicycles.

62. My coworker likes swiss cheese.

63. r. j. reynolds is the name of our supervisor.

64. I've never been to the caribbean ocean.

65. My favorite book was *charlotte's web*.

66. My favorite movie is *star wars*.

67. Do you subscribe to *entrepreneur* magazine?

68. I'm going to join mothers against drunk drivers.

Add commas to the following sentences to punctuate them correctly.

69. Fred please answer me.

70. Sorry Joan did you say something?

71. Yes but I guess you weren't listening.

72. Actually I was listening thinking and typing at the same time.

Add the correct punctuation to the end of each of the following sentences.

73. Wait, come back

74. Show this display to the manager

75. Is there another way to do this

76. I doubt it

Add dashes or quotation marks to each of the following sentences to punctuate them correctly.

77. Melanie was waiting at least I thought she was.

78. Come on, said Sharon, let's leave her.

79. I'm right here, Melanie called out.

80. This report the sales summary must be completed before you leave.

Add semicolons and colons to the following sentences to punctuate them correctly.

81. Here are the supplies you ordered stamps, pens, pencils, paper, and a typewriter ribbon.

82. Please pay the bill use my company credit card.

83. The meeting starts at 2 00.

84. The bus was late so I was late for work.

Choose the correct prefix or suffix to add to the words in parentheses. Choose from *I-*, *re-*, *in-*, *im-*, *un-*, *-ful*, *-er,* or *-ment*. Write the new word in the space provided.

85. I want an _____conditional commitment.   _____

86. Her dress was color_____.   _____

87. Please _____write this now.   _____

88. Sam is not a team play_____.   _____

Write these sentences in inverted order. Use the space provided to write your answers.

89. You can see the end at last. _____

_____

90. He waved goodbye, smiling at me. _____

_____

91. I tripped, not paying attention to where I was going. _____

_____

92. He saw the mail carrier, looking out the window. _____

_____

Choose the most effective sensory or spatial details to complete the following sentences. Write your answer in the space provided.

93. The day was (bright and sunny) (light).   _____

94. Place the box (there) (in the corner).   _____

95. The surface of the road was (slippery and icy) (wet). _____

96. Set the book (here) (on the edge of your desk).   _____

For answers **97** to **106,** refer to the paragraph below.

(1) Home computers have revolutionized the way we work and play at home. (2) Like the radio and television before it, the home computer is becoming a mainstay in American homes. (3) With computers, families can create, store, manipulate, and transmit information. (4) They can access information on any conceivable topic from medical information, to hobbies, to products and services. (5) As more families purchase computers. (6) The market is continuing to grow. (7) This means that software manufacturers are constantly creating new computer programs, and programs such as educational games and interactive computer "books" are increasingly available. (8) Once feared as a possible threat to the book industry, computer books now add a new dimension to reading and give readers a sense of being a part of the story, instead of being outside it. (9) Computer games have changed the way we play as well. (10) Role-playing games and interactive games transmitted over modems now allow two or more players to play against one another, even when they are separated by long distances. (11) But it's not all fun and games. (12) Computers teach new skills and helps develop others. (13) Even in games, word processing, spreadsheets, and data management skills all may come into play. (14) Educational games teach more traditional skills, such as math and reading, in fun ways. (15) Helpful new programs also teach adults and give them easier and faster ways to accomplish tasks. (16) Many people now use computer programs to help them compute their taxes. (17) The programs check the returns for mistakes and even mail the returns to the IRS. (18) The availability and use of computers in homes will continue to grow, as more people realize their value and take advantage of this developing technology.

97. Sentence 2.   <u>Like the radio and television before it</u>, the home computer is becoming a mainstay in American homes. Which of the following is the best way to write the underlined portion of the sentence?

  a. Like the radio and television before it, the home computer is becoming a mainstay in American homes.

  b. Like the radio and television before them, the home computer is becoming a mainstay in American homes.

  c. Like the radio and television before those, the home computer is becoming a mainstay in American homes.

  d. Like the radio and television before us, the home computer is becoming a mainstay in American homes.   _____

98. Sentence 2.   Like the radio and television before it, the home computer <u>is becoming</u> a mainstay in American homes. Which of the following is the best way to write the underlined portion of the sentence?

  a. is becoming   **c.** having become

  b. are becoming   **d.** have becoming   _____

99. Sentences 3 and 4.   With computers, families can create, store, manipulate, and transmit information. They can access information on any conceivable topic from medical information, to hobbies, to products and services. Which of the following is the most effective combination of sentences 3 and 4?

  a. . . . information they: can access . . .

  b. . . . information, although they can access . . .

  c. . . . information, but they can access . . .

  d. . . . information; they can access . . .

100. Sentences 5 and 6.   As more families purchase computers. The market is continuing to grow. The most effective combination of sentences 5 and 6 would include which of the following groups of words?

  a. . . . purchase computers the market . . .

  b. The market is continuing to grow when more families purchase computers.

  c. . . . purchase computers, the market is . . .

  d. As more families purchase computers; the market is . . .

101. Sentence 11.   But <u>it's</u> not all fun and games. Which of the following is the best way to write the underlined portion of the sentence?

  a. it's

  b. its

  c. what is

  d. that is   _____

102. Sentence 12.   Computers teach new skills <u>and helps develop others</u>.

Which of the following is the best way to write the underlined portion of this sentence?

    a. and helps develop others

    b. but help develop others

    c. and help develop others

    d. and help develop other   _____

103. Sentence 14.   Educational games teach more traditional skills, such as math and reading, in fun ways. What correction should be made to this sentence?

    a. Educational games teach more traditional skills, such as math and reading, in fun ways.

    b. Educational games taught more traditional skills, such as math and reading, in fun ways.

    c. Educational games teach more traditional skills; such as math and reading, in fun ways.

    d. Educational games teach more traditional skills—such as math and reading—in fun ways.   _____

104. Sentence 15.   Helpful new programs also teach adults and give them easier and faster ways to accomplish tasks. Which of the following is the best way to write this sentence?

    a. Helpful new programs also teach adults and give them easier and faster ways to accomplish tasks.

    b. Helpful new programs also teach adults, giving them easier and faster ways to accomplish tasks.

    c. Helpful new programs also teach adults, but give them easier and faster ways to accomplish tasks.

    d. Helpful new programs also learn adults and give them easier and faster ways to accomplish tasks.   _____

105. Sentences 16 and 17.   Many people now use computer programs to help them compute their taxes. The programs check the returns for mistakes and even mail the returns to the IRS. The most effective combination of sentences 16 and 17 would include which of the following group of words?

    a. . . . compute their taxes, the programs check . . .

    b. . . . compute their taxes; the programs check . . .

    c. . . . compute their taxes, although the programs check . . .

    d. . . . compute their taxes, if the programs check . . .   _____

106. Sentence 18.   The availability and use of computers in homes will continue to grow, as more people realize their value and take advantage of this developing technology. Which of the following is the best way to write this sentence?

   a. The availability and use of computers in homes will continue to grow, as more people realize their value and take advantage of this developing technology.

   b. The availability and use of computers in the home will continue to grow, as most people realize their value and take advantage of this developing technology.

   c. The availability and use of computers in the home will continue to grow, as more people realize their value and took advantage of this developing technology.

   d. The availability and use of computer in the home will continue to grow as more people realize their value and take advantage of this developing technology.

Final Checkup Answer Key

1. Mr. Smith
2. manager
3. He
4. Dayton
5. You're
6. mentor's
7. It's
8. They're
9. Will
10. feel
11. was
12. look
13. has given
14. told
15. learn
16. let
17. Q
18. S
19. C
20. E
21. or
22. but
23. If
24. and
25. report
26. problem areas
27. Tony, question
28. notebook
29. Employee complaints are taken seriously.
30. More women work here than men.
31. Female employees make up 60 percent of our workforce.
32. Some women receive less pay than men do for the same work.
33. us
34. him
35. themselves
36. I
37. are
38. was
39. Success
40. experiences

41. Each
42. none
43. Few
44. Either
45. they
46. These
47. this
48. This
49. delayed
50. patiently
51. really
52. good
53. An
54. the
55. an
56. an
57. longer
58. friendlier
59. this
60. bad
61. Bob's Bicycles (circle B,B)
62. Swiss (circle S)
63. R.J. Reynolds (circle R,J,R)
64. Caribbean Ocean (circle C,O)
65. *Charlotte's Web* (circle C,W)
66. *Star Wars* (circle S,W)
67. *Entrepreneur* (circle E)
68. Mothers Against Drunk Drivers (circle M,A,D,D)
69. Fred, please answer me.
70. Sorry, Joan, did you say something?
71. Yes, but I guess you weren't listening.
72. Actually I was listening, thinking, and typing at the same time.
73. Wait, come back. or Wait, come back!
74. Show this display to the manager.

75. Is there another way to do this?
76. I doubt it.
77. Melanie was waiting—at least I thought she was.
78. "Come on," said Sharon, "let's leave her."
79. "I'm right here," Melanie called out.
80. This report—the sales summary—must be completed before you leave.
81. Here are the supplies you ordered: . . . .
82. Please pay the bill; . . . .
83. 2:00
84. The bus was late; . . . .
85. unconditional
86. colorful
87. rewrite
88. player
89. Can you see the end at last?
90. Smiling at me, he waved goodbye.
91. Not paying attention to where I was going, I tripped.
92. Looking out the window, he saw the mail carrier.
93. bright and sunny
94. in the corner
95. slippery and icy
96. on the edge of your desk
97. a
98. a
99. d
100. c
101. a
102. c
103. d
104. b
105. b
106. d

Final Checkup Evaluation Chart

If you missed questions:	*Pay particular attention to:*
1–8	Lessons 1 and 2
5–8	Lesson 3
9–16	Lessons 4, 5, and 6
17–28	Lesson 8
29–32	Lesson 8
33–36	Lesson 9
37–44	Lesson 10
45–56	Lessons 11 and 12
57–60	Lessons 12 and 13
61–68	Lesson 14
69–84	Lesson 15
85–88	Lesson 16
89–106	Lessons 18 through 20

Exercise Answers

EXERCISE 1

A.
1. An employee is someone who works at a (job.)
2. An employer is someone you work for.
3. Some employers use [humor] to settle (disagreements.)
4. A boss, or supervisor, gives (orders.)
5. Some people work in plants or shops.
6. Bosses like workers to be on (time.)
7. Often, workers must use a (time card.)
8. (Skills) are needed in every workplace.
9. Some (skills) can be learned through (training.)
10. Employers expect workers to be serious about their (jobs.)

B.
1. People who buy from a (business) are (customers.)
2. Sales to (customers) make (money) for a (business.)
3. Sales help pay for the (salaries) of (workers.)
4. All employees should treat (customers) well.
5. Communication is an important job (skill.)
6. Many workplaces have (training.)
7. Training may also be called (classes) or (workshops.)
8. Classes can teach (workers) communication (skills.)
9. A class may also teach how to use a (telephone) to make a (sale.)
10. Classes in computer (training) are popular today.

EXERCISE 2

A.
1. drive-in, weekend
2. airplane, storm
3. pilot, crew
4. passenger, controls
5. landing, airport

B.
1. copilots, meals, passengers
2. years, attendants, airplanes
3. San Francisco, Chicago
4. day, flight, hours
5. attendants, nurses
6. people, flight
7. excitement, jobs
8. trips, work, problems
9. journeys, passengers
10. cabins, room, comfort
11. aisle, seat, side
12. Travel, air, days
13. crew, travelers, courage
14. Pilots, landmarks, ground
15. Transportation, aircraft, time
16. trip, New York, Los Angeles, hours
17. flights, meals

EXERCISE 3

A.
1. New Orleans
2. Dr. Laura Miller
3. Washington Street
4. City Construction
5. American Red Cross
6. Social Security Office
7. President Bill Clinton
8. Rowe's Housekeeping Department

B.
1. Sears Tower, John Hancock Building
2. Missouri, Jefferson City
3. Pacific Ocean, October
4. Ann's, Canada, Christmas
5. Io, Jupiter
6. General Colin Powell, Gulf War

EXERCISE 4

A.
1. Arizona
2. Phillips
3. July
4. Plumbing
5. United States
6. September
7. Memphis
8. New York
9. Statue of Liberty
10. Empire State Building

Exercise Answers

B. 1. They have many plants in the state of Michigan.
2. Henry Ford made auto production easier.
3. The Model T was one of Ford's first cars.
4. You can see Ford's early cars at the Henry Ford Museum in Michigan.
5. The Fords today look much different from those Henry Ford made.

EXERCISE 5

A.
1. bushes
2. computers
3. copies
4. classes
5. memos
6. benches
7. bakeries
8. taxes
9. cities
10. ladders
11. disks
12. heroes
13. ladies
14. staplers
15. planks
16. babies
17. tickets
18. wrenches

B.
1. jeans
2. ties
3. colors
4. Suits
5. dresses
6. shoes
7. coworkers
8. hats
9. shirts
10. businesses, uniforms

EXERCISE 6

A.
1. clocks
2. loaves
3. tomatoes
4. faxes
5. pianos
6. crutches
7. desks
8. sisters
9. machines
10. cabinets
11. branches
12. classes
13. movies
14. selves
15. coins
16. shelves
17. halves
18. floors
19. shoeboxes
20. scarves

B.
1. partners, problems
2. Husbands, wives
3. brothers, sisters
4. workers, lives
5. Fights, troubles
6. Battles, sexes

EXERCISE 7

A.
1. Streaks
2. claps, schools
3. women, children
4. umbrellas, feet
5. crutches
6. teeth
7. styles
8. managers
9. Clerks
10. Customers, umbrellas

B.
1. men
2. women
3. data
4. ZIP Codes
5. strategies
6. curricula
7. feet
8. geese
9. potatoes
10. checks
11. mice
12. ideas

EXERCISE 8

A. 1. There were several crises in the office last month.
2. I stood so long on the showroom floor that my feet began to ache.
3. no change
4. no change
5. Yesterday deer nearly ran into my car.
6. no change
7. no change
8. no change
9. "The next thing you know," he said, "someone will ask me to cook oxen!"
10. That noise is from the workmen repairing our roof.

EXERCISE 9

A. 1. daughters-in-law
2. analyses
3. great-uncles

Exercise Answers

4. encyclopedias
5. countrymen
6. golf courses
7. cactuses, cacti
8. self-starters
9. double plays
10. drive-ins
11. forget-me-nots
12. teeth
13. series
14. funguses, fungi
15. moose
16. salmon
17. geese
18. handfuls, handsful
19. women
20. scissors
21. axes
22. chassis

B. 1. great-grandparents
2. trout
3. commanders in chief
4. bacteria
5. congresswomen
6. Chinese
7. armfuls, armsful
8. dictionaries
9. fishermen
10. stimuli

EXERCISE 10

A. 1. I, he
2. I, him, it
3. she, this, her
4. them, their
5. they, me, them
6. We, their
7. I, their, them
8. You, you, I, them

B. 1. They
2. them

3. He/She
4. They
5. their
6. It

EXERCISE 11

A. 1. them   6. She
2. They   7. She, them
3. it   8. it
4. him, her   9. They
5. it   10. you

B. 1. official   7. award
2. reporter   8. man
3. organization   9. man
4. mechanic   10. winners
5. People   11. companies
6. president   12. suggesters

EXERCISE 12

A. 1. his   6. his
2. her   7. their
3. his or her   8. his or her
4. he   9. her
5. her   10. his

B.   **Sample Answers**
1. Some photos do not do justice to their subjects.
2. The lens is in its case.
3. Most professionals take good care of their equipment.
4. That printer works in her basement.
5. The snapshots fell out of their frames.
6. A tripod definitely has its uses.
7. The photographer won awards for his pictures.
8. That bracelet is her favorite piece of jewelry.
9. Those toys are their old ones.
10. A fresh battery is needed for the time mechanism to work on that clock.

Exercise Answers

EXERCISE 13

A.
1. <u>People</u> (Everyone)
2. <u>friends</u> (Several)
3. <u>socks</u> (neither)
4. <u>Jose and Lucinda</u> (Both)
5. <u>socks</u> (Several)
6. <u>friends</u> (All)
7. <u>socks</u> (Each)
8. <u>socks</u> (Both)
9. <u>friends</u> (All)
10. <u>socks</u> (Many)

B.

Pronoun	Number
1. Many	plural
2. few	plural
3. Everyone	singular
4. Somebody	singular
5. others	plural
6. anyone	singular
7. both	plural
8. Each	singular
9. Each	singular
10. Neither	singular
11. something	singular
12. everyone	singular

EXERCISE 14

A.
1. our
2. your
3. your, her
4. your, his
5. My
6. Its
7. Our, your
8. My, their
9. your, his
10. his

B.
1. mine
2. yours
3. hers
4. his
5. Their
6. ours
7. Its
8. yours
9. hers
10. his
11. theirs
12. our

EXERCISE 15

A.
1. he's
2. it's
3. we'd
4. I've
5. she'll
6. you're
7. I'd
8. they've
9. I'll
10. I'm

B.

	Across	Down
	5. they're	1. it's
	6. he's	2. we're
	9. he'll	3. we'd
	10. you've	4. you'll
	11. I've	7. she's
	12. you'd	8. they'd
	13. she'll	11. I'll

EXERCISE 16

A.
1. she'd
2. they've
3. isn't
4. weren't
5. I'll
6. it's
7. couldn't
8. you'll
9. we've
10. didn't

B.
1. aren't — are not
2. he's — he is (or has)
3. can't — cannot
4. wouldn't — would not
5. it's — it has (or is)
6. don't — do not
7. wasn't — was not
8. haven't — have not
9. you're — you are

C. Sample Answers
1. I wouldn't do that if I were you.
2. I wasn't satisfied with your product.
3. I'll pick you up at the bus station.

EXERCISE 17

A.
1. they're
2. you're
3. There
4. You're
5. It's
6. their
7. It's, you're
8. their

Exercise Answers

9. Your, their

10. their

B.   **Sample Answers**

1. The printer had its paper jammed.

2. It's time for our sales meeting.

3. Did you bring your tools?

4. You're going to need them.

5. Their sales were off this month.

6. They're coming to the meeting late.

7. There will be a video shown first.

EXERCISE 18

A.   1. its

2. they're

3. Their

4. Your

5. whose

6. You're

7. its

8. their

9. they're

10. there

11. You're

12. It's

13. their

14. Who's

15. they're

16. their

17. it's

18. whose

19. its

20. their

21. Whose

22. they're, there

EXERCISE 19

A.   1. the store's atmosphere

2. Mr. Haskins' help

3. the student's choices

4. the shirt's color

5. the clerk's job

6. the sweaters' design

7. the man's inquiry

8. the boys' floor

9. the children's toys

10. the elevator's noise

11. the telephone's ringing

B.   1. clothes'

2. manager's

3. salespeople's

4. boys'

5. Helen's

6. son's

7. Jim's

8. dresses'

EXERCISE 20

A.   1. elevator's

2. man's

3. groups'

4. pilot's

5. president's

6. visitors'

7. twins'

8. employees'

9. door's

10. hero's

11. computer's

12. assistant's

13. editors'

14. women's

15. son-in-law's

16. oxen's

17. friend's

18. club's

19. group's

20. seminar's

B.   1. sweep's

2. cleaner's

3. jobs'

4. job's

5. people's

6. work's

7. employer's

EXERCISE 21

A.   1. copies

2. copy's

3. copies'

4. heroes

5. heroes'

6. hero's

7. woman's

8. women's

9. women

Exercise Answers

10. shelves
11. shelves'
12. shelf's

B. 1. Zoo's
2. Mexico's
3. Runners
4. Workers'
5. Hordes
6. Players'
7. Mothers
8. Men's
9. Stocks

EXERCISE 22

A. 1. ladies
2. streets'
3. boys
4. boxes
5. worker's

B. 1. singular possessive
2. plural
3. plural possessive
4. plural
5. plural
6. singular possessive
7. singular possessive
8. singular possessive
9. plural
10. singular possessive
11. singular possessive
12. plural possessive
13. singular possessive

EXERCISE 23

A. 1. possessive
2. plural
3. possessive
4. possessive
5. plural
6. possessive
7. plural
8. possessive

9. possessive
10. plural
11. possessive
12. possessive
13. plural
14. plural

B. 1. Students
2. others
3. articles
4. readers
5. cooks
6. author's
7. family's
8. demonstrations
9. methods
10. teacher's
11. cooks
12. expert's
13. Bakers
14. Students'
15. recipes

EXERCISE 24

A. 1. is
2. repairs
3. cut
4. hammer
5. may feel
6. work
7. may change
8. tow
9. check
10. adjust

B.   Sample Answers
1. A dipstick is used to check oil.
2. Service station managers give orders to mechanics.
3. A hose sometimes needs replacing.

4. Dead batteries cause cars to stop running.
5. The tires are flat.
6. His windshield wipers need to be replaced.
7. A tune-up is needed if a car is running rough.
8. The passenger side of the car has a dent.
9. Her mechanic is on vacation.
10. The garage door is locked.

EXERCISE 25

A. 1. are
2. were used
3. is
4. found
5. lay
6. train
7. attend
8. study
9. help
10. gain

B. 1. gather
2. are
3. found
4. buried
5. seem
6. was
7. touched

EXERCISE 26

A. 1. joined
2. was
3. became
4. used
5. hid
6. looked
7. fooled
8. was

Exercise Answers

B. **Sample Answers**

1. Many important activities <u>stopped</u> during the flood.
2. I <u>got</u> paid at the end of the week.
3. Jennifer <u>is</u> a talented employee.
4. The smiling faces of coworkers <u>greeted</u> her after the award presentation.
5. That tall, imposing building <u>is</u> the terminal.
6. Meetings with middle managers <u>can be</u> very useful.

EXERCISE 27

A.
1. sounded
2. sounds
3. smelled
4. smelled
5. grew
6. grow
7. taste
8. tastes, make
9. feels
10. felt

B. **Sample Answers**

1. We grow vegetables in our garden in the summer.
   My son has grown two inches this year.
2. Those villages sound the civil-alert siren every month to test it.
   New cars sound so much quieter than old ones.
3. You can smell the landfill two miles away on a hot day.
   Those new perfumes smell like insect spray.
4. The boxer could feel the pain as he hit the floor.
   Do you feel well enough to go to work today?

EXERCISE 28

A.
1. <u>had gotten</u>
2. <u>had opened</u>
3. <u>were looking</u>
4. <u>should help</u>
5. <u>could find</u>
6. <u>should know</u>
7. <u>must ask</u>
8. <u>is stacking</u>
9. <u>May help</u>
10. <u>Would direct</u>
11. <u>are shelved</u>
12. <u>Does carry</u>
13. <u>is located</u>
14. <u>have helped</u>
15. <u>were turning</u>
16. <u>Did get</u>
17. <u>could look</u>
18. <u>had found</u>
19. <u>must pay</u>
20. <u>will add</u>
21. <u>has bagged</u>
22. <u>is handling</u>
23. <u>will be leaving</u>

EXERCISE 29

A.
1. were considered
2. have come
3. do use
4. are being studied
5. have been discovering
6. is called
7. is described
8. may perform
9. is supported

B. **Sample Answers**

1. They were arriving in a limo.
2. She was entering the side door.
3. They have stayed in that hotel before.
4. Sam is working downtown.
5. Tom has not participated in the study.

EXERCISE 30

A.
1. date
2. were started
3. were held
4. have become
5. are shown
6. have been added
7. can be seen
8. have been participating
9. are found
10. will remain

B.
1. <u>have eaten</u>
2. <u>are seen</u>
3. <u>can be</u>
4. <u>have been known</u>
5. <u>could take</u>
6. <u>must save</u>
7. <u>may need</u>
8. <u>will have</u>
9. <u>might be</u>

Exercise Answers

EXERCISE 31

A. 1. was accepted **P**
2. divided **A**
3. settled **A**
4. were bought **P**
5. were purchased **P**
6. looked **A**
7. gave **A**
8. was advertised **P**
9. notified **A**
10. was cooked **P**
11. was served **P**

B. 1. The cooks threw out any burnt food.
2. Our club conducted a review of the breakfast.
3. Several people suggested a few improvements.
4. The treasurer counted the money.
5. The club considered the breakfast a triumph.

EXERCISE 32

A. 1. claimed past
2. wanted past
3. remained past
4. considered past
5. look present
6. find present
7. place present
8. add present
9. swirl present
10. will sink future
11. will discover future
12. will strike future

B. 1. Many people will start their visit at Coloma.
2. Town names recall miners' lives of long ago.
3. Rough and Ready attracted adventurers.
4. Only a few Gold Rush towns remain.

EXERCISE 33

A. 1. depended past
2. burn present
3. worry present
4. import present
5. is present
6. will cost future
7. have present
8. lies present
9. say present
10. had past
11. will heat future

B. 1. included   7. burn
2. was   8. will use
3. are   9. will work
4. delivered   10. will be
5. passed   11. Will, be
6. shoveled

EXERCISE 34

A. 1. started past
2. remember present
3. will recognize future
4. change present
5. substituted past
6. remains present
7. recorded past
8. will photograph future
9. uses present
10. will tell future

B. **Sample Answer, in the Past**
Dark clouds filled the sky. The wind increased in speed. The lifeguard whistled the swimmers out of the lake. Large waves crashed noisily on the beach. The first drops dotted the pale sand. People quickly scrambled for cover. With blankets over their heads for protection, they ran for their cars.

Exercise Answers

EXERCISE 35

A.
1. work   present
2. are employed   present
3. was   past
4. tells   present
5. cared   past
6. brought   past
7. married   past
8. will celebrate   future
9. are planning   present
10. will provide   future

B.
1. She bought a new bicycle.
2. Grandmother wants to keep fit.
3. She will enjoy the scenery around her retirement home.
4. I will go riding with her on weekends.
5. I bought a used bike myself.

EXERCISE 36

A.
1. submitted
2. liked
3. mopped
4. erased
5. tried
6. handled
7. photocopied
8. gazed
9. flapped
10. denied
11. applied
12. beeped

B.
1. Meg realizes she must work more efficiently.
2. Sometimes she hurries too much.
3. Then she makes unnecessary mistakes.
4. Meg planned to complete her project by Wednesday.
5. She worried about finishing it on time.
6. Luckily, she completed it on schedule.

EXERCISE 37

A.
1. were
2. could
3. wanted
4. knew
5. work
6. is
7. learning
8. hope
9. will welcome
10. will send

EXERCISE 38

A.
1. has asked
2. have guessed
3. has delivered
4. have gathered
5. has opened
6. has displayed
7. have enjoyed

B.   **Sample Answers**
1. The IRS answered both of my questions about taxes.
2. I have hoped to meet you for a long time.
3. I earn $5,000 a year at my part-time job.
4. The company never replied to my letter.
5. Paul has hurried home every day this week.
6. My company's stock has dipped to below $30 a share.

EXERCISE 39

A.

Present	Past
1. admire	admired
2. worry	worried
3. clean	cleaned
4. shelve	shelved
5. prepare	prepared
6. hurry	hurried
7. stir	stirred
8. stop	stopped
9. ship	shipped

Past With *Has*

A.
1. has admired
2. has worried
3. has cleaned
4. has shelved
5. has prepared
6. has hurried
7. has stirred
8. has stopped
9. has shipped

Exercise Answers

B. 1. drummed   5. sipped
     2. like   6. called
     3. completed   7. pushed
     4. mailed   8. nudged

EXERCISE 40

A. 1. start; (is) starting; started; (have, has) started
     2. continue; (is) continuing; continued; (have, has) continued
     3. ache; (are) aching; ached; (have, has) ached
     4. glide; (is) gliding; glided; (have, has) glided
     5. help; (is) helping; helped; (have, has) helped

B. 1. has succeeded   6. has practiced
     2. has failed   7. has suffered
     3. has struggled   8. has endured
     4. have applauded   9. have prepared
     5. have watched   10. have cared

EXERCISE 41

A. 1. found   4. gave
     2. taken   5. begun
     3. ate   6. spoken

B. 1. saw   4. have written
     2. has spoken   5. came
     3. has done

C. Sample Answers
     1. The voters have chosen a Republican for President in four of the last five elections.
     2. Reading the Bible has taught me how to cope.
     3. My husband has gone fishing with some friends.

EXERCISE 42

A. 1. grew
     2. kept
     3. blew

     4. drove
     5. brought
     6. kept
     7. said
     8. knew

B. 1. I tell them not to run.
     One ran anyway.
     He has run away from me again.
     2. In the summer, the sun sets at about 9 o'clock at night.
     It set at 9:05 today.
     It had set at 9:04 yesterday.
     3. I hear the sounds of the waves.
     I heard a cry in the wind.
     I have heard cries of distress, but this was just a seagull.

EXERCISE 43

A.

	Present	Past	Past With Has
1.	take	took	has taken
2.	speak	spoke	has spoken
3.	choose	chose	has chosen
4.	know	knew	has known
5.	grow	grew	has grown
6.	fly	flew	has flown
7.	find	found	has found
8.	think	thought	has thought
9.	bring	brought	has brought

B. 1. have given   5. have found
     2. said   6. took
     3. has chosen   7. thought
     4. broke   8. grew

EXERCISE 44

A. 1. dove   7. felt
     2. realized   8. forsook
     3. began   9. brought
     4. given   10. held
     5. wrote   11. put
     6. gave   12. gave

Exercise Answers

B. 1. fought
    2. flown
    3. gotten
    4. worked

EXERCISE 45

A. 1. helping verb
    2. helping verb
    3. main verb
    4. helping verb
    5. main verb
    6. helping verb
    7. main verb

B. 1. will be
    2. are
    3. are being
    4. have been
    5. am
    6. can be
    7. is
    8. am

EXERCISE 46

A.
1. Are	7. have been
2. will be	8. is
3. are	9. were
4. was	10. are
5. has been	11. are
6. will be	12. are being

B.   **Sample Answers**
1. In the morning, I am still half asleep.
2. The moon is full tonight.
3. The videotapes are on a shelf in the family room.
4. Was my tax return accurate?
5. The people in Mexico were friendly to us.
6. Who will be the next President?
7. You are being a pain in the neck.
8. I was being silly too.

EXERCISE 47

A. 1. are
    2. is

3. Are
4. aren't
5. Being
6. to be

B. 1. Her company has always been known for finding solutions to unusual problems.
2. She was also looking for someone with leadership qualities.
3. She found that person; José has just been offered the position of project manager.
4. In addition to creativity, the ability to work independently will certainly be important in this job.

EXERCISE 48

A.
1. has	6. have
2. haven't	7. have
3. has	8. have
4. has	9. haven't
5. have	

B. 1. I think I should have worn my glasses.
2. My friend Matt has given me valuable hints.
3. Each shot has a different quality.
4. I have heard the sounds of arrows.
5. Some arrows have a hiss like a snake.
6. My whole arm has begun to tremble.
7. My arrow must have landed by the target.

EXERCISE 49

A.
1. does	6. didn't
2. Didn't	7. had done
3. did	8. did
4. Do	9. Does
5. did	10. doesn't

B.
1. do, did	7. Did
2. did	8. does
3. did	9. do, did
4. do	10. did
5. done	11. Did
6. Do	12. done

Exercise Answers

EXERCISE 50

A.
1. has
2. has
3. did
4. have
5. has
6. were doing
7. have
8. had
9. did have
10. did
11. has
12. have
13. has

B.
1. did
2. is having
3. had
4. had done or has done
5. does

EXERCISE 51

A.
1. can't
2. won't
3. wouldn't
4. haven't
5. weren't
6. isn't
7. doesn't
8. aren't
9. don't
10. didn't
11. couldn't
12. hadn't
13. hasn't
14. wasn't

B.
1. weren't
2. didn't
3. aren't
4. don't
5. isn't
6. can't
7. haven't
8. won't
9. doesn't
10. shouldn't
11. wasn't
12. hadn't
13. weren't

EXERCISE 52

A.
1. set
2. lays
3. left
4. let
5. sat
6. laid
7. Let
8. left

B.
1. laid
2. setting
3. laid
4. left
5. sat
6. leave

EXERCISE 53

A.
1. sit
2. lain
3. set
4. risen
5. raise
6. lies
7. sit
8. set
9. raises
10. laid
11. rose

B.   Sample Answers
1. Lay the baby on the bed between pillows. The baby can lie there safely.
2. My son just can't sit still. Set the table down in that corner over there.
3. My wife and I rise at seven every morning. Start the fire while I raise the tent.
4. The stock market has risen again. Our landlord has raised our rent again.

EXERCISE 54

A.
1. Let
2. lets
3. leave
4. left
5. teaches
6. learn
7. lend
8. borrowed
9. learn
10. taught
11. left

B.   Sample Answers
1. Don't let the dog out without his collar. The Thomases leave their dog with us when they're away.
2. I wish I could lend you the money. I wish I could borrow the money from you.
3. My family taught me a lot about life. I learned how to accept other people, for example.
4. The open door has let the cold air in. Joel has left his car lights on.

EXERCISE 55

A.
1. laid
2. set
3. rose
4. lent
5. Let
6. sit
7. teach
8. lie

Exercise Answers

9. lent   11. raise
10. Let

B. 1. laid   5. rose
2. has taught   6. sat
3. left   7. learn
4. has learned

EXERCISE 56

A. 1. not a sentence   4. sentence
2. not a sentence   5. sentence
3. not a sentence   6. not a sentence

B. 1. teams/played
2. They/passed
3. coaches/shouted
4. Juan/played
5. brother/was
6. everyone/cheered
7. team/won

C. **Sample Answers**
The manager called me into his office and taught me a lesson.
I learned a good lesson from my manager.
My worst assignment was to speak in front of a group including the manager.

EXERCISE 57

A. 1. ? question   5. . statement
2. ! exclamation   6. . command
3. . statement   7. ? question
4. ! exclamation

B. 1. They look very costly.
2. How beautiful they still are!
3. Hold them carefully.
4. Should we insure them?
5. Don't bump your head.

EXERCISE 58

A. 1. Follow my lead.   command
2. Use your head to get ahead in life.   command
3. Good managers listen to employees.   statement

4. Wow, this is exciting!   exclamation
5. We call this sport "shooting the rapids."   statement
6. Your vote can make a difference.   statement
7. Oh no, we're going to crash!   exclamation
8. When do we leave for the meeting?   question
9. Bring me the files on the desk.   command
10. I'd like to do this again.   statement

B. **Sample Answers**
1. statement — Not everyone likes daytime television.
2. question — Are you one of those people?
3. command — Try it sometime.
4. exclamation — I love it!

EXERCISE 59

A. 1. statement   5. command
2. command   6. statement
3. statement   7. question
4. question   8. exclamation

B. 1. Did ghostwriting exist in ancient Rome?
2. There is still a need for ghostwriters.
3. Do some businesspeople need ghostwriters to write their speeches?
4. Consider being a ghostwriter yourself.
5. I could make a lot of money ghostwriting.
6. That isn't possible! or, I don't think that is possible!

EXERCISE 60

A. 1. The unhappy young man
2. The keys
3. Piles of books
4. Some dirty shirts
5. Old papers
6. Cards from last night's game
7. The room

Exercise Answers

8. A <u>giant</u> clean-up <u>job</u>
9. <u>His</u> <u>work</u>
10. The <u>object</u> of his <u>search</u>
11. A <u>weary</u> <u>Ken</u>
12. The <u>enormous</u> <u>task</u>
13. <u>His</u> <u>old</u> <u>dog</u>
14. <u>Ken</u>

B.   **Sample Answers**
My least favorite work (assignment) is making phone calls. (I) don't like to talk on the phone. The (problem) with commuting is the traffic. Every day too many (cars) and (busses) cram into too little highway space.

EXERCISE 61
A.   1. This (library)
2. (People) of all ages
3. Many (adults)
4. (Groups) of teenagers
5. (Pictures) by local photographers
6. A famous (artist)
7. Several local (clubs)
8. Travel (films) about faraway places
9. The (library)
10. A community (volunteer)
11. Old and new (CDs)

EXERCISE 62
A.   1. It | requires strength and stamina.
2. You | are lifting bricks all day long.
3. Your hands and arms | may become tired.
4. Detailed, precision work | is a part of the job.
5. Bricklayers | sometimes create elaborate patterns with bricks.
6. Some people | may call bricklaying an art form.
7. Bricklayers | are also called masons.
8. The job of mason | includes tile layers and cement masons, as well.
9. Some brick, tile, and cement masons |

are working as independent contractors.
10. They | pay all their own expenses up front.
11. Their fees | are paid once the full job has been completed.

B.   **Sample Answers**
The man next door <u>invented a new kind of paintbrush</u>. We <u>collected more newspapers for recycling this month</u> than last. I <u>worked overtime all day Saturday</u>. I just <u>completed a sixty hour work week</u>. We <u>started a savings account for my overtime earnings</u>.

EXERCISE 63
A.   1. (identified) 80 facial expressions
2. (are) signs of different feelings
3. (share) many kinds of smiles and expressions
4. (will trigger) a broad smile
5. (cause) some very interesting grins
6. (express) fear or surprise
7. (use) smiles for courtesy and respect, too
8. (has proven) a connection between feelings and posture
9. (walk) with a slouch
10. (have) straighter posture
11. (will skip) along lightly

EXERCISE 64
A.   1. Its shape <u>doesn't change every night.</u> does change
2. The moon's surface is actually <u>reflecting sunlight.</u>   is reflecting
3. We <u>could barely see the moon last night.</u> could see
4. A thin crescent <u>was dimly glowing in the night sky.</u>   was glowing
5. The clouds <u>had nearly made the moon invisible.</u> had made
6. It <u>didn't rise until very late.</u>   did rise

Exercise Answers

7. I have never seen an eclipse of the moon.
have seen

8. The earth's shadow will sometimes cover the moon's surface.   will cover

9. The moon can also cast a shadow over the earth.   can cast

10. Eclipses of the earth have often frightened people.   have frightened

11. They could not understand this strange occurrence.   could understand

EXERCISE 65

A. 1. abacus/is
2. abacus/has
3. counters/are used
4. civilizations/used
5. Egyptians-Chinese-Romans/counted
6. abacus/is
7. Computers/became

B.   **Sample Answers**
A. 1. I work in an office.
2. An employee of ABC Company hired me.
3. My boss has taught me a lot.
4. The happiest day in my career was Monday.
5. The truck driver drove safely to the warehouse.
6. The dispatcher has an office on the third floor.

EXERCISE 66

A. 1. A big rodeo │ takes place in July.
2. This event │ is held in Alberta.
3. It │ is the Calgary Exhibition and Stampede.
4. This festival │ lasts ten days.
5. More than 850,000 people │ come to Calgary.
6. Rodeo champs from all over │ participate.
7. Everyone │ marches in a parade.
8. Many events │ are scheduled during the rodeo.

9. Races with chuck wagons │ are popular.
10. Tourists │ enjoy rope throwing too.

B. 1. The biggest and most famous rodeo │ is held in Calgary.
2. Great rodeo performers │ rope steers and ride bucking horses.
3. Newspapers, radio stations, and television networks │ cover the events.
4. Visitors │ watch events and wander around.
5. They │ eat at the many restaurants and buy souvenirs.
6. Tourists and locals │ enjoy the sights and sounds.
7. Many performers │ have colorful saddles and fancy outfits.
8. Performers and spectators │ find opportunities for dancing.

C.   **Sample Answers**
1. The clerk stocks and cleans the shelves.
2. Computers and faxes help.
3. The team discusses and votes.

EXERCISE 67

A. 1. Is the Mississippi River used for transportation?
The Mississippi River is used for transportation.
2. Is Mount Kilimanjaro located in Africa near Kenya?
Mount Kilimanjaro is located in Africa near Kenya.
3. Is Rainbow Bridge, a natural bridge, located in Utah?
Rainbow Bridge, a natural bridge, is located in Utah.
4. Is the Verrazano Narrows Bridge a suspension bridge?
The Verrazano Narrows Bridge is a suspension bridge.

B. 1. Does the management listen to new ideas?

Exercise Answers

2. The <u>telephone</u> <u>did ring</u> this morning.
3. <u>Will</u> this <u>store</u> <u>close</u> at 6 P.M.?
4. <u>You</u> <u>are going</u> to the store.
5. <u>Is</u> <u>Gary</u> a transfer student?

EXERCISE 68

A. 1. Large <u>hailstones</u> <u>did fall</u> last night.
2. <u>You</u> <u>have seen</u> darker thunderclouds than these.
3. <u>They</u> <u>are getting</u> closer and closer.
4. That <u>tree</u> <u>was struck</u> by lightning.
5. <u>I</u> <u>may listen</u> to the weather report.

B.

Simple Subject	Simple Verb
1. clouds	came
2. storms	do occur
3. raindrops	beat
4. Joan	was caught

EXERCISE 69

A. 1. <u>Will</u> (you) please <u>tell</u> me the time?
2. Why <u>does</u> (he) <u>want</u> the time?
3. <u>Is</u> (it) four o'clock yet?
4. <u>Has</u> (she) <u>missed</u> her appointment?
5. <u>Is</u> your (watch) very accurate?
6. <u>Do</u> (you) <u>have</u> a watch of your own?
7. <u>Will</u> (you) <u>buy</u> me one?
8. Why <u>should</u> (we) <u>do</u> that?
9. Where <u>is</u> my (watch?)
10. <u>Have</u> (I) <u>lost</u> my new watch?

B. 1. A loud (shout) <u>came</u> from the street.
2. My (sister) <u>ran</u> to the window.
3. Below the window <u>stood</u> (Rosa.)
4. In her eyes <u>were</u> (tears.)
5. In her hand <u>lay</u> her (watch.)
6. There <u>was</u> a (problem) with the spring.
7. There <u>was</u> no other (watch) like it.
8. On the back <u>were</u> her (initials.)
9. At the corner <u>was</u> a repair (shop.)
10. Quickly <u>ran</u> (Rosa) toward it.

C. 1. Jane raced around the corner.
2. Was Jane late for work?
3. In her office stood Jane's boss.
4. Jane was in trouble.

EXERCISE 70

A. 1. Sam <u>put</u> the apron on.
2. He <u>took</u> out some flour.
3. He <u>took</u> out some milk.
4. He <u>took</u> out other ingredients.
5. Sam <u>mixed</u> the flour and the milk.
6. He <u>added</u> the other ingredients.
7. Sam <u>made</u> some bread.
8. Sam <u>set</u> the oven at 350°.
9. He <u>baked</u> the bread.
10. Juanita <u>helped</u> Sam.
11. Juanita <u>cooled</u> the bread.
12. Then Juanita <u>wrapped</u> the bread.

B. **Sample Answers**
1. customer
2. question
3. muffins, cookies, wheat bread, rye, etc.
4. bagels
5. one, two, three, etc.
6. coffee, tea, etc.
7. butter
8. jam

EXERCISE 71

A. 1. <u>Jim</u> (and) <u>Donna</u>
2. <u>Jim</u> <u>helps</u> with the baking (and) <u>Donna</u> <u>serves</u> the customers.
3. in the basement (or) in the pantry
4. in the kitchen (and) in the dining area
5. <u>Joe</u> <u>fixed</u> my hard drive last spring, (but) <u>it</u> <u>needs</u> work again.
6. task (or) activity
7. <u>photography</u> (and) <u>volleyball</u>
8. at the gym (or) in her darkroom
9. <u>Andy</u> <u>is</u> a good artist, (but) <u>Marnie</u> <u>is</u> even better.
10. <u>sketches</u> (and) <u>draws</u>
11. <u>I</u> <u>like</u> to eat in the cafeteria, (but) my <u>friend</u> <u>prefers</u> to bring her lunch.

Exercise Answers

12. ride the bus (or) drive cars

B.   Sample Answers

1. My wife and I were married two years ago.
2. No one but me can do that job.
3. I can drive or take the train to work.
4. I was proud and happy to become a new father.
5. I applied for a loan at the bank but didn't get it.
6. Turn up the television, or stop talking.

EXERCISE 72

A.
1. and	7. and
2. but	8. both, and
3. so	9. but or yet
4. but	10. or
5. for	11. because
6. either, or	12. Neither, nor

B.
1. and	5. Neither, nor
2. Both, and	6. so
3. either, or	7. Both, and
4. but, also	

EXERCISE 73

A.
1. It	6. He
2. They	7. They
3. They	8. She
4. It	9. He
5. He	

B.
1. Lauren and I	4. We
2. She, I	5. They
3. Charlie and she	6. Charlie and I

EXERCISE 74

A.
1. us	4. them
2. us	5. us
3. her	

B.
1. me	8. them
2. us	9. her
3. us	10. him
4. me	11. him
5. me	12. them
6. them	13. her
7. me	

EXERCISE 75

A.
1. him	6. them, me
2. us	7. us
3. her, me	8. them
4. her, me	9. her, me
5. him	10. him

B.

1. Besides her and me, no one else knew the secret.
2. Nadia was meeting with them and me.
3. Some more packages came for you and us.
4. Here are some responses from her and them.
5. Correct.

EXERCISE 76

A.
1. He	6. she
2. him	7. him
3. them	8. she
4. he	9. He
5. it	10. They

B.
1. me	6. us
2. They	7. He
3. them	8. him
4. me	9. them
5. I	10. him

EXERCISE 77

1. Her boss gave concert tickets to us.
2. The couple in the second row were Phyllis and I.
3. We watched the musicians tune their instruments.
4. All of us couldn't wait for the concert to begin.
5. Between the stage and me stood an usher.
6. The people who play trumpets sat closest to Phyllis and me.

Exercise Answers

7. Phyllis and I enjoyed the concert.

8. The orchestra played the *Grand Canyon Suite* for us.

9. The music sounded very pleasant to me.

10. The next day she told her boss about the concert.

EXERCISE 78

A.
1. (itself) printer
2. (yourselves) you
3. (themselves) women
4. (myself) I
5. (himself) Bob
6. (ourselves) We
7. (itself) group
8. (herself) Mrs. Zack
9. (myself) I
10. (themselves) citizens
11. (himself) carpenter
12. (herself) boss

B.
1. ourselves
2. himself
3. themselves
4. themselves
5. ourselves
6. themselves
7. himself
8. ourselves

EXERCISE 79

A.
1. calls
2. move
3. say
4. knows
5. laugh
6. sound
7. imitate
8. calls
9. refer

B.
1. gets
2. enjoy
3. find
4. becomes
5. interest
6. amuses
7. remember

EXERCISE 80

A.
1. looks
2. lead
3. are
4. lies
5. pick
6. walks
7. roars
8. is
9. bump
10. rise

B.
1. glide
2. seems
3. are
4. take
5. soar
6. are
7. help
8. is
9. use
10. constructs

EXERCISE 81

A.
1. send
2. attend
3. brings
4. begins
5. win
6. arrives
7. cook
8. stay
9. have

B.
1. welcome
2. eat
3. correct
4. makes
5. close
6. set
7. plays
8. dresses
9. correct
10. correct
11. like

EXERCISE 82

A.
1. No one   Singular
2. everybody   Singular
3. Few   Plural
4. Several   Plural
5. Somebody   Singular
6. Others   Plural
7. Everyone   Singular
8. Many   Plural
9. Someone   Singular
10. Both   Plural

B.
1. know
2. fit
3. knocks
4. are
5. sees
6. arrives
7. bring
8. buy
9. sings
10. plays

EXERCISE 83

A.
1. Everyone has
2. None think
3. Everyone is
4. Most are
5. Few contain
6. All equals
7. many are
8. Each has
9. One needs
10. Each uses

Exercise Answers

11. <u>Anybody</u> <u>is</u>
12. <u>All</u> <u>needs</u>
13. <u>No one</u> <u>thinks</u>
14. <u>both</u> <u>are</u>
15. <u>Neither</u> <u>has</u>
16. <u>Everyone</u> <u>requires</u>

17. <u>No one</u> <u>is</u>
18. <u>Most</u> <u>is</u>
19. <u>Many</u> <u>waste</u>
20. <u>Some</u> <u>use</u>
21. <u>Everyone</u> <u>learn</u>

EXERCISE 84

A.
1. works
2. helps
3. takes
4. is
5. have
6. is
7. does
8. is
9. work
10. travel

B.
1. has
2. have
3. has
4. has
5. have
6. has
7. have
8. have
9. has
10. has

EXERCISE 85

A.
1. shows
2. are
3. is
4. are
5. is
6. require
7. is
8. attract

B.
1. Maps of this state show all the important roads.
2. Many people in our town do not travel far from home.
3. Bicycles with ten gears appear frequently.
4. The use of bicycles has increased recently.
5. A bicycle rider without proper skills is dangerous.

EXERCISE 86

A.
    S   V
1. Jobs <u>for outgoing types</u> include costumed telegram delivery, and flower or balloon delivery.
             S
2. Zany costumes, <u>some homemade,</u>

        V
  can replace uniforms.
    S   V
3. Smiles, <u>as well as money,</u> are part of the payment.
    S   V
4. Children, especially <u>young ones,</u> love clowns.
    S   V
5. Clowns—<u>with sad or funny faces</u>—will be welcomed at most children's parties.
    S   V
6. Clowns, <u>on their off days,</u> may entertain their own children at home.
            S
7. Almost anyone <u>with a sense of humor</u>
         V
  can become a costumed delivery person.
    S   V
8. Few people, <u>believe it or not,</u> make really good clowns.

B.
1. are
2. helps
3. put
4. make
5. is
6. require
7. want

EXERCISE 87

A.
1. are
2. is
3. seem
4. do
5. does
6. is
7. are
8. was
9. Are
10. is

B.
1. <u>patents</u> have been
2. <u>dogs</u> are
3. <u>they</u> Are
4. <u>collie</u> *correct*
5. <u>bulldog</u> comes
6. <u>dogs</u> *correct*
7. <u>they</u> Are
8. <u>we</u> *correct*
9. <u>way</u> is
10. <u>we</u> don't

Exercise Answers

EXERCISE 88

A.
1. Have (you) heard
2. Is (it)
3. Does (it) have
4. is (fruit) called
5. have (you) eaten
6. Does (it) look
7. Is (fruit)
8. Is (this)
9. is (fruit)
10. Should (it) be eaten

B.
1. Here | There is
2. There is
3. Here | There are
4. There are
5. Here | There is

C.
1. Money and receipts were inside the drawer.
2. A plaque is above the bookshelves.
3. A cabinet and a wastebasket are alongside the desk.
4. My colleagues are down the hall.

EXERCISE 89

A.
1. fine blue
2. this warm
3. three vivid green
4. this favorite
5. That, lovely
6. sorry, this special
7. Helpful
8. Two, several

B.
1. That (night)   which one
2. kindly (custodian)   what kind
3. next (morning) which one
4. woolen (scarf)   what kind
5. happy (woman)   what kind
6. thank-you (card)   what kind
7. thoughtful (Mr. Moss)   what kind

C.   Sample Answers
1. second shift   business letter
   two employees
2. steel factory   international fax
   three supervisors

3. carpenter's union   in-house memo
   four managers

EXERCISE 90

A.
1. Arabian horses
2. Canadian lumber
3. Spanish lace
4. Australian beef
5. Danish furniture
6. Egyptian jewelry
7. Turkish carpets
8. Swiss watches
9. Grecian sandals

B.
1. Two German officials met the English consul.
2. The hostess wore Indian jewelry and Chinese silk.
3. The Peruvian guests liked the Alaskan salmon.
4. The European visitors heard Puerto Rican music.
5. He liked Canadian bacon with his eggs.

EXERCISE 91

A.
1. Chinese
2. Spanish
3. Hawaiian
4. French
5. Indian
6. Ukrainian
7. Welsh
8. Italian
9. American
10. Russian

B.
1. Ecuadoran baskets
2. Scottish kilt
3. Swedish rug
4. Irish team
5. Canadian lakes
6. German cars
7. Egyptian river
8. Mexican jewelry
9. Bolivian minerals
10. Jamaican singer

EXERCISE 92

A.   Sample Answers
1. new books—10. We received a shipment of new books.
2. decorative ornaments—11. Our shop sells decorative ornaments.

Exercise Answers

3. lovely seashells—12. We also carry lovely seashells.

4. back storeroom—13. Some items are kept in the back storeroom.

5. popular audiotape—14. This is our most popular audiotape.

6. angry customer—15. One angry customer walked out because we had no more of these audiotapes.

7. special poster—16. This customer is looking for a special poster.

8. gray dolphin—17. It has a picture of a gray dolphin.

9. opposite wall—18. The poster is hanging on the opposite wall.

B.
1. (skillful)
2. (many) European
3. (several)
4. (famous) English
5. Australian
6. British
7. North American
8. (colorful) (young)

EXERCISE 93

A.   Sample Answers
1. busy day
2. colored paper
3. employee's time card
4. regular customer
5. country music
6. city bus
7. office building
8. dim lobby
9. stormy weather
10. summer vacation
11. good salary
12. next check

B.
1. ancient wooden
2. fine ancient (Grecian)
3. (American) scientific
4. many numerous
5. Several new
6. beautiful (Roman)
7. important (European)
8. Other this historical

C.
1. remarkable
2. priceless
3. joyful
4. foolish
5. hopeless
6. wonderful
7. valuable

EXERCISE 94

A.
1. a
2. an
3. The
4. the
5. an
6. a
7. an
8. the
9. the
10. an

B.   Sample Answers
1. The showroom was full of cars.
2. An auditor looked at our books.
3. A recommendation was sent to personnel.
4. The hospital just added a new wing.

EXERCISE 95

A.
1. these
2. this
3. These
4. those
5. That
6. these
7. those
8. this
9. these
10. this

B.
1. Those fax machines are broken.
2. That electronic dictionary holds over 10,000 words.
3. I hope to buy one of these small laptop computers.
4. I'd like to have some of these new technologies in my home.
5. The boys from that team are on the bus.

EXERCISE 96

A.
1. Those
2. these
3. This
4. Those
5. this
6. That
7. those
8. These

Exercise Answers

9. That
10. this
11. Those

B.
1. Personally, I prefer these sailboats.
2. This harbor is very busy.
3. Have you ever ridden on one of those ferries?
4. I once took a boat to that island.
5. Look at those oyster boats docked at the pier.

EXERCISE 97

A.
1. that way
2. those cooks
3. These eggs
4. This restaurant
5. Those customers
6. this morning
7. this problem
8. that moment
9. This customer
10. those eggs
11. that plate
12. these eggs
13. those eggs
14. these eggs
15. These kinds

B.
1. This
2. Those
3. these
4. This
5. this
6. those

EXERCISE 98

A.

Descriptive Word	Comparing Two Things	Comparing Three or More Things
large	larger	largest
nervous	more nervous	most nervous
smooth	smoother	smoothest
splendid	more splendid	most splendid
shiny	shinier	shiniest
intelligent	more intelligent	most intelligent
rough	rougher	roughest
wide	wider	widest
early	earlier	earliest
creative	more creative	most creative

B.
1. narrower
2. prettier
3. nicest
4. most difficult
5. most attractive
6. more expensive
7. smallest
8. neater

EXERCISE 99

A.

Description	Two Things	Three or More Things
1. hungry	hungrier	hungriest
2. brilliant	more brilliant	most brilliant
3. tidy	tidier	tidiest
4. angry	angrier	angriest
5. athletic	more athletic	most athletic
6. huge	huger	hugest
7. kind	kinder	kindest
8. delicious	more delicious	most delicious
9. thin	thinner	thinnest
10. simple	simpler	simplest

B.
1. gloomiest
2. more mysterious
3. windiest
4. shabbiest
5. more ambitious
6. more cheerful
7. sunnier

EXERCISE 100

A.

Description	Two Things	Three or More Things
1. much	more	most
2. far	farther	farthest
3. little	less	least
4. bad	worse	worst
5. good	better	best

B.
1. more
2. farther
3. least
4. better
5. best
6. worst
7. farther
8. worse
9. farthest
10. most
11. less
12. best
13. more

EXERCISE 101

A.
1. taller, tallest
2. happier, happiest
3. easier, easiest
4. more careful, most careful
5. higher, highest
6. keener, keenest
7. less, least; littler, littlest
8. worse, worst

Exercise Answers

9. more loyal, most loyal
10. cleaner, cleanest
11. sturdier, sturdiest
12. more curious, most curious

B.
1. more ferocious   7. little
2. sharper   8. More
3. smaller   9. faster
4. more sensitive   10. quick
5. largest   11. keener
6. most dangerous   12. earliest

EXERCISE 102

A.
1. carefully (explain)   how?
2. (demonstrate) first   when?
3. closely (watch)   how?
4. gently (guide)   how?
5. slowly (learned)   how?
6. (can master) first   when?
7. (is) slowly   how?
8. (are taken) seriously   how?

B.
1. outside (sold)   where?
2. patiently (waited)   how?
3. quickly (rose)   how?
4. soon (shaded)   when?
5. then (noticed)   when?
6. uncomfortably (stood)   how?
7. immediately (moved)   when?
8. there (improved)   where?

EXERCISE 103

A.
1. (politely) answered
2. (definitely) had
3. (outside) sat
4. (steadily) improved
5. (alone) started
6. (Now) has
7. (always) deals
8. (frequently) holds
9. (rapidly) spreads
10. (quite) is

B.   **Sample Answers**
1. People lined up eagerly.
2. Customers definitely liked the jewelry.
3. Many people bought placemats first.
4. The goods were displayed everywhere in the store.
5. Bowls were arranged attractively on tables.
6. Sales continued briskly.
7. Vases were put on shelves continually.
8. Sara and her employees worked tirelessly.
9. The sale closed profitably.
10. The customers left the store reluctantly.

EXERCISE 104

A.
1. Yesterday   6. Later
2. cautiously   7. so
3. clumsily   8. down
4. clearly   9. quickly
5. very   10. swiftly

B.
1. quietly walked
2. Soon saw
3. clumsily hopped
4. slowly moved
5. near came
6. suddenly stopped
7. hopefully watched
8. occasionally care
9. silently watched
10. away hopped

EXERCISE 105

A.
1. Eagerly   6. quite
2. inside   7. carefully
3. Extremely   8. Soon
4. very   9. silently
5. Then   10. here

B.
1. here   6. outside
2. very   7. too
3. excitedly   8. overhead
4. later   9. extremely
5. now   10. rather

Exercise Answers

EXERCISE 106

A.

Adverb	Comparing Two Actions	Comparing Three or More Actions
cheerfully	more cheerfully	most cheerfully
hard	harder	hardest
fast	faster	fastest
gently	more gently	most gently
firmly	more firmly	most firmly
excitedly	more excitedly	most excitedly
eagerly	more eagerly	most eagerly
politely	more politely	most politely
likely	more likely	most likely

B.
1. quickly
2. faster
3. more slowly
4. sooner
5. angrily
6. more politely
7. most likely
8. more respectfully
9. most easily
10. more eager

EXERCISE 107

A.

Adverb	Comparing Two Actions	Comparing Three or More Actions
1. late	later	latest
2. happily	more happily	most happily
3. early	earlier	earliest
4. carefully	more carefully	most carefully
5. soon	sooner	soonest
6. easily	more easily	most easily
7. high	higher	highest
8. loudly	more loudly	most loudly
9. fast	faster	fastest
10. clearly	more clearly	most clearly

B.
1. nearest
2. sooner
3. more closely
4. latest
5. faster
6. most loudly
7. higher
8. fastest
9. more slowly
10. more efficiently

EXERCISE 108

A.
1. Many people of various ages
2. Fuzzy, yellow balls
3. The fans in the stands
4. A skillful woman
5. Her young, eager opponent
6. Her wooden racket
7. The weary player on the other side
8. A brisk wind
9. The great speed of the ball
10. A firm backhand
11. The younger player
12. The proud winner of the tennis match

B.
1. played courageously in the hot summer sun
2. served well at the beginning
3. returned sharply
4. crossed quickly
5. were playing soon
6. enjoyed really
7. improved greatly
8. began cautiously performed beautifully

EXERCISE 109

A.
1. nicely
2. daintily
3. suddenly
4. heartily
5. dutifully
6. slowly
7. oddly
8. kindly

B.
1. quiet corner
2. noisily rang
3. cheerfully spoke
4. soft voice
5. loudly speak
6. excited Madge
7. happily cried

C. Sample Answers
1. The snow fell softly on the windshield of the truck.
2. The product had a rough texture.
3. Always carry the testing materials gently.
4. Accessing a web site is simple if you practice.

Exercise Answers

EXERCISE 110

A.
1. steadily
2. really
3. well
4. quick
5. nervous
6. anxiously
7. carefully
8. sure
9. closely
10. gradually
11. really

B.
1. really
2. really or surely
3. surely
4. sure
5. really or surely
6. sure
7. really or surely
8. real
9. real

EXERCISE 111

A.
1. beautiful
2. surely
3. really
4. carefully
5. eager
6. useful
7. abundantly
8. quick
9. delightful

B.
1. Edison successfully extracted the rubber from goldenrod.
2. Today scientists think highly of his results.
3. They are sure Edison was right.
4. Goldenrod is a very useful plant.
5. It can be harvested easily.
6. Its small yellow flowers smell fragrant.

EXERCISE 112

A.
1. well
2. badly
3. well
4. badly
5. well
6. badly
7. well
8. good
9. well
10. bad
11. badly
12. badly

B.
1. Marnie restocks better than Lois.
2. The assembly plant's roof is leaking worst of all.
3. I like spring better than fall.
4. Have you ever seen worse weather than this?

EXERCISE 113

A.
1. good   noun
2. well   verb
3. bad   noun
4. good   noun
5. well   verb
6. good   noun
7. well   verb
8. good   noun
9. badly   verb
10. bad   noun

B.
1. better
2. badly
3. worse
4. worst
5. well
6. better
7. best
8. bad
9. good
10. better

EXERCISE 114

A.
1. go badly
2. want badly
3. well enough
4. shops well
5. dresses badly
6. wear well
7. looks bad
8. go well
9. badly do want
10. should fit well

B.
1. bad
2. good/bad
3. well
4. good/bad
5. good/bad
6. well
7. well
8. well
9. good/bad
10. good/bad
11. good
12. badly

EXERCISE 115

A.
1. there i
2. first california utah new mexico
3. some i england's
4. uncle phil mt. rushmore
5. u.s. senate washington, d.c.
6. japanese tokyo
7. the japan china
8. australia september
9. i

B.
1. Many people in North America speak the English language.
2. Many people in Canada speak French as well as English.
3. The official language of Mexico is Spanish.
4. Sarita A. Ramírez, from Mexico City, can speak English.

Exercise Answers

5. She will tour the United States in August.
6. Sarita's tour is sponsored by the Latino Foundation.

EXERCISE 116

A.
1. karl waetzel austrian
2. president clinton
3. martin's video arcade
4. vancouver british columbia
5. may july
6. kenya west germany china
7. *tonight show*
8. high note musical agency
9. st. olaf's avenue lee
10. middle ages
11. southeast asia
12. spain

B.
1. a. Mediterranean Sea
   b. Mediterranean country
2. a. Atlantic Ocean
   b. Atlantic coastline
3. a. Russian dressing
   b. Russian Revolution

EXERCISE 117

A.
1. It's a Wonderful Life
2. New York Times
3. "The Way We Were"
4. "The Old Gumbie Cat"
5. Auto Shop Owners
6. What Color Is Your Parachute?
7. "Working Smarter, Not Harder"
8. "The Monkey's Paw"
9. A Fistful of Dollars
10. "Down in the Valley"

B.   Sample Answers
1. Webster's Dictionary
2. Amistad
3. "Three Marlenas"
4. USA Today
5. Romeo and Juliet
6. Sports Illustrated

7. "Driven to Succeed"
8. "The Raven"

EXERCISE 118

A.
1. Beauty and the Beast
2. "Tree at My Window"
3. Till We Meet Again
4. Mayor Tom Bradley
5. "The Noise of Waters"
6. Queen Elizabeth
7. The Milwaukee Journal
8. "The City in the Sea"
9. General George Patton
10. Reader's Digest

B.
1. the natural
2. out africa
3. star wars the empire strikes back return jedi
4. on road again
5. the san francisco chronicle
6. the battle hymn republic
7. american gothic
8. this old house
9. a mother's tale
10. death salesman

EXERCISE 119

A.
1. The Old Man and the Sea
2. Member of the Wedding
3. "Bridge Over Troubled Water"
4. The Last Emperor
5. "Casey at the Bat"
6. "The Legend of Sleepy Hollow"
7. "The Midnight Ride of Paul Revere"
8. In Search of Excellence
9. The Joy of Cooking
10. "Yesterday"
11. U.S. News and World Report
12. National Geographic

B.
1. senator
2. president   senator
3. congressman   mrs.

Exercise Answers

4. queen
5. dr.   mrs.   prime minister
6. mrs.
7. ambassador
8. judge
9. princess

EXERCISE 120

A.
1. Ⓙune 9, 1999
2. Ⓜiss Ⓙennifer Ⓜacy
3. 684 Ⓜararoneck Ⓐve.
4. Ⓓr. Ⓕrancis Ⓐ. Ⓣooley
5. Ⓣhurs., Ⓝov. 21
6. Ⓖen. Ⓡaymond Ⓜadison
7. Ⓜon., Ⓙan 5
8. 1701 Ⓜeeting Ⓗouse Ⓡd.
9. Ⓜs. Ⓗannah Ⓚ. Ⓔberhardt
10. Ⓜr. and Ⓜrs. Ⓙules Ⓒhavitz

B.
1. Dr.	6. Dr.	8. Prof.
2. Blvd.	7. a. Oct.	9. Col.
3. St.	b. Nov.	10. Ave.
4. Jr.	c. Wed.	
5. L.	d. Fri.	

EXERCISE 121

A.
1. Mon.—Dec. party
2. Tues.—Dr. J. Lopez
3. Wed.—go to P.O.
4. Thurs.—Jan. report
5. Fri.—Elm St. fair
6. Sat.—Ill. taxes due

B.
1. Sgt. E. A. Nichols
R.R. 3
Danville, VA 24541
2. Dr. Sidney D. Morris
58 Pinetree Dr.
Dallas, TX 75252
3. Marjorie S. Hull
2 Ocean Rd., Apt. 5
San Jose, CA 95122
4. Rev. J. Jones
P.O. Box 200
Kingsport, TN 37664

EXERCISE 122

A.
1. day, Jeb
2. Evans, are
3. hand, Donna
4. careful, Wayne, of
5. bedroom, Sal
6. remember, Vicki, to
7. think, Mr. Evans, that
8. Donna, this

B.   Sample Answers
1. No, I've never applied for a credit card.
2. Oh, I'm not sure.
3. Yes, I've been denied credit.
4. No, I don't know what collateral is.
5. Well, you could read about it in books.

EXERCISE 123

A.
1. I will be leaving on Monday, August 8.
2. I will return on Thursday, August 11.
3. Along the way, I will stop in Harrisburg, Pennsylvania.
4. I will also go through Parkton, Maryland, on my way south.
5. My destination is XYZ Company, 62 Putnam Street, Williamsburg, Virginia.
6. On August 10, 1999, I will deliver my report there.

B.

126 Mulhaven Road
Lancaster, Pennsylvania 17062
July 5, 1999

Mr. Tom Snyder, Sales Manager
XYZ Company
62 Putnam Street
Williamsburg, Virginia 23185

Dear Mr. Smith:

I received your letter dated Tuesday, July 3. I am preparing copies of my report for your staff. They will be ready by Friday, August 5, or I can bring them with me on August 11. I will look

Exercise Answers

forward to our lunch at the Traveller's Stop Restaurant, 1711 Brandywine Boulevard, Williamsburg. I have confirmed its location. It is right near the expressway. I will meet you there at noon, August 11.

Sincerely,

Ms. Adrienne Taft
Sales Manager

EXERCISE 124

A.
1. Nora, Jim, and Paco are in charge of the news.
2. I handle the editorials, and Len draws the cartoon.
3. Ben, the best writer on the staff, is the editor.
4. Jo, our photographer, takes pictures of special events, assemblies, and sports.
5. Phil lays out the copy, and Ellen proof-reads.
6. A newspaper requires hard work, but we enjoy it.
7. Sam interviews people, takes notes, and writes stories.
8. He interviewed Ed Flynn, the police chief.
9. Mr. Flynn, by the way, has led a very interesting life.
10. He explores caves, but he also enjoys gourmet cooking.
11. I eat franks and beans, macaroni and cheese, or pizza.

EXERCISE 125

A.
1. 1900, but
2. miner, one   quickly, has
3. mountains, once   communities, are
4. towns, however, are
5. Tourists, hikers, and
6. miners, people   profit, use
7. course, as   knows, a

8. Otherwise, the
9. days, however, plastic

B.
1. Well, I washed all the dirt out of the pan, Karl.
2. Although this looks like gold, it may only be pyrite.
3. If you wait, I'll get my magnifying glass.
4. Would you carry the tweezers, the jar, and my old hat?

EXERCISE 126

A.
1. walk, Emily
2. Avenue, along Thirty-fifth Street, and
3. interesting, but
4. Yes, but
5. area, the garment district, is
6. shoes, we'll
7. Elton, maybe
8. Unfortunately, I
9. go, but
10. camera, sunglasses, and

B.
1. along, workers
2. know, Emily, that
3. Avenue, another
4. garment, Emily
5. wear, men's wear, sportswear, and
6. visit, but
7. Historically, this
8. district, a busy place, employs
9. now, it
10. Institute, a school, is
11. design, fabric, and
12. Incidentally, don't
13. Where, may I ask, are

EXERCISE 127

A.
1. Once there were millions of them! (exclamation)
2. Imagine what a sight they were. (command)
3. Are there many buffalo herds today? (question)

Exercise Answers

4. There are still herds in some areas. (statement)

5. They are protected by the federal government. (statement)

B. 1. Didn't you set your alarm? (question)
2. Well, of course I did!   (exclamation)
3. Why didn't you get up?   (question)
4. I didn't hear the alarm.   (statement)

EXERCISE 128

A. 1. Some examples of jobs for the future might include: . . . .
2. If you start a home secretarial business, you might need new equipment: . . .
3. A word processing business might provide typing for various businesses: . .
4. There are several advantages to home businesses: . . . .
5. There are also a few disadvantages: . . . .
6. Some of the products we sell are: . . . .

B. 1. 5:00   3. 3:45   5. 3:29
2. 1:30   4. 11:56

C. 1. To Whom It May Concern:
2. Dear Mr. Abbott:
3. Dear Editor:
4. Gentlemen:

EXERCISE 129

A. 1. Whales are not fish; they are mammals.
2. Mammals breathe air; therefore, whales breathe air.
3. Some people draw the whales; others photograph them.
4. The West Coast is whale country; whale watching is best there.

B. 1. Sir: 6. 10:00 10:00
2. none   7. long; they
3. states: Washington   8. boats; they
4. winter; therefore   9. circles; these
5. day; some   10. alert; they

EXERCISE 130

A. 1. I told Charles about an article called "Dreams Do Come True."
2. "Was it good?" asked Charles.
3. "Yes, Charles," I answered, "it was taken from a book."
4. "The book is quite good," I said.
5. "It sounds interesting," commented Charles.
6. "I like books on business advice," he added.
7. "Would you like to borrow this book?" I asked.
8. Charles nodded and said, "That would be great."
9. He turned to the chapter called "A Good Start."
10. "I think you'll like it," I said, "because it is so helpful."

B. 1. "I think I'll take a walk," said Mike.
2. "I'll stay here and read," I replied.
3. correct
4. "That's interesting," I said, "because his wife is in the Air Force."
5. correct

EXERCISE 131

A. 1. Work, eat, and sleep—these are all I do.
2. Wine, women, and song—now that is a phrase whose time is past.
3. Take down the ladder—it's right behind you.
4. I will go—if I can get ready in time.
5. This job—my first—is a challenge.
6. That sign—the red and white one— shows our logo.

B. 1. I wish I could—never mind—I changed my mind.
2. I agree—I think—with your basic point.
3. This should go—no, wait—that's not right.
4. John won't like this—but he'll never know.

Exercise Answers

EXERCISE 132

A. 1. renew
2. unable
3. inhumane
4. impossible
5. undo
6. inland

B. 1. agreement
2. tester
3. painful
4. treatment
5. excitement
6. plumber

C. 1. helpful
2. Inaction
3. renegotiate
4. entertainment
5. recall
6. plentiful

EXERCISE 133

A. **Sample Answers**
1. coworker
2. lunchroom
3. structure
4. lobby
5. workshop
6. piano

B. 1. condo, apartment
2. career, job
3. angry, mad
4. boss, supervisor

C. **Sample Answers**
1. Dawn is a coworker.
Dawn is a colleague.
2. I'm going to the cafeteria.
I'm going to the lunchroom.
3. This structure was solidly built.
This building was solidly built.

EXERCISE 134

A. **Sample Answers**
1. undependable
2. seldom
3. luck
4. imperfect
5. outgoing
6. late

B. 1. common, unusual
2. tardy, punctual
3. promptly, delayed
4. exit, enter

C. **Sample Answers**
1. Joan is the most dependable worker I know.
Joan is the most undependable worker I know.
2. I habitually eat lunch at 12:30.
I seldom eat lunch at 12:30.
3. I have such misfortune.
I have such luck.

EXERCISE 135

A. 1. meet
2. meet
3. meat
4. die
5. dye
6. There
7. Their
8. They're

B. **Sample Answers**
1. I bought a blue shirt.
The wind blew hard last night.
2. The pair of socks I bought shrunk.
Do you have a pear in your lunch?
3. Did you peek at your performance rating?
At what point did our business peak?
4. He rode the bus to work.
The road was under construction.
5. This fax uses plain paper.
Has his plane arrived?

Exercise Answers

6. She displayed a lot of patience dealing with that customer.
He brings the patients back to their rooms.

EXERCISE 136

A.
1. anybody
2. anywhere
3. anything
4. any
5. anyone
6. never
7. any
8. anybody

B. Sample Answers
1. I'm never a bad sport.
2. It isn't any of my business, but some people are bad sports.
3. They never give congratulations when you do well.
4. I had no idea free throws would be so difficult.
5. There is nothing better than sinking a jump shot.
6. I didn't know anything could be such fun.

EXERCISE 137

A.
1. anything
2. can
3. anyone
4. either
5. anywhere
6. was
7. anybody
8. Almost
9. were
10. any

B.
1. I couldn't find either of them upstairs.
I could find neither of them upstairs.
2. They haven't ever escaped before.
They have never escaped before.
3. There are (almost) no places left to look.
There are hardly any places left to look.

EXERCISE 138

A.
1. sieve
2. conceive
3. receive
4. believe
5. retrieve
6. deceive
7. perceive

B.
1. receive
2. believe
3. conceive
4. perceive

C. Sample Answers
1. I received an *A* on my paper.
2. I believe you overslept.
3. Did you deceive your friend?
4. She was relieved that she didn't lose her car keys.

EXERCISE 139

A.
1. quality
2. quaint
3. quarter
4. equal
5. equator

B.
1. phase
2. Physical
3. phobia
4. phone
5. Phillipe

C.
1. ride
2. wrist
3. wrong
4. right
5. wrap

EXERCISE 140

A.
1. plain (circle i)
2. play (circle y)
3. Honor (circle H)
4. failed (circle i)
5. peak (circle a)
6. honest (circle h)
7. breach (circle a)
8. stay (circle y)
9. write (circle w)
10. sail (circle i)

B.
1. heat
2. main
3. tray

Exercise Answers

4. Honestly
5. claims
6. Eat
7. pray
8. tainted

EXERCISE 141

A.
1. are
2. are
3. are
4. are
5. are
6. need
7. have
8. enjoy
9. want
10. hope

B.   Sample Answers
1. Both Linn and Kate are taking night courses.
2. Both my supervisor and the plant manager come in at 6 A.M.
3. Both the time clock and the wall clock run late.
4. Our bowling league and theirs win many games.

EXERCISE 142

A.
1. appear
2. help
3. are
4. likes
5. was

B.
1. Both Don and I want a business someday.
2. Either my friends or Don is calling tonight.
3. Neither Don nor I have enough money now.
4. Both an independent business and a franchise cost money.
5. Either these buildings or that building rents offices.
6. Not only my boyfriend but also I like country music.

EXERCISE 143

A.
1. He jumped into his clothes and rushed down the stairs.
2. Ben's wife smiled at him and offered him some orange juice.
3. Ben gulped down the juice and ate rapidly.
4. Ben's wife told him to slow down and reminded him it was Saturday.
5. Ben had thought it was a work day and was relieved.

B.
1. (opened) the newspaper and (began) to read
2. (leaned) back in his chair and (closed) his eyes
3. (walked) outside and (enjoyed) the sun
4. (relaxed) and (appreciated) the lunch break
5. (clapped) his hands and (laughed) merrily
6. (danced) and (sang) for the children
7. (read) the book last night and (took) it back to the library today.

EXERCISE 144

A.
1. Wolves and foxes are also members of the dog family.
2. Raccoon dogs and dholes come from Asia.
3. Huskies and malamutes like very cold climates.
4. My boyfriend and I like all different breeds of dogs.

B.
1. Dalmatians lived as mascots in firehouses and ran beside the engines to fires.
2. Newfoundlands have thick coats and make good retrievers.
3. Most breeds enjoy the water and can swim well.

EXERCISE 145

A.
1. Travel by ship appeals to me, and travel by plane would also be enjoyable.
2. Once sea journeys were on sailing ships, but now most sea passengers travel by ocean liner.
3. Would you like to sail around the world, or would you rather fly?

B.
1. two
2. two
3. one
4. one
5. two

Exercise Answers

EXERCISE 146

1. He considered a borrowed one, but his friend favored a used one instead.
2. A truck would do, or a van might be a possibility.
3. The van would be more comfortable, and he could also use it as a camper.
4. A hot dog truck was for sale, and it gave him a new idea.
5. The windows and awning looked funny, but he liked them anyway.
6. His friend suggested rebuilding the interior, or Sandy could just use it to sell hot dogs.
7. They laughed at the truck, but Sandy bought it anyway.

EXERCISE 147

A.
1. Amelia Earhart flew airplanes, and she flew with great skill.
2. She flew across the United States alone, and she crossed the ocean alone.
3. People admired Amelia, or they thought she was crazy.
4. She crossed the ocean, but she did not realize her dream.
5. She tried to fly around the world, but she disappeared.

B.
1. Jacqueline was an expert pilot, and she set many records.
2. Do not combine.
3. Do not combine.
4. She often flew alone, but sometimes she flew with a partner.

EXERCISE 148

A.
1. In Maine, rivers and lakes freeze.
2. Cars, trucks, and buses cross the Kennebec River on a drawbridge.
3. Winter weather prevents river traffic and causes delays.
4. In spring, ice blocks the river waters and rams the bridge.

5. Huge boats hit the ice at full power, and they break it up.

B.   Sample Answer

The Snohomish and the Yankton are icebreakers. These large, powerful boats work together as a team. The work is dangerous and requires skill. These boats are fitted with sharp blades in the front. The blades cut and break the ice.

EXERCISE 149

A.
1. (b)
2. (b)
3. (a)
4. (a)
5. (a)

B.   Sample Answers

1. My favorite times of the day are coffee break, lunch, and quitting time.
2. Graphics or pictures in advertisements are visual, attention-getting, and persuasive.
3. Some benefits of this job are insurance, flextime, and maternity leave.
4. Phones, faxes, and photocopy machines can be found in nearly every office today.

EXERCISE 150

A.

1. Myths, legends, surround
   S   S   V

2. Mozart, wrote, performed
   S   V   V

3. Mozart, sister, were
   S   S   V

4. kings, queens, heard
   S   S   V

5. violin, piano, were
   S   S   V

6. Mozart, family, traveled
   S   S   V

7. emperor, empress, met
   S   S   V

Exercise Answers

       S   S   V

8. operas, concerts, entertain

       S   V   V

9. music, played, sung

       S   S   V

10. girlfriend, I, saw

B.
1. one
2. two
3. two
4. one
5. two
6. two
7. two
8. two
9. one
10. one

EXERCISE 151

A.
1. They enjoy visit
2. catacombs attracts inspire
3. paths tombs date
4. Funerals services were held
5. San Callisto San Sebastiano are
6. builders cut dug
7. invaders uncovered destroyed
8. Historians investigate study
9. writings paintings decorate
10. pictures show tell

B.
1. two
2. one
3. two
4. two
5. one
6. two
7. one
8. one
9. one

EXERCISE 152

A.
1. The pony express did not last long, but it was important.
2. The telegraph system reached Missouri, but it stopped there.
3. Mail was carried by ships, or it was sent by wagon train.
4. These methods were slow, and better service was needed.
5. Riders rode two thousand miles, and each trip took 10 days.
6. The horses had to be quick, or the riders did not use them.
7. The riders rode in relays, but each horse went 15 miles.
8. Most riders rode 75 miles, but some rode farther.
9. The mail was picked up in Missouri, and it was taken rapidly to California.
10. Early trips took 10 days, but later the trips were shorter.

B.

      S   V   S

1. Life in the pony express was hard, and it

   V

was lonely.

      S   V   S

2. The West was a wilderness, and stations

   V

were miles apart.

      S   V

3. The riders changed horses quickly, and

       S   V

then they rode off.

      S   V

4. They rode under any conditions, and

       S   V

their bags held the mail.

      S   V   S

5. Workers packed the mail, and it usually

   V

arrived safely.

       S   V   S

6. The company tested many riders, but it

   V

chose only the best.

     S   V   S

7. A few riders became famous, and legends

   V

began about some.

     S   V   S   V

8. Delivery of the mail was fast, but mail was lost once.

      S   V

9. The telegraph started, and the pony

Exercise Answers

        S   V

express ended.

            S   V   S

10. Mail service continued, but people still

        V

remember the pony express.

EXERCISE 153

A.
1. D		8. D	
2. S		9. S	
3. D		10. D	
4. D		11. S	
5. S		12. S	
6. D		13. S	
7. D			

B.
1. D	4. D
2. I	5. D
3. D	

EXERCISE 154

A.
1. when they are full
2. since fuel became expensive
3. as long as they are cruising
4. that fly long distances
5. When a jet takes off
6. which climb vertically
7. if the currents are suitable

B.
1. I gulped down breakfast, since I had to leave for work early.
2. I dried my shirt, which was still in the washing machine.
3. It was time to move when the clock read 6:15.
4. I took the train that was for early commuters.
5. Sometimes I get blisters, because I have a mile walk to the train station.
6. The sun came out after it rained in the morning.

EXERCISE 155

A. **Sample Answers**
1. She wanted to rent a tape that was a popular movie.
2. She had to hurry because the store would soon close.
3. Her friend Anita stopped her while she was jogging down the sidewalk.
4. Together they crossed the street when the light changed.
5. They sprinted through the door as fast as they could.
6. Chloe quickly found the tape that she wanted.

B.
1. Because computers seldom make errors
2. which make most of the detailed drawings
3. who require precise calculators
4. that control the engine and the instrument panel
5. (no dependent thought)

EXERCISE 156

A. **Sample Answers**
1. The company's tax refund was late because the state had problems with its computer.
2. The furniture in the office was covered while we painted the reception area.
3. City streets become slippery when freezing rain falls.
4. You know it is dangerous if you cannot see through the fog.
5. I remained at work until I got my paycheck.
6. The meeting began again when everyone got quiet.

B.
1. When four people play tennis
2. If only two play
3. (has no dependent thought)
4. Since players had no rackets then
5. Because they hit the ball this way

Exercise Answers

6. (no dependent thought)

7. (no dependent thought)

EXERCISE 157

A. 1. You want to avoid stilted writing that sounds impersonal and may turn off a potential customer.

2. Practice speaking what you write, so that you can see if your writing sounds conversational.

3. Being too casual can also be a problem, since it may make your customer feel unimportant.

B. 1. Whereas management has recently taken the request under advisement, they will be able to deliver their response in the near future.

2. While reading your writing out loud can help make it sound more conversational, it also helps you spot mistakes, such as bloating or grammar errors.

EXERCISE 158

A. 1. Samantha watched the ketchup oozing across the floor.

2. From the freezer, he removed a fish that was sixteen inches long.

3. On her head the customer wore a felt hat that was much too large.

4. We saw the tour bus pulling off the highway at the exit.

B. 1. Each crew knows just how to handle its machine. Each crew knows how to handle just its machine.

2. Only one vehicle can travel 180 miles per hour. One vehicle can travel only 180 miles per hour.

3. Only some vehicles are built from a few materials. Some vehicles are built from only a few materials.

4. Just five vehicles completed 50 laps. Five vehicles completed just 50 laps.

EXERCISE 159

A. 1. Bus drivers carry all kinds of passengers, young, old, rich, and poor.

2. Bus drivers are responsible for the safety and comfort of their passengers.

3. Many bus drivers work part-time, putting in only twenty to thirty hours per week or even less.

4. Some bus drivers work split shifts, driving several hours in the morning and several hours in the evening.

B. **Sample Answer**

The long, green bus pulled up to the curb and squealed to a stop. The front door opened, making a whooshing sound. Three passengers got off, a tall, red-headed student with a black cap, an elderly gentleman with a cane, and a young businesswoman. Then two new passengers boarded, and the bus pulled away again.

EXERCISE 160

1. In the 1840s many women were courageous and adventurous.

2. Wives of whaling-ship captains waited patiently and bravely.

3. The families of sea captains sometimes sailed with them for years at a time.

4. The women wrote in their diaries daily, thoughtfully, and faithfully.

5. They told of strange sights, adventures, and tragedies.

6. The people aboard the ship had adventures on the ocean and in foreign ports.

7. Sometimes storms raged fiercely and destructively.

EXERCISE 161

A. 1. (Walking down the aisles,)

2. (practicing on stage)

3. (dressed in a tuxedo)

4. raised

5. (Waving his baton,)

Exercise Answers

6. <u>gleaming</u>
7. <u>booming</u>
8. <u>crashing</u>
9. (<u>filling</u> the auditorium)
10. (<u>Clapping</u> their hands,)
11. (<u>Facing</u> the audience,)

B. 1. <u>doctor</u> <u>dedicated</u> to his profession
2. <u>patients</u> <u>suffering</u> from illnesses
3. <u>Using</u> <u>scientific approaches</u> <u>he</u>
4. <u>books</u> <u>describing</u> his medical procedures

EXERCISE 162

A. 1. Focusing his camera lens, the photographer took a picture.
2. The circus featured lions jumping through fiery hoops.
3. The fans applauded the runners racing toward the finish line.
4. The doctor bandaged the athlete's leg injured in the game.
5. My husband washed his car parked in the driveway.

B. 1. Looking over the report, the manager found a mistake.
2. Using the intercom, the dispatcher called the dock supervisor.
3. She couldn't read the fax written in a foreign language.
4. Running down the street, I almost missed the bus.
5. I applied for the job advertised in the newspaper.
6. The mechanic found the socket lying on the floor.

EXERCISE 163

A. 1. The guide, Mr. Yakub, showed the American television crew around.
2. The bazaar, a kind of open market, was exciting.
3. Many animals, mostly sheep and goats, are sold here.
4. Camels, the ships of the desert, are traded too.
5. The buyers, nomadic herdsmen, look for bargains.
6. The merchants, clever sellers, look for business.
7. Kashgar, an oasis city, is in the Takla Makan Desert.
8. Long ago Kashgar was on an important trade route, the Silk Road.
9. A famous traveler, Marco Polo, once stopped here.
10. The people of Kashgar are Uighers, descendants of a Turkish group.

B.
1. <u>mountains</u> (the Pamirs)
2. <u>carts</u> (popular means of transportation)
3. <u>Donkeys</u> (traditional beasts of burden)
4. <u>Poplars</u> (graceful trees)
5. <u>fruit</u> (melons and oranges)
6. <u>goods</u> (oil and meat)
7. <u>bells</u> (desert necessities)
8. <u>bargaining</u> (favorite pastime)

EXERCISE 164

A. 1. systems for creating and keeping control over group activities—governments.
2. county, municipality, township, school district, special district—groups.

B. 1. Benefits—such extras as paid vacations, sick leave, medical insurance, and retirement plans—are often generous in government jobs.
2. Tuition assistance, help with the cost of higher education, is often a benefit in state government jobs.

EXERCISE 165

A. 1. <u>Oak Park</u> a suburb of Chicago
2. <u>father</u> a doctor

Exercise Answers

3. <u>sports</u> boxing and football
4. *Star* a newspaper in Kansas City
5. *In Our Time* a collection of his short stories
6. <u>novels</u> *A Farewell to Arms* and *For Whom the Bell Tolls*

B. 1. Alone in a rowboat, he caught a giant fish, a marlin.
2. Sharks, a menace to fishermen, attacked and devoured the marlin.
3. Ernest Hemingway wrote a short novel, *The Old Man and the Sea*, based on this true story.

EXERCISE 166

A. 1. sentence   4. sentence
2. fragment   5. fragment
3. fragment

B. 1. Job-related computer bulletin boards are good places to read about jobs or to post a résumé.
2. Many computer bulletin boards cater to local communities, so jobs listed would likely be local jobs.
3. Commercial (fee-based) information services provide another alternative for job seekers.
4. Most libraries provide free access to the Internet, along with assistance or training in Internet use.

EXERCISE 167

A. 1. In prehistoric times, people tied skins around their feet.
2. An early shoe, the sandal, was worn in Egypt, Greece, and Rome.
3. Sandals were made from hard leather or plant fibers.
4. When people wanted warmth, they wore soft leather shoes.
5. Boots were originally used for hunting.

B. 1. Moccasins were made of animal skins, and they were comfortable.

2. Heeled shoes originated in the 1400s, and they were wooden.
3. Heels were helpful because they kept feet from mud and water.
4. Some shoes had pointed toes, while others had platforms.

EXERCISE 168

A.   **Sample Answers**
1. I walked to work that beautiful autumn day.
2. I arrived at the doctor's office, where I work.
3. Yesterday I took a bus downtown.
4. Correct
5. My brother and his family were in the waiting room.

B. 1. He isn't awake yet because his alarm wasn't set.
2. I enjoy work that takes me outside.

EXERCISE 169

A. 1. Correct
2. Many people work in service jobs. Some are waiters, waitresses, clerks, and food service providers.
3. Some jobs were lost when computers began to be used. Others were created.
4. People must sometimes retrain for new jobs. Sometimes they must return to school.

B. 1. We need to deal with change and be flexible.
2. Change is a part of life; everything changes over time.
3. Change can be fun, if we have the right attitude.
4. By accepting change, we make it our ally; it can no longer threaten us.

EXERCISE 170

A. 1. Correct
2. Farms are small. Most farmers are very poor.

Exercise Answers

3. The people of India speak many indigenous languages. Most educated Indians also speak English.

B.   Canada is a huge country. It lies to the north of the United States. Canada has English-speaking people and French-speaking people. It also has many immigrants from Asia, Africa, and Europe. To many U.S. natives, Canada is a vacationland. The country is also our most important trading partner.

EXERCISE 171
Sample Answers

1. Our first project was vegetable soup. Chopping all those vegetables was a lot of work.
2. The next lesson was chili, but I cut back on the amount of hot peppers.
3. Spaghetti can be made with tomato sauce, or you can substitute tomato paste and water.
4. Soon we will learn to bake. I just love the smell of fresh bread!
5. There are never any leftovers. The students in our class always eat up their projects.
6. Someday I will be a chef, and people from all over will flock to my restaurant.

EXERCISE 172

A. 1. Conflicts at work can result in more than hurt feelings; they may involve job loss as well.
2. Most conflicts can be worked out. You won't always be able to solve every problem, but you can find ways to compromise.
3. Believe it or not, conflicts can be useful; they can help build relationships.
4. Negative reactions can be discussed, and they can lead to better understanding.

5. Conflict gives you a reason to think about your behavior. When you do, you may see some things you want to change.
6. Perhaps your communication skills could be improved, and you could use some training in that area.
7. You could attend a seminar or class; one that deals with both communication and conflict would be a good choice.

EXERCISE 173
Sample Answers

1. The firefighters prepared quickly.
2. The fire chief, Jake Reynolds, gave orders.
3. The fire truck raced through busy traffic.
4. The brave firefighters turned on hoses.
5. The building, a red brick house, smoked.
6. Hearing the sirens, a crowd gathered.
7. One person, John Dannon, was injured.
8. Soon an ambulance arrived.
9. Covered with soot, the firefighters looked exhausted.
10. A firefighter climbed up a ladder.
11. Police patrolled the noisy crowd.
12. A newspaper reporter took pictures of the burning building.

EXERCISE 174

A. 1. As time passed, he became an experienced pilot. He wanted to be the first person to fly nonstop across the Atlantic Ocean. He planned the flight for months.
2. Lindbergh accomplished what he set out to do. He broke the world record for a nonstop airplane flight. Many honored Lindbergh for his achievement.

B. 1. He did not have enough supplies.
2. He made a successful nonstop flight.

C. 1. People on the ground cheered and applauded.
2. When he landed in France, Lindbergh was very tired.

Exercise Answers

EXERCISE 175

Sample Answers

1. I like looking at maps and drawing them.
2. My cousin has a road map of Europe.
3. She likes to plan the car trip that she hopes to take one day.
4. It's fun comparing old and recent maps of the same place and seeing the differences.
5. I imagine traveling to all the places on the map.
6. You can hardly recognize the shapes of the continents on the old maps.
7. Map makers get highly accurate pictures of the earth from satellites.
8. Cartographers make our maps and study them.

EXERCISE 176

Sample Answers

1. Most comets are faint, fuzzy, and difficult to recognize.
2. Comets are gigantic clouds of gas and dust.
3. The only solid part is the comet's nucleus—a lump of ice, dirt, and stones.
4. The brightest comets can sprout enormous tails, which can be tens of millions of miles long.
5. The ancient Chinese thought comets brought famine, sickness, and war.
6. Comets cannot be seen clearly if it is cloudy.
7. Halley's Comet appears every seventy-six years.
8. My grandmother saw Halley's Comet through a telescope when she was young.
9. Halley's Comet will appear next around the year 2061.

EXERCISE 177

Sample Answers

1. Emily Dickinson wrote poetry that was never published during her lifetime.

2. She lived in Amherst, Massachusetts.
3. She carefully observed nature.
4. In her poetry she described a snake, a bird, and a storm.
5. On scraps of paper, she wrote poems about life and death.
6. She had an original way of rhyming words, punctuating lines, and capitalizing.
7. Her poem about March is very imaginative.
8. Admirers of Emily Dickinson enjoy reading the story of her life.
9. Her father was a successful lawyer and a member of Congress. However, he treated her sternly.

EXERCISE 178

Sample Answers

1. Is the medical profession opening up?
2. In years past almost all doctors were men, but today more women are enrolling in medical school.
3. More young black and Hispanic people are studying to be doctors.
4. In the future, many of these students will be dedicated doctors.

EXERCISE 179

A. 1. b.   2. c.

B. 1. There will be a showing of a film about smoke alarms.
2. Rosa hit a home run, winning the game for her team.

EXERCISE 180

2. Voice mail is a very efficient way to leave messages.
3. There are standard rules of etiquette for using voice mail.

EXERCISE 181

A. 1. a
2. b
3. c

Exercise Answers

B.   **Sample Answers**

1. Instead, show poise and class by practicing restraint.
2. Speak to the person privately, ask him to change his behavior, and withhold criticisms until you are alone.

EXERCISE 182

A. 1. Many American swimmers have won world fame.
2. The United States has many famous skyscrapers.
3. Brazil and Portugal had a close relationship.
4. Night owls stay up late.

B.   **Sample Answers**

1. Even a bad job is often better than no job.
2. a. A bad job gives you some income.
   b. A bad job gives you work experience.
   c. A bad job can often be made better.
   d. A bad job may lead to a better job.

EXERCISE 183

A.   A new program is enriching the lives of senior and young citizens. Children and adults at a young/old day care center are going to art classes, storytelling, cooking sessions, and games. Each child and adult has a special "buddy" that he or she spends time with. This program promises to give young and old a lot of hugs and to provide them with lasting friendships.

B.   **Sample Answers**

1. Supervised training allows new employees to learn the correct way to do their jobs. Supervised training gives new employees a chance to practice and learn from their mistakes.
2. Your heart will be healthier. You will feel more lively and energetic.

EXERCISE 184

I remember the first time I saw the ocean at dawn. Frothy breakers crashed on the deserted beach. Driftwood bleached as white as bone littered the cool, damp sand. The sea's distant surface shone like a mirror. At first, the sun was only a tiny, red lump piercing the blue-black sky. As it rose, it began to look like a molten lead coin. A breeze as faint as a sleeping baby's breath rustled the dune grass behind me. The day had just begun.

Sentences 2, 5, 9, and 10 should be omitted.

EXERCISE 185

A.   After   Above me
        For example   Then
        Just as

B. 1. For instance   2. Behind
        In addition   Outside
        Just as   beyond
                           Far
                           Inside

3. Before
   White
   Then
   behind
   Finally

EXERCISE 186

A. 1. (2)   5. (8)
        2. (1)   6. (6)
        3. (4)   7. (3)
        4. (7)   8. (5)

B.   **Sample Paragraph**

The ranch hands at Big K Dude Ranch wake up before sunrise to begin their chores. First they feed and groom the horses. Then after a big breakfast, they put bridles and saddles on the horses. They take the tourists on riding tours. By late afternoon, they arrive back at the ranch with the tourists tired and sore, but happy. In the evenings, the ranch hands play guitar and sing around the campfire.

Exercise Answers

EXERCISE 187

A. 1. First 3. Next 5. soon
2. Then 4. After 6. Now

B. 1. First
2. Next
3. Then
4. Finally

C. (Have your instructor read your paragraph.)

EXERCISE 188

A. **Sample Answers**

Yesterday	and
First	Soon
Then	Later
Next	

B. (Have your instructor read your narrative paragraph.)

EXERCISE 189

A. **Sample Answers**

At first	Then
Now	Later
Eventually	finally

B. 1. 3 5. 1
2. 5 6. 6
3. 2 7. 4
4. 7

Elena devised a summer exercise program for herslef. First, on Mondays, she would swim in the park pool. After that, she would ride her bike. On Wednesday evening Elena's bowling team meets. On Thursday, she would jog one mile. Late Friday afternoon she played tennis. Finally, on the weekend, she would lift weights.

EXERCISE 190

A. **Sample Answers/Describing a Car**
1. shiny black finish
2. low, sleek lines
3. hum of the engine
4. red and black pinstriped interior
5. fuzzy, soft feel of the cloth seats.

B. **Sample Answers/A Good Boss**
1. Well-trained
2. Good listening skills
3. Good speaking skills
4. Patient
5. Approachable
6. Fair
7. Good writing skills
8. Aware of work requirements
9. Sense of humor
10. Respectful to subordinates

EXERCISE 191

A. **Sample Answers/Your Favorite Restaurant**
1. Hearing – nice background music
2. Sight – oceanview
3. Smell – food smells spicy
4. Taste – food is delicious
5. Touch – frosted mugs

B. **Sample Answer**

I have a favorite restaurant. It has great food and good service. The music is lovely background while I quietly talk to a friend. I like to sip a root beer served in a frosted mug and watch the ocean while I wait for my delicious meal.

EXERCISE 192

A. **Sample Answers**
1. woof, woof, arf, arf of barking dogs
2. soft, fluffy fur
3. fresh, cool water
4. bulky, brown and black German Shepherd mix
5. white mice scurried

B. **Sample Answer**

I once worked with a person who had one year left on the job before retire-

Exercise Answers

ment. This person worked the same job for 35 years. It was her first and only job. Although she was well informed about her job and did it well, she never wanted to make any changes or improvements. When I joined the staff, it was very stifled and people were discouraged. After she retired, things became more progressive.

EXERCISE 193
A. 1. left, directly ahead, right
2. left to right
3. toward

B.   **Sample Answer**

My office is near the front entrance of our building. From my left window I can see the lobby, with dozens of people scurrying around. To my right is another smaller desk with my computer on it. Sometimes my coworkers borrow my computer, and we chat as they work. At my feet, under my desk, I keep a small space heater. I use it on very cold days, when a draft comes in from the lobby.

EXERCISE 194
A.   In downtown Chicago, the buildings are close together, and it is easy to get from one to another quickly. On your lunch hour you can walk outside and enter a world of choices for places to go and things to do. You can run across the street and catch a quick cup of coffee and a sandwich. Then you might go to the corner, turn right, and be at your favorite department store. Here you can pick up a pair of earrings or perhaps a new tie. You might want to drop your clothes off at the cleaner's next door. In front of you, you might see a street vendor with some lovely jewelry to sell. Behind you might be a street musician offering soothing sounds for busy shoppers. All too soon, your

lunch break will be over. You'll walk back down the street to your office building, pleased with all you've done in just an hour.

B.   (Have your instructor read your letter.)

EXERCISE 195
(Have your instructor read your descriptive paragraph.)

EXERCISE 196
A.   **Sample Answers**
Person's Name/Physical Appearance/Interests
John: dark/cars
stocky/sailing
in good shape/plays sports
bearded/parties
Tim: tall/investments
fair/photography
glasses/watches sports
not in good shape/loner

B. 1. A computer is like a typewriter because you can type on both of them.
A computer is different from a typewriter because a computer has a screen, and the screen allows you to edit your mistakes before they are printed.
2. A bus and a car both provide transportation.
A car can carry only a few people, while a bus carries many.
3. A boss and an employee are both workers.
A boss can give orders, but an employee must follow them.

EXERCISE 197
A. 1. automobile   6. automobile
2. motorcycle   7. automobile
3. both   8. both
4. motorcycle   9. both
5. both

Exercise Answers

B.   Sample Answers
Working at Home and Working From
a Business Location

Similarities

    often do same work in both locations

    can get same pay

    often work with same types of equipment

    (computer, fax)

Differences

must be dressed for work; can work from home in casual attire

must take breaks at designated times at work

can take breaks at any time at home

children or visitors may cause distractions at home

EXERCISE 198

	Typewriter	**Computer**
Comparisons	1. Has letter and number keys	1. Has letter and number keys
	2. Has space bar and return bar	2. Has space bar and return bar
	3. Can create letters and other documents	3. Can create letters and other documents
Contrasts	1. Has been used in business since the late 1800s	1. Has been used since the mid-1900s
	2. Uses only ribbons for printing	2. May use dry ink cartridges
	3. Uses no silicon chips	3. Uses silicon chips to store information
	4. Prints paper right in machine	4. Printed pages go through separate machine (printer)
	5. Can print only one type style	5. Can print any number of different typefaces (fonts)

EXERCISE 199

A.

	Type of Instrument	**Tone**
flute	woodwind	high pitch
tuba	brass	low pitch

	How It Is Played	**Size**
flute	by blowing across a hole	small, slender
tuba	by blowing into a mouthpiece	large

Exercise Answers

B.   Sample Answers
1. Both have printed pages and are bound. Unlike a book, which is published once, a magazine is published at regular intervals.
2. Both a table and a desk are pieces of furniture at which you sit. However, a table consists mainly of a top without the sides and the drawers that a desk has.
3. Both a memo and a letter are forms of business communication. A mcmo has a different form than that of a letter.
4. Both a nail and a screw are used in construction. However, a nail is inserted with a hammer, and a screw is inserted with a screwdriver.

EXERCISE 200

(Have your instructor read your paragraph.)

EXERCISE 201

A.   1. First   3. On the whole
       2. Then   4. Finally

B.   1. Example: how to prepare for an interview
       2. Example: To prepare for an interview, you must think about many things.
       3. Details about the paragraph:
          —Find out about job requirements.
          —Think about skills you can bring to the job.
          —Find out about the company (use the library).
          —Dress neatly and conservatively.
          —Smile.
       4. first, then, on the day of
       5. Sample Paragraph
          To prepare for an interview, you must think about many things. First, you must find out about the job you are applying for. What are the requirements? What skills do you have that you can bring to this job? Then, find out about the company, if you can. Check the library

for details. Knowing background information about the business helps you impress an interviewer. On the day of the interview, dress neatly and conservatively. Be sure to wear your smile.

EXERCISE 202

A.   1. (5)
       2. (1)
       3. (3)
       4. (4)
       5. (2)
       6. (6)

B.   (Have your instructor read your explanatory paragraph.)

EXERCISE 203

A.   Sample Answers
1. Watching television is a relaxing way to spend an evening.
2. One of the worst mistakes humans can make is to destroy the wilderness.
3. Day care for employees' children reduces employee stress.
4. The minimum wage should not be raised if that means fewer jobs.
5. The budget for exploring outer space should not be cut.

B.   Sample Answers
1. Watching television is a relaxing way to spend an evening.
   a. It doesn't demand too much thought.
   b. You can lie back or watch from some other comfortable position.
   c. You can be together with family members and discuss the television shows.
2. One of the worst mistakes humans can make is to destroy the wilderness.
   a. Today many people enjoy spending time in the wilderness.
   b. We must save some wilderness for our children and their children.

Exercise Answers

c. Animals and plants require the wilderness to survive, and our survival depends on theirs.

3. The budget for exploring outer space should not be cut.
   a. It appeals to our sense of adventure.
   b. It adds to our knowledge of the universe.
   c. It leads to new and practical developments here on earth.

EXERCISE 204

A.   Sample Answers

1. women's sports. Women's sports should be supported much more by fans.
2. television advertising. Advertisements on television should be more strongly regulated.
3. workplace equipment. Workplace equipment should be up-to-date in order to expect the maximum performance from employees.
4. voting. Some people who don't vote are actually doing us all a favor.
5. dieting. Too much emphasis is placed on dieting these days.

B.   Sample Answers

Topic sentence—Advertisements on television should be more strongly regulated.

Supporting details—

too many commercials now

interrupt shows far too often

often commercials are sexist or offensive in some other way, some appeal to children, make them want toys and food they should not have

airwaves belong to everyone, not just to those who can afford to pay to advertise their products

EXERCISE 205

A.   A good mentoring relationship should involve a seasoned employee taking a new or younger employee under his or her wing. Mentors should usually be older employees with experience. They should like to help young people who show potential. A mentor should help an employee learn the "ropes" of a job—the values, established procedures, etc. A mentor should also give advice about paths to success and warn of pitfalls. A good mentor will often "go to bat" for his or her employee and help secure raises or promotions. ~~I had a mentor once myself.~~

B.   Sample Paragraph

People being mentored need to do their part to learn about the realities of their business or trade. They should go over their job descriptions with their boss or personnel manager. They should read all manuals related to their job. They should talk to and listen to ideas from other employees. They should check out the competition for ideas. They should learn all about the job description of the position for which they are next in line. They should become aware of unspoken rules of behavior, such as dress codes, office friendships, and not conducting personal business on company time.

Correlation Chart of *English Workout: Language Skills for the Workplace* to SCANS

	English Workout: Language Skills for the Workplace **Exercises**
Resources—Allocates time, money, material and facilities, and human resources	To the Student Exercises 10, 36, 37, 121, 122
Interpersonal skills	Exercises 17, 18, 31, 37, 44, 52, 97, 99, 106, 172, 181
Information	Exercises 20, 22-25, 44, 54, 56, 95, 180
Systems	Exercises 1, 6, 11, 19, 20, 28, 30, 33, 35, 110, 126, 156, 159, 164
Technology	Exercises 95, 149
Basic skills	Check What You Know Final Checkup Exercises 1-178, 185, 187-192, 201-205
Thinking skills	24, 27, 29, 38, 41, 42, 46, 51, 53, 57-60, 62, 64, 68, 69, 77, 94, 109, 123, 133-135, 138, 147, 149, 154, 159, 160, 162, 173-177, 179-184, 186, 189, 193-196, 200
Personal qualities	To the Student Exercises 5, 13, 29, 40, 44, 63, 79, 83, 127, 157, 169, 181, 190